POPE PIUS XII LIB., ST. JOSEPH COLLEGE
3 2528 01324 5644

S0-CKV-008

Training for Professional Child Care

Beverly Gulley
Jacqueline Eddleman
Douglas Bedient

Southern Illinois University Press
Carbondale and Edwardsville

Printed in the United States of America
Designed by Cindy Small
Production supervised by Natalia Nadraga

Library of Congress Cataloging-in-Publication Data

Gulley, Beverly.
Training for professional child care.

Includes bibliographies and index.
1. Child care—Study and teaching. I. Eddleman, E. Jacqueline. II. Bedient, Douglas. III. Title.
HQ778.5.G85 1987 362.7'12 86–26151
ISBN 0–8093–1331–6

The paper used in this publication meets the minimum requirements of American National Standard for Information Sciences
– Permanence of Paper for Printed Library Materials, ANSI Z39.48-1984.

Contents

Figures

Tables

Foreword

Although providing care for infants and young children is exciting and satisfying, it has never been an easy task. Today, more than ever, when so many children require some form of care outside the home, it is vital that individuals be adequately trained to meet the challenge and demand for appropriate and high-quality care. This book was written as an answer to the challenge. It provides teachers, careproviders, and others involved in the fascinating world of child care with a practical approach to developmental care, understanding of children, and activities to enrich and improve the lives of children and families as they participate in child care programs. Through choice of activities and through an annotated bibliography after each chapter, the book also attempts to familiarize learners with important research and literature in the field.

A great deal of study, exploration, and on-site activity has gone into the creation of the book. Originally, it was conceived and developed as a series of workshops for a training project involving child care workers in southern Illinois. Choice of topics and training materials was based on the findings of a 1977 survey conducted by the Office of Child Development of the Illinios Department of Children and Family Services, a random sampling of day care centers by the same office, and a 1981 regional survey of careproviders in southern Illinois. Thus, the needs, problems, and major concerns of child careproviders were always kept in the forefront during development of the series that ultimately grew into this book.

Input from other important sources also aided in the development of the materials and activities. Careproviders, representatives of the Department of Children and Family Services, instructors, and human development professional staff at Southern Illinois University at Carbondale served on an advisory council, while the developed materials were reviewed and evaluated by the Department of Children and Family Services, an area validation team, and Dr. Mary Ellen Durrett of the University of Texas at Austin.

The materials have been thoroughly and vigorously tested. They were originally used in the training of approximately three hundred child careproviders. Observations and experiences of the trainees, as well as of experts and professionals during the training process, were then considered, and revisions were made on the basis of input and use for the future training of careproviders in Illinois. In essence, then, the book is the final product of valuable input, practical applications, and further input collected over a period of more than four years.

Reports and feedback from a wide variety of individuals who have utilized the series indicate that they have found the topics and materials comprehensive, practical, and —what is more—easy to use. Moreover, the materials have been welcomed because they are designed for use in different types of child care settings, including child care centers and family day care within the home.

Finally, the Department of Children and Family Services supports the use of materials in this book for the delivery of high-quality training to child careproviders. The department and the authors hope that the book will be a valuable source of interest, enrichment, and improvement in child care training, child care services, and child and family life in Illinois and throughout the country.

Gordon Johnson
Director
Illinois Department of Children and Family Services

Preface

THE overall purpose of this book is to provide information and ideas to be used in the training of teachers in early childhood development programs. It can be used for preservice or in-service training for other groups, such as family day careproviders, residential child care workers, parents, or foster parents, but it has primarily been prepared for those who work or plan to work in group child care settings. We have observed that high-school teachers and community college instructors have found the information and the related materials useful in their child development and child care courses. The book is written in practical language and offers a step-by-step approach to training child careproviders.

The book was originally written and developed as part of a Title XX Training Project for child care workers that was funded by the Illinois Department of Children and Family Services, the Illinois Department of Public Aid, and the U.S. Department of Health and Human Services. The concepts herein resulted from a survey of child care workers in Illinois and the expertise of many individuals who were involved in the training and evaluation of these professionals. The material has been used in numerous training sessions for child careproviders and others who work with young children in Illinois, and its effectiveness has been tested and evaluated extensively.

The information included in this book is a result of three writings. First written and used for training in 1981 and 1982, the material was revised again at the end of 1982 and used for training from 1982 to 1985. The book went through its final rewriting in 1985–86, with revisions based on thoughtful comments from individuals, too numerous to count, who had used the training materials.

Though written for the trainer the book can be used by anyone who wants to know more about appropriate ways of working with children, primarily in preschool-aged groupings. The reader can expect to find information that relates to many aspects of child development and child care. The reader can also expect assistance in eliciting discussions during training sessions and will find activities that involve the learners during and after the training sessions.

The overall goal of this book is to provide child careproviders with the knowledge and skills necessary to care for children in a highly professional manner. The book was written with the intent of making teaching easy. The material can be presented in a number of different ways, but the information is most beneficial when utilized to address individual training situations in a child care setting.

The structure and the features of the book make it unique and efficient for training. It is written in simple yet professional language and addresses the most current and typical concerns of teachers of young children. The book is divided into fifteen training chapters that are designed to provide an almost cookbook approach to teaching.

Each chapter begins with a brief introduction to the training topic followed by the objectives for the chapter. Key ideas or main points are provided as an overview of the primary concepts covered in the training session. The remaining content is subdivided by topics and subtopics in order that the trainer can more easily utilize the material. The chapters are written so that the trainer can teach directly from the book as it is or can adapt the information to an individual style of teaching. In general, the book is written in the first person and recognizes that "we," the trainer and learner, are in the profession together working as a team for the benefit of children.

Within each chapter are activities that assist the trainer in moving the training from the didactic mode to the application mode. Each chapter contains question starters that are designed to elicit thought and discussion from the participants. Questions are posed and possible responses are provided so that the trainer can more easily generate discussion within the group setting. The trainer is also encouraged to add more questions and responses as the needs arise.

The chapters contain two additional kinds of activities designed to encourage participation in the training process. Learning activities are interspersed throughout each unit and are written to encourage involvement in the application of information being covered. They also provide an alternate approach to encourage learner participation. At the end of each chapter is a number of enrichment activities that participants are encouraged to do as follow-up learning activities. The enrichment activities are designed to provide additional experiences whereby participants can apply the information included in the training session to their individual situations and circumstances.

The book is interspersed with charts and figures that are used to further illustrate and reinforce important points. The chapters can be taught without the reproduction of the chart and figures, but they do add another dimension to the training.

At the end of each chapter is an annotated bibliography listing the current publications relative to each topic. These bibliographies can be used to provide direction for further background reading for the trainer and those involved in the training session. The comprehensive Table of Contents was so designed in order that the trainer could easily locate all the information that is covered in each chapter.

It is expected that each chapter will take about 2 to 2 1/2 hours to cover. However, since each trainer and each group is different, the sessions will vary in length. Because the chapters are subdivided into topical areas, the trainer can easily adjust the training schedule to the needs of the group.

To accommodate the practical nature of writing, the words "he" and "she" are used interchangeably throughout the book. We hope that we have provided a balance in our usage of the gender words. In addition, the words "teacher," "careprovider," and "child care worker" are used interchangeably in the book, but for the purposes of this book refer to individuals who work with prekindergarten children, usually in group child care settings.

In summary, the reader and/or trainer should find the book an efficient means of providing preservice and in-service training to teachers of young children. It was written by individuals who have themselves used the material for training purposes and who after years of experience in training teachers wrote the book to accommodate the growing need to provide training to this group of professionals. The book is easy to use, yet complete, and is one response that addresses this need for training materials.

Acknowledgments

THERE are many people who have made contributions to the writing and publication of this book. We, the authors, are sensitively aware that no one person is able to compile a manuscript of this nature without the assistance of many individuals. We would like to recognize those individuals and thank them for their contributions.

In the initial stages of the conceptualization of these materials a number of people played a role in identifying important knowledge and skills needed by teachers of young children. In particular Miriam Klimstra and Beverly Howie, licensing representatives for the Illinois Department of Children and Family Services, met diligently with the authors and provided their expertise in identifying concepts that they thought should be included. Jain Sherrard and Catherine D'Amico, who had expertise in curriculum development, made major contributions to conceptualizing, writing, editing, and facilitating the production of the original manuscript. Several graduate students in Human Development provided their input and assisted in gathering information: Janet Jones, Paula Marks, Natalie Kretzmann, Ijlah Haaq, and Joyce Pettijohn.

In addition to the three authors, other individuals made important contributions to the writing of first drafts of the original chapters. Their contributions to specific chapters and the original titles of the chapters are listed below:

Jain Sherrard: The Child Care Professional, Effective Communication with Children, Observation of Children

Natalie Kretzmann: Normal Child Development, Developmental Assessment of Children, Part 2, Parent Education, Dimensions of Play, Child Abuse: Understanding and Action, Learning Environments

Linda Corder: Dimensions of Play, Learning Environments

Dr. Carolyn Haessig: Nutrition for Children

Dr. Peter Sherrard: Effective Staff Communication

Other individuals who added their expertise to the initial conceptualization and worthiness of the training materials were those who served as content validation consultants: Dr. Mary Jo Oldham, Southeast Illinois Community College; Mary Ellen Abell, John A. Logan Community College; Linda Corder; Duane Gard; and Sue Whitlock.

We would especially like to acknowledge the contributions that Dr. Mary Ellen Durrett, University of Texas at Austin, made to the evaluation and validation of the original materials. She also provided encouragement and support to complete the project.

The Illinois Department of Children and Family Services has provided continued support and encouragement over the years. Special appreciation is extended to Gordon Johnson, Director, and Gregory Coler, former Director, and Judy Hansen-Zaleski, Jerry Metzger, and Nathan Gibson, all staff of the Staff Training Development Office.

Our special gratitude goes to Helen Austin and Nillofur Zobairi for their assistance in typing, editing, and patience in seeing this project to completion. They spent many hours beyond what was expected and have taken as much pride in the finished product as the authors. To you we are especially thankful.

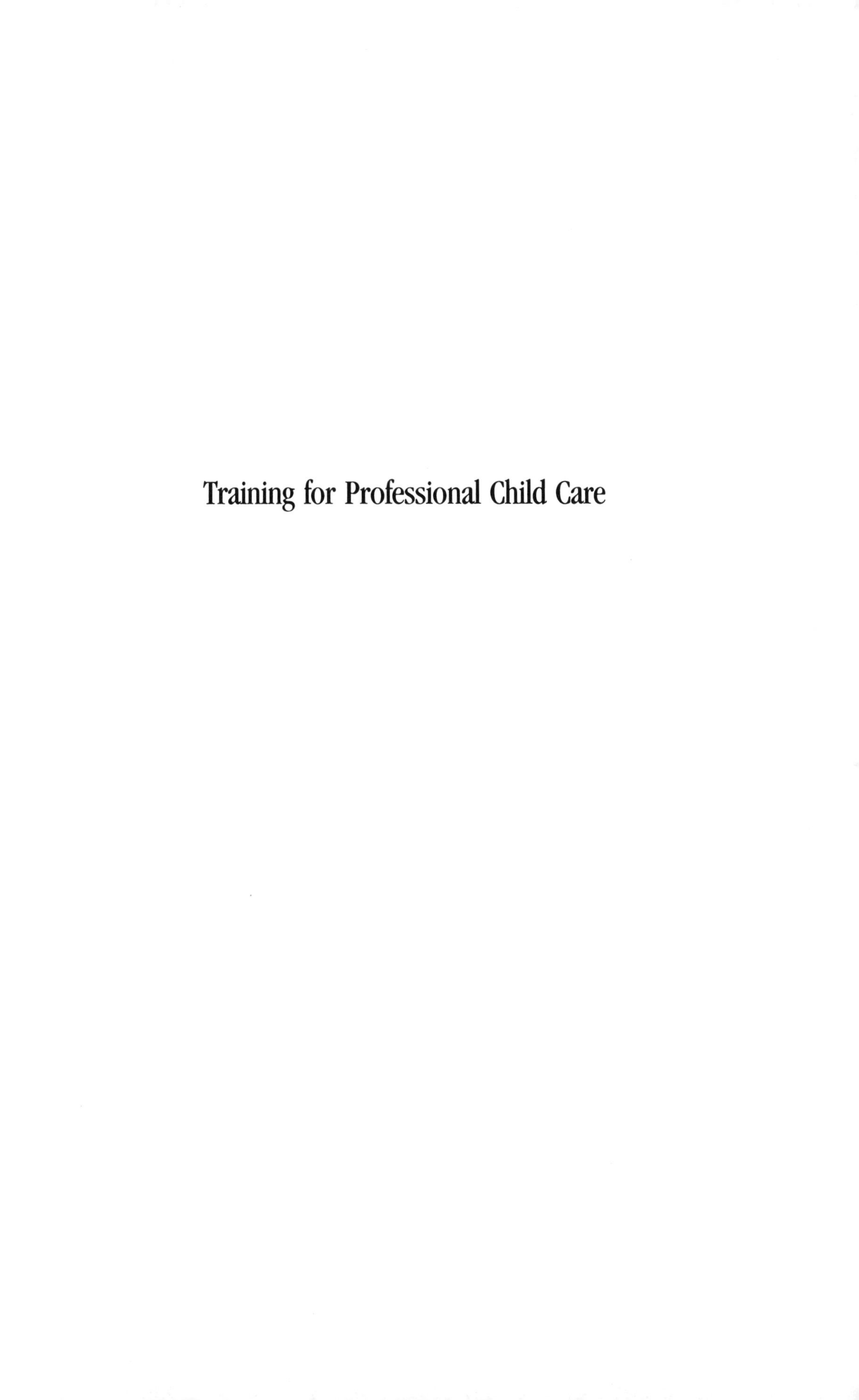

Training for Professional Child Care

1 Professionalizing Child Care

IN recent years the professional status of early childhood educators has been a foremost concern of those in the child care profession. This concern has been fostered by the growing ranks of mothers working outside the home and by early childhood professionals themselves (Ade, 1982; Caldwell, 1984; Hostetler & Klugman, 1982; Silin, 1985). The call for professionalization of this field has resulted in attempts to define professional child care and establish the meaning of quality child care. It has also resulted in serious attempts to analyze why stress and burnout permeate child care jobs and what steps can be taken to cope with stress and prevent burnout. Finally, this movement has encouraged professionals to examine the need to become advocates for children and families.

Objectives

The overall purpose of this chapter is to recognize the importance of professional child care and the ways in which careproviders can have a positive impact on the lives of children and families. In this chapter we will review the current status of the child care profession, identify characteristics of those who provide quality child care programs, analyze causes of stress and burnout in child care, and recommend ways in which we can better cope with these problems. We will also address the reasons why child care professionals should serve as advocates for children and families, and suggest strategies to accomplish this advocacy role.

Key Ideas

Child care is a profession that is growing rapidly and is consequently in need of persons who are trained to meet the growing demands for quality child care outside the home. The quality of child care depends to a great extent on the way in which child careproviders view themselves as essential human service professionals. Thus, the need to professionalize child care is essential if the quality of children's programs is to be improved.

To improve the quality of child care, we must understand what it means to operate a quality program and acquire the skills that are needed to provide good care for children. We also need to be aware that child care is stress-producing, but that there are ways to cope with stress and thus make the job of caring for children more enjoyable and rewarding.

In addition to recognizing the need to professionalize the field of child care and to understand what is involved in quality child care, we have a legal and moral responsibility to serve as advocates for children in the public arena. Knowing how we can advocate for children is part of our responsibility as child care professionals.

The Child Care Profession

The child care profession has changed significantly in recent decades. Just a few years ago, when the economy was more stable, most mothers stayed at home with their children. The traditional nuclear family—dad, the breadwinner, and mom, home with the children—was the most typical description of the family. Relatives, older siblings, close friends, and neighbors were often available to help with the care of children.

Times have changed radically, and these changes have affected almost every adult and child in the country. Today, almost 50% of all American mothers with children under the age of 6 are either employed or looking for work, which means that more than 7 million children are in need of child care. Most of the auxiliary care is provided by nonrelatives, and much of it is outside the home.

Parents in the United States currently spend about 10 million dollars a year on a variety of child care arrangements—including church nurseries, employer sponsored centers, government funded facilities, and private facilities. There is every reason to believe that the child care business will continue to grow substantially during the remainder of this century. Projections indicate that by the last decade of the century 66%, or two-thirds, of the nation's mothers will be in the work force. The Urban Institute predicts that by 1990, 10.5 million children will be cared for by someone other than their parents.

In spite of the growing demand for child care outside the home, the child care profession is not substantially recognized by the public as a profession worthy of respect. In 1977, the Department of Labor's *Dictionary of Occupational Titles (DOT)* was still assigning a low skill level to "day care workers," and even recent upgrading of the status of these workers does not accurately reflect the comprehensive nature of the job (Hostetler & Klugman, 1982). Child careproviders often work for minimum wage or not much higher and are frequently referred to as "babysitters." Yet providing child care is a profession that encompasses a vast network of human service professionals. The profession is obviously important; it is also difficult, challenging, and worthy of continual expansion.

Characteristics of Quality Child Careproviders

The dictionary defines a profession as "a principal calling, vocation, or employment requiring specialized and often long and extensive academic preparation." If we think of ourselves as professionals in a growing profession, we should have a clear understanding about what constitutes professional child care.

A number of personal characteristics and skills constitute a child care professional. We should know what they are if we intend to develop professionally.

Question Starter: What characteristics and skills do we need to be child care professionals? (Responses may include: sense of humor; stamina; creativity; flexibility; patience; dependability; love for children.)

The characteristics and skills we need to provide quality child care are many and comprehensive. The job we do is a comprehensive service that supplements the care given to children by their families

(Caldwell, 1984). We must continue to make every effort to clarify who we are and what we do if we are to be recognized as professionals.

Learning Activity: Develop the concept of the child care professional by asking participants to specify and define characteristics which they consider to be important to the child care profession. Use the categories specified here to further delineate the desirable characteristics: general characteristics, such as cooperation, dependability, and enthusiasm; personality, such as poise and sense of humor; control of the learning environment, such as discipline, guidance, and attention to health and safety; teaching skills, such as planning, preparation, motivation, and organization; and professional attitude.

Characteristics of Quality Child Care Programs

A definition of professionalism includes not only who we are, but what we do. Having excellent facilities, equipment, menus, and curricula is important but is no substitute for what actually happens to children in our care. What is really important is the quality of the experiences we provide for children when we are with them.

One way of analyzing what constitutes an effective early childhood program is to identify what it is that we want children to be able to do. Although not limited to this list, we should be aware of some of the primary goals for children. We want children to develop and maintain a positive feeling about themselves and their abilities to create and to learn, and to be able to expand their awareness of the world through their sensory experiences. We want them to develop language through listening, speaking, and dramatic play activities, which form the basis for reading, writing, and other communication skills. We want them to attain maximum physical growth and health through motor activities and proper nutrition and to understand their own strengths and limitations. We want them to be able to express verbal and nonverbal feelings and to show respect for the rights and properties of others. Finally, we want them to become self-directing and to enjoy and respect life.

Once we have identified what we want children to accomplish, we are in a better position to identify what comprises a quality child care program. The overall goal of a quality program is the creation of a growth-fostering environment. In general, program quality depends on the characteristics and training of the staff, the physical setting, and the overall support provided by society in general.

Learning Activity: Ask participants to complete the following phrases with statements that reflect quality programming for children: (*a*) The child care staff cares for children by . . . (*b*) Programs and program activities are offered that . . . (*c*) Child care staff relates to family and community by . . . (*d*) The facility and programs are designed to meet the varied demands of children, families, and staff by . . . Discuss individual responses in the group setting.

The characteristics of a quality child care program have been identified by the National Association for the Education of Young Children (*Accreditation Criteria and Procedures,* 1984), with input from teachers, administrators, and other early childhood experts. These guidelines are used for the accreditation of child care centers and address the areas of curriculum, staff-child and staff-parent interactions, staff qualifications and development, administration, physical environment, health and safety, nutrition and food service, and evaluation. Caldwell and Hilliard

(1985) have also defined components of quality child care that are useful in planning and evaluating programs.

Job Burnout

Working with young children can be enjoyable, exciting, and fulfilling; it can also be enervating and frustrating. There are major stress-producing components inherent in child care no matter how ideal the working situation. Therefore, no one really questions the presence of stress in child care work.

Question Starter: What are some of the stress-producing aspects of caregiving? (Responses may include: staff conflict; long hours; low pay; low status; noise and confusion; ungrateful parents.)

Hyson (1982) identifies the primary causes of stress in child care. First, too much change contributes to confusion that can lead to stress. For example, young children themselves provide variety: they are predictably unpredictable. The nature of preschool programs themselves is often unpredictable, since there is no prepackaged curriculum on which teachers can rely, and because some of the important ingredients of early childhood education, such as free play, often result in unpredictable behavior.

Second, frustrating barriers can cause stress. Child care certainly has its share of frustrations and roadblocks to the achievement of goals. For instance, we generally assume that it is our responsibility to help children succeed. When children become frustrated and are not successful, we may blame ourselves. When parental goals do not mesh with staff goals, parents can become obstacles to achieving goals. Conflicts with staff can inhibit goal achievement as well. Of course, low pay, restricted mobility, and lack of job security are very real barriers to the attainment of personal goals.

Third, pressures to achieve can lead to stress. The job of caring for children does not carry with it high status and the usual indicators of achievement, such as high salary. Therefore, we may assume inordinate demands for personal perfection and may go out of our way to have the very best bulletin boards, newsletters, parent conferences, and so forth.

Fourth, separation and loss can be stress-producing. As teachers of young children, we tend to develop special bonds with those in our care. When children grow older and move into the school-age years, the separation may be particularly disturbing if we feel that these are "our" children.

Too much stress can lead to burnout. In fact, the incidence of burnout in the child care profession is very high, often contributing to 30%-50% turnover in staff each year (Seiderman, 1978). Because of the inherent nature of our stressful jobs, we need to be aware of the symptoms and stages of burnout.

Seiderman (1978) identifies some of the early signs of burnout. These include tardiness, absenteeism, low energy levels, complaining, preoccupation with job details, and inappropriate and overimaginative discussions about children. With the appearance of these signs we may suspect that burnout is occurring, especially when there is no apparent cause for the development of these attitudes and behaviors.

As burnout progresses, additional symptoms appear. Some of these are anger, defeatism, depression, chronic headaches, susceptibility to illness, boredom, gossiping, irritability, low morale, cynicism, increased criticism of the program and the administration, and resentment of children. In the final stages we may resign or be terminated or become so demoralized as to merely go through the act of providing care for children.

Question Starter: What are some of

the ways in which we can reduce stress in our lives? (Responses may include: learn and practice relaxation techniques; communicate concerns to colleagues and superiors; be assertive about the job when necessary.)

Several steps can be taken to cope with stress so that burnout can be prevented (Hyson, 1982). The first step is to reduce some of the uncertainty about the job. For example, we can plan the curriculum to provide both structure and flexibility. Next, we can strive to regain and maintain autonomy. Sometimes direct and assertive confrontation is a very powerful way of gaining control of a situation that has gotten out of hand. Furthermore, we can maintain internal equilibrium so that a certain amount of control is exerted over the job. Equilibrium may be achieved through exercise, relaxation techniques, and the support of family and friends.

Seiderman (1978) recommends ten steps that child care facilities can take to combat staff burnout. First, since burnout is a problem inherent in child care work, we should establish policies and procedures that reflect an understanding of this fact. Second, we should establish open communication systems so that we have an opportunity to voice opinions and participate in the decision-making process. Third, we should be involved in operational problem solving and in making decisions about our own environment and working conditions. Fourth, we should pay particular attention to working conditions, including wages, benefits, and praise and recognition. Fifth, we need change in routine and rhythm, which we can accomplish by infusing our jobs with new and stimulating projects and activities. Sixth, we can encourage joy and laughter. Seventh, we can work for flexible job responsibilities that can provide some variety and help prevent boredom. Eighth, we can renew our skills and attitudes by taking courses, attending workshops, or engaging in social activities. Ninth, we all need to have successful experiences. Tenth, we need to feel that we can occasionally be responsibly selfish.

We must make every effort in our jobs both personally and programmatically to address the problem of burnout. We can prevent burnout when we consciously take steps to minimize conditions that are conducive to its occurrence.

Child Advocacy

The growing concern about the professional status of child care has encouraged us to develop an awareness of the need to become advocates for children. We need to ask ourselves what it means to be an advocate for children. It means, first of all, that we make every effort to clearly understand and respect ourselves and our profession by being aware of its history and knowledge base (Ade, 1982; Silin, 1985). It also means that we understand what quality child care is, and that we take a stand in its favor. Advocacy means that we place a value on what we do and then help the public to understand the value of the work. Finally, advocacy means that we make public officials aware of the needs of children and families and work to elect public officials who are sympathetic to children and families.

Question Starter: How do we start to make a difference for children and ourselves? (Responses may include: being informed; joining professional organizations; forming coalitions; communicating with legislators.)

Willer (1983) suggests several ways in which we can affect public policy. We can be informed about state and national legislation that directly affects our jobs and the children and families we serve. Newspapers and magazines often discuss current legislation, but the best source is information discussed in professional literature provided by publications such as *Childhood Education, Young Children, Child Care Information Exchange, Report on Preschool Programs,* and *Day Care U.S.A. Newsletter.*

We can join professional organizations that have a natural interest in child care issues and lobby on behalf of children and families. Professional organizations keep us informed about current research, practices, and advocacy issues in our field. The Children's Defense Fund, the Child Care Action Campaign, the National Association for the Education of Young Children, the Association for Childhood Education International, and the National Coalition for Campus Child Care are some of these organizations.

We can join with other people and other organizations to build coalitions that work for legislation supporting quality child care. In this way, we are better able to build large and effective networks of people who share a similar interest in the welfare of children.

Finally, we can communicate directly with our legislators about issues related to children and families. Writing letters, making phone calls or personal visits, and sending telegrams are some of the ways to accomplish this task. Moreover, we can solicit help from parents, boards, and the community by encouraging each of these groups to communicate their concerns in the same manner.

Learning Activity: Develop the concept of advocacy by asking small groups of participants to select a current issue of concern to the child care profession and compose a letter to a legislator that addresses this issue. Encourage participants to be specific and precise. When finished, have them read their letters aloud for comments and feedback.

In effect, we should use all the means available to become advocates for children. We must remember that advocacy is a lifetime investment of effort and energy that will only be realized when every person involved in child care makes a contribution.

Summary

In this chapter we have explored the status of the child care profession and examined the characteristics of quality child care programs and child care professionals. We have looked at stress and burnout in the child care profession, identified symptoms of burnout, and examined ways in which we can better cope with stress and combat burnout. Most importantly, perhaps, we have explored ways to become advocates for children. A more complete awareness of each of these issues will hopefully help each of us become better teachers of and advocates for children.

Enrichment Activities

1. Using the characteristics and skills of child care professionals, identified in the unit, specify at least four areas in which you would like to improve. Plan strategies for improvement and record your progress in making these improvements. The format below can be used:

Desired Improvements	Improve cooperation with staff.
Strategies for Improvement	Work jointly, constructively, and loyally with staff by taking into consideration and acting upon their ideas when appropriate.
Record of Success	Solicit ideas about parent meetings from a colleague and implement them.

2. Select a child care issue currently before the United States Congress or state legislature. Compose a letter to your legislative representative that comprehensively addresses this issue. Share it with colleagues, parents, and board members and solicit their support.
3. Rolc play a telephone call to a legislator that addresses the same child care issue. Anticipate possible reactions and plan strategies for addressing them. Better yet, call or visit your legislator and address this issue firsthand.
4. Examine yourself and your child care facility and identify possible symptoms and conditions that can lead to burnout. Explore steps you can take to combat potential burnout. Be specific and record specific adjustments you can make to deal with potential stress-producing factors.

Bibliography

Ade, W. (1982). Professionalism and its implications for the field of early childhood education. *Young Children, 37* (3), 25–32.

The term professional is defined, and reasons are given to explain why the field has not attained true professional status. Two levels of early childhood education are identified, and it is observed that at least five major changes must occur before the goal of professionalization can be realized—especially at the prekindergarten level. These five changes in turn depend on sociological criteria such as a sound and systematic knowledge base, support from society, and the type and nature of professional services offered.

Allen, K. E. (1983). Children, the congress, and you. *Young Children, 38* (2), 71–75.

Useful advice is given on how to effectively advocate for raising the status of children. Included are tips on how to write to one's Congress member, on letting one's expertise show on matters pertaining to children, on getting to know legislators and their staff, and on making professional affiliations known. Teachers are asked to support their beliefs with their time, energy, and money.

Caldwell, B. M. (1983). How can we educate the American public about the child care profession? *Young Children, 38* (3), 11–17.

The author points out that the public view of child care is limited because of confusion regarding terminology associated with child care, negative connotations of terms such as "day care" and "institutionalized child care," and distorted press coverage. She urges child care professionals to attain self-understanding, demand quality, seek business support, launch their own media campaigns, and become active advocates for children.

Caldwell, B. M. (1984). What is quality child care? *Young Children, 39* (3), 3–8.

Defining professional child care as a comprehensive service, the author emphasizes that quality programs should foster children's development physically, intellectually, socially, and emotionally. It is imperative that child care professionals educate the public about their profession. They can do this by demonstrating the connection between child care and other human services. They can show the public the positive aspects of quality child care. And they can commit themselves to research dealing with both the process and the products of child care programs.

Caldwell, B., & Hilliard, A. G. (1985). *What is quality child care?* Washington, DC: National Association for the Education of Young Children.

The authors explore the true meaning of professional care for young children. They examine society's lack of child orientation and public unwillingness to pay for quality.

Feeney, S., & Kipnis, K. (1985). Professional ethics in early childhood education. *Young Children, 40* (3), 54–56.

Introducing a survey by the National Association for the Education of Young Children, the authors point to ambiguities concerning ethics in early childhood education. Problems in five areas generally arise: personal, legal, employment, social theory, and professional ethics. A code of ethics could simplify the decision-making process. The writers urge early childhood educators and philosophers to study standards for their profession and identify ethical conflicts most likely to be faced by practitioners.

Fernandez, H. C. (1980). *The child advocacy handbook.* New York: Pilgrim Press.

A book that can be of help to anyone who cares for children and is interested in becoming an advocate for them. The basic ingredients for advocacy are simple but important: caring, knowing, and acting. Practical suggestions are offered on how systems can be changed in favor of children. Actual examples are presented to show that action on behalf of children does work. Information is given on resources, materials, and national and local organizations that work for children.

Honig, A. S., & Lally, J. R. (1975). How good is your infant program? Use an observation method to find out. *Child Care Quarterly, 1,* 196–207.

The authors give a useful list of caregiver behavior and character traits that can be checked or self-checked. An observation instrument is provided for discovering areas in which improvement or further training is needed.

Hostetler, L. (1983a, February). Putting our child care skills to work in advocacy. *Child Care Information Exchange,* pp. 25–29.

In this encouraging article for child advocates, the author lists and discusses fifteen skills possessed by early childhood professionals that can be used to influence policies on behalf of children and families.

Hostetler, L. (1983b, March/April). How-to guide for advocates. *Child Care Information Exchange,* pp. 25–29.

The author stresses the increasing need for child advocacy, and suggests ways in which success can be accomplished. She discusses means of making the public aware of children's programs; getting acquainted and keeping in touch with those who can influence change; actively involving policy makers; using nontraditional methods to arouse interest; and involving staff and parents.

Hostetler, L., & Klugman, E. (1982). Early childhood job titles: One step toward professional status. *Young Children, 37* (6), 13–22.

The paper reports on a pilot study project by the Illinois Association for the Education of Young Children and the President of the National Association for the Education of Young Children. The study focuses on the status and perception of early childhood personnel, whose dissatisfaction with their status was reflected in the findings. Results show low salaries and discrepancies between employer/employee perceptions of fringe benefits and staff turnover. The authors point out that the central issue of self-definition and self-analysis can be dealt with, in part, by established nomenclature. Based on survey responses, a "nomenclature hierarchy" is recommended, along with various task descriptors. Establishing nomenclature is only one step toward professionalization. Professional standards and systems of evaluation are, of course, essential.

Hymes, J. L. (1975). *Early childhood education: An introduction to the profession.* Washington, DC: National Association for the Education of Young Children.

This book traces the development of the early childhood profession and explains why teaching young children is satisfying. It provides an introduction and overview of the profession.

Hyson, M. C. (1982). Playing with kids all day: Job stress in early childhood education. *Young Children, 37* (2), 25–32.

The author identifies the causes of stress in child care educators, discusses the effects of stress, and suggests ways—both individual and collective—of coping with stress.

Jorde, P. (1982). *Avoiding burnout: Strategies for managing time, space, and people in early childhood education.* Washington, DC: Acropolis Books.

This book details an account of elements that cause both job-related and personal burnout, as well as ways of controlling these factors. It provides practical information, self-assessment devices to recognize personal strengths and weaknesses, and suggestions on how to manage time, space, and other people.

Katz, L. G., & Ward, C. H. (1978). *Ethical behavior in early childhood education.* Washington, DC: National Association for the Education of Young Children.

This concise book explores the dilemmas of the early childhood profession. It provides useful information on resolving these dilemmas.

Kontos, S., & Stevens, R. (1985). High quality child care: Does your center measure up? *Young Children, 40* (2), 5–9.

Three recent studies measuring child care quality and its influence on children's development and behavior found that children in high quality centers show more positive behavior, vocalize better with adults, and have higher test scores in language development than do children in medium- or low-quality child care.

Martin, M. P., & Klaus, S. L. (1974). *Worker burnout among child protective service workers.* National Center on Child Abuse and Neglect.

This study details the scope, causes, characteristics, and effects of worker burnout. Means of alleviating and combatting burnout are also explored. A useful list of resources and organizations is provided in the appendix.

Melton, G. B. (1983). *Child advocacy: Psychological issues and interventions.* New York: Plenum.

The importance of child advocacy is explored, and a wide assortment of relevant research is reviewed. Advocacy strategies are discussed, and it is suggested that child advocacy can, in fact, become an integral part of regular helping services.

Montessori, S. (1985, May). How to lobby for child care. *Child Care Information Exchange,* pp. 9–10.

Practical advice is offered on how to dress, talk, and behave when lobbying on behalf of children.

Seiderman, S. (1978). Combatting staff burn-out. *Day Care and Early Education, 5* (4), 6–9.

This thoughtful article examines in detail the conditions leading to staff burnout and the symptoms that characterize it. Ten important steps to combat burnout are explained and analyzed. Administrators and teachers should find the article both informative and helpful.

Silin, J. G. (1985). Authority as knowledge: A problem of professionalization. *Young Children, 40* (3), 41–46.

Professionalization may have both positive and negative effects. Factors that must be considered are the teacher's knowledge as authority, ambiguities regarding appropriate knowledge and curriculum for young children, and the influence of current educational and/or technological trends on institutionalized kindergartens. The modern technical/scientific approach discourages dealing with values and is often based on the work of theorists, while what is needed is a knowledge base tested by practitioners. Problems of professionalization in the field include a devaluation of the historical involvement of early childhood in educational reform, increased social control, less sympathetic involvement with children, and loss of control in designing and implementing curricula.

Willer, B. (1983). Expanding our child advocacy efforts: NAEYC forms a public network for children. *Young Children, 38* (6), 71–74

Child advocacy is an important component of early childhood education. The article takes a look at public policy goals related to children's needs and suggests strategies to realize these goals. Immediate goals may require strategies such as lobbying and coalition building, while long-term goals can be attained through advocacy networks, selection of decision makers, and the promotion of child and family needs.

Wilson, L. C., & Headley, N. (1983). *Working with young children.* Washington, DC: ACEI Publications.

Parents, teachers, and administrators will find this small booklet helpful and practical. It deals with currently available programs and who provides them, and examines qualities that make a good program, characteristics of good caregivers, parent involvement, financing, housing, licensing, and regulation.

Zigler, E., & Finn, M. (1981). From problem to solution: Changing public policy as it affects children and families. *Young Children, 36* (4), 31–32, 55–59.

The struggle to improve the status of children and families in the United States is an ongoing one. The author describes the problems, risks, and constraints involved, and discusses prerequisites to forming and changing public policies. Educators are urged to unite their efforts and knowledge to develop support strategies and bring about changes in the nation's attitudes and policies regarding children.

2

Understanding Children

AS teachers of young children, we are required to understand the growth and development of the child from birth through the preschool years. The information presented in this chapter is based on the premise that in order to work effectively with children, we must understand their growth and development at each age in the functional areas: physical/motor, cognitive, language, and social/emotional. In order to respond appropriately to children at each developmental level, we also need to know the types of activities and materials that are suitable for children at various ages and stages.

Objectives

In this chapter we not only will identify characteristics of normal child development but will analyze why it is important for us to understand typical developmental milestones. We will define the physical/motor, cognitive, language, and social/emotional developmental areas and study the development of the child in each of these areas from infancy to 5 years of age. In the context of this approach, we will discuss appropriate adult responses to the development of the child at each age level.

Key Ideas

Child development encompasses the physical/motor, cognitive, language, and social/emotional areas. The concept of normal child development is somewhat misleading because there is a normal age range for developmental milestones to occur. There are also several principles of development that are consistent for all human beings: development proceeds in an upper to lower cycle, and from the central area to the outer extremities; development is orderly and continuous but the rate of development varies; and normal development is affected by hereditary and environmental influences.

Understanding normal child development provides us with information that helps us to be more responsive and nurturant to children. It enables us, first of all, to have realistic expectations of children. It helps us to make judgments about whether a particular behavior is appropriate or inappropriate for a particular child. Understanding the precise developmental status of a child helps us plan activities to stimulate her current stage of development, as well as anticipate the next phase in her development.

Patterns of Development

Question Starter: How would you define child development? (Responses may include: there is no such thing; children have certain skills at specific ages; only generalizations about child development exist.)

One of the best ways to approach an understanding of child development is to recognize that there is a range of development that is normal for each age and stage. We must also acknowledge that there is no such thing as the average child. For example, if we measured the height of a hundred 3-year-olds, we would find a range of heights with only a few children conforming to the exact norm or average. All children are individuals and develop at different rates in different areas.

Children also approach new learning skills with their own individual needs, abilities, and sense of timing. For example, some children learn to walk as early as 9 months, while others do not begin to walk until 15 months; both are considered normal. Verbally skilled toddlers learn to use two-word sentences when they are 18 months old, but most children accomplish this task around 2 years of age. All of these children are in the range of normal. On the other hand, the child who can speak in short sentences at 15 months is very precocious indeed, while the child who cannot speak in two-word sentences at age 3 may be delayed developmentally. Other factors, such as vision, hearing, and psychological and emotional problems that may be contributing to a possible delay, should then be explored.

Our understanding of children is enhanced when we comprehend several broad concepts about development. We should know, for example, that development proceeds from the head to the toes. That is, children have control over their backs before they have control over their legs; they are able to sit up before they are able to walk. Development also proceeds from the central part of the body to the outer extremities. In other words, children master some control of the central parts of their bodies before they are able to manipulate their fingers.

When we know that growth and development are orderly and continuous, we are better able to understand why children can master certain skills before others. This understanding helps us to plan activities that children can do at certain stages in their development.

Although development is orderly and continuous, the rate of development varies with the individual. Some children develop more quickly than others in certain areas, but their development follows a pattern similar for all children.

Heredity and environment also influence development, making each child a unique individual. Every person develops according to an individual timetable dependent upon that person's hereditary and environmental background.

Rationale for Understanding Child Development

Question Starter: Why is it important to understand normal child development? (Responses may include: having realistic expectations; understanding specific behaviors; recognizing developmental stages; planning activities; recommending or taking corrective measures.)

Understanding normal stages of development and abilities that correlate with specific ages provides us with more realistic expectations of children. This knowledge reduces the frustration and anger that can result from expecting too much from children. For example, if we expect to teach a 3-year-old to recognize numbers on flash cards in a fifteen minute period, we will both fail. If we push children to become toilet trained before they are ready, they are likely to get frustrated and stop trying.

Socioeconomic and cultural factors also influence the development of a child. Toilet training is expected much earlier in some cultures than in others. Knowing that these differences are normal, and allowing for them, can improve our work with children.

Understanding normal stages of development and expectations at various ages helps us formulate correct and helpful responses to children. For example, when a toddler asserts his newfound independence and use of language by giving a firm no, an astute teacher understands that this is a normal response. When we know that toddlers experience a stage of autonomy that manifests itself in negative behavior, we are able to respond to it as a developmental need rather than as a behavior problem. On the other hand, when a 5-year-old uses no frequently, we know that this behavior is inappropriate for his age.

It is also important to know how the developmental areas are related to each other. Each developmental accomplishment is important and provides the foundation for emerging skills. For example, children need the experience of creeping, which has its own purpose, separate from walking. Not only is creeping a mode of transportation, but it strengthens eye-hand coordination and the development of large muscle coordination. Therefore, we would not want to encourage a child to walk before she becomes proficient at creeping. We need to know what the developmental milestones are at the typical ages because each stage of development has its own essential purpose. Our goal as teachers of young children is to help them move through each stage at optimal levels.

Finally, being aware of development at all ages assists us in understanding why children behave in certain ways. Even when we do not work with children of various ages, having information about each developmental stage helps us better understand the needs of the children in our care. For example, even though we may not work with infants or toddlers, knowing about development at those ages provides an understanding of the children with whom we work.

It is also particularly critical to understand that the learning patterns and social behaviors established during a child's first 2 years of life form the foundation for future learning and behavior. If we understand how children get to where they are, we can approach their current situation with knowledge, and be more responsive to them. To illustrate, if a 3-year-old is unusually withdrawn and easily frustrated, we may find that he did not receive appropriate physical and emotional care as an infant and consequently has not developed secure relationships with people. Understanding the need for secure attachments during infancy can help us respond more appropriately to the 3-year-old child.

By recognizing the patterns of normal child development, we are more aware of what children should be able to do at a particular stage and anticipate what should follow. As a result, we can plan activities to stimulate children's current abilities and plan for the newly emerging skills that will follow. For example, since most 2-year-olds are beginning jumpers, we would plan activities that help develop that skill, such as providing objects of varying heights and widths so that children can practice jumping. Moreover, information about child development provides a framework for knowing when to begin encouraging the development of new skills. For instance, when we know that 4-year-olds should be able to draw a simple man, we can encourage the 3 1/2-year-old to draw a face.

Understanding normal child development also enables us to identify developmental characteristics that vary from typical patterns, and plan activities or corrective measures early in the child's life. The earlier we are aware of developmental delays, the more we can help the child in that particular area. When we know that a child is unusually precocious, we can do much to encourage optimal development.

As adults who spend a lot of time with children, we have the opportunity and responsibility to provide more than physical care. While much of children's development emerges naturally, all of it can be stimulated and enriched. Thus, when we understand normal child development, we become better teachers of young children. First, we have more realistic expectations of children. Second, we understand better the reasons for their behavior. Third, we are able to plan appropriate activities for children. Finally, we learn to recognize advanced or delayed development and are better prepared to take appropriate steps to help children.

Normal Child Development

We will approach the study of normal child development by identifying typical characteristics of children at various ages, and appropriate adult responses, in the context of the four developmental areas described below. We will investigate each area of development for the child at various ages: the infant (birth to 24 months); the 2- to 3-year-old; the 3- to 4-year-old; and the 4- to 5-year-old.

Physical/motor development refers to the large and small muscles of the body. Large muscle development refers to gross motor development: walking is a gross motor skill. Small muscle development refers to fine motor development: stacking small cubes or blocks is a fine motor skill.

Cognitive development includes knowing, learning, or the thought processes. It is those behaviors that develop from rather simple reflex responses to extremely complex logical reasoning. It encompasses imagery, perception, thought, reasoning, reflection, problem solving, and all verbal and other learned behaviors.

Language development includes receptive language (comprehension) and expressive language (saying words). Children develop receptive language before expressive language.

Social/emotional development refers to the development of personality characteristics, social interaction skills, and self-help skills such as eating, dressing, and toileting. The development of an attachment to significant others (mother, father, careprovider) is particularly critical to positive social/emotional growth in the early years.

Learning Activity: Divide participants into four groups and assign each group one of the following age categories: infancy (birth–24 months); 2–3 years; 3–4 years; 4–5 years. Ask participants to identify developmental characteristics of children in each of the developmental areas in their assigned age group and chart them on newsprint or paper. The Normal Child Development Guide in table 1 summarizes the major milestones in a child's life and can be used as a reference to check responses and as a guide for the remainder of the unit.

Birth to 24 Months

Infancy is the period from birth to 24 months. During this early period of development the child will grow and change more than at any other time in his entire life. It is also the period of time when the child's development is most affected by the circumstances of his life. If experiences are positive, the child has an excel-

Table 1. Normal Child Development Guide:
Major Milestones in a Child's Life

	Physical/Motor	Cognitive/Learning	Language	Social/Emotional
Definition	Development of large body muscles (gross motor) and small body muscles (fine motor).	Development of knowing (includes imagery, perception, thought, reasoning, reflection, problem solving, and all verbal behavior). Its development in infancy is particularly inseparable from the development of the senses and motor skills.	Development of language that is both understood by the receiver and verbally expressed.	Development of those behavior patterns, beliefs, standards, and motives that are valued by, and appropriate in, one's own cultural group and family. It includes self-help skills of eating, dressing, and toileting. Attachment is also a key factor in social/emotional development; it is a social relationship essential to positive growth.
Birth to 6 weeks	Gross—When lying on stomach lifts head 45°. Fine—Follows object with eyes 45°. Gets fist to mouth.	Reflex behavior.	Undifferential crying (general signaling). Simple sounds. Discriminates range of sounds.	Looks toward eyes of person holding him. First smile.
6 weeks to 3.5 months	Gross—When lying on stomach lifts head and chest, supporting self with forearms. In sitting position, head is steady. Hands usually open. Fine—Follows objects with eyes a range of 180°. Brings hands together.	Coordinates various simple systems (hand-mouth coordination, hear-eye coordination). Sucks at sight of bottle or breast. Watches own hands. Explores toys by banging, sucking, pulling. Recognizes familiar people; smiles more readily to mother.	Cooing including "u" or "oo" sounds. Attends to speaking voice. Differentiated crying (specific signaling). Laughs, squeals.	Enjoys being propped up. More responsive to surroundings, looks alert, smiles socially.
3.5 to 6 months	Gross—Rolls over. Bears some weight on legs. Kicks vigorously. Gets feet to mouth. Sits with support.	Brings toys played with in hands into field of vision to see and manipulate. Observes objects as small as a	Turns to voice. Plays with sound.	Likes to be played with, spoken to, be near people. Very pleasant. Lively curiosity. Resists toy pull. Plays

Table 1. (*continued*)

	Physical/Motor	Cognitive/Learning	Language	Social/Emotional
	Head steady. Fine—Reaches for and grasps objects routinely. Transfers objects from hand to hand.	raisin. Hand-mouth coordination refined.		peek-a-boo. Works for toy out of reach. Increased interest in objects.
6 to 9 months	Gross—Sits without support. Stands, holding on. Pulls to stand. Pulls self to sitting position. Creeps or crawls. Fine—Stretches arms out to be taken. Grasps raisin between thumb and finger. Bangs cubes held in hand.	Interested in making simple things happen (cause-effect). When object disappears looks to see where it has gone and tries to recover it. Stranger anxiety emerges.	Combines consonant and vowel sounds, "ma-ma," "da-da" (babbles). Vocalizes satisfaction and recognition of people. Imitates sounds. Responds to sound. Attaches meaning to first words. "Talks," makes noises to attract attention. (Indicates wants by moving body toward objects or person. Reaches, leans, creeps.)	Eats finger foods. Drinks from cup with help. Vocalizes at mirror image. Holds bottle. Abrupt mood change. Differentiated smiling. Cries when mother leaves. Withdraws from strangers. Likes frolicky play.
9 to 12 months	Gross—Walks, holding onto furniture. Stands alone. Walks alone. Stoops and recovers. Creeps upstairs. Fine—Grasps raisin between thumb and index finger with overhand grasp.	Interested in hinged objects (doors, books). Puts things in and out of containers. Looks for objects out-of-sight (object permanence). Shows interest in pictures.	Vocalizes "da-da" or "ma-ma" specifically. Babbles using patterns of pitch, stress, rhythm, and intonation. Responds to words (example: "where is daddy?"). Understands five to six words. May say two to three words. Understands "no" or inflection of "no." Shakes head for no. Obeys simple requests (example: "Give me your cup"). Responds to music vocally.	Holds spoon with help. Moves constantly during diaper changes. Plays pat-a-cake. Repeats performance that is laughed at. Recognizes self in mirror. Waves "bye-bye." Stops when told "no." Indicates wants in ways other than crying (pointing, gesturing naming). Plays ball.

12 to 15 months	Gross—Walks backward. Rolls ball. Seats self on small chair. Kneels without support. Walks, pulls toy. Fine—Stacks two blocks. Dumps raisin from bottle without demonstration.	Practices learning-to-learn skills (example: scribbles spontaneously). Increasingly practices simple skills on objects (cause-effect).	Says three words other than "ma-ma," "da-da." Responds to name. Tries to sing along. Tries to repeat new words after adult.	Drinks from cup without help. Uses spoon, spilling little. Imitates housework. Imitates adults. Kisses on request. Shows or offers a toy. No longer shy with strangers.
15 to 18 months	Gross—Walks up and down steps holding on. Climbs in and out and up. Runs. Opens cabinets and drawers. Fine—Stacks four cubes.	Continues to practice simple skills on objects. Tries out new behaviors to reach some goal. Intentionally finds new solutions to new problems.	Vocabulary of twenty or more words. Points to named pictures. Points to one to three named body parts. Adds new words more rapidly. Listens to simple stories. Combines many sounds using correct intonation.	Removes simple garments. Understands simple rules. Expresses negativism; tests, resists adult. Desires to be independent. Sometimes aggressive. Becomes frustrated easily. Eager to please.
18 to 24 months	Gross—Walks up and down stairs alone, using one hand. Kicks ball forward. Throws ball overhand. Jumps in place. Fine—Stacks eight cubes. Copies vertical line within 30°.	Can picture events in mind and follow through with them. Can try out solutions to problems in mind and discard ones that do not work. Object permanence is fully developed, knows something exists even when not visible.	Vocabulary expands rapidly. Combines two different words. Names pictures of simple objects. Follows simple directions. Elaborate monologues fade.	May put on simple clothing with supervision. Washes and dries hands. Negativism begins to decrease.
2 to 3 years	Gross—Climbs stairs alone using both feet per stair. Pedals tricycle. Walks backward, sideways. Tip-toes. Balances on one foot, one second. Jumps eight inches on both feet. Runs well. Fine—Imitates vertical line. Copies O. Imitates a bridge with three cubes. Scribbles with straight	Differentiates words from objects. Creates mental images of objects not present. Begins make-believe play. Egocentric. Differentiates between one and many. Picks longer line. Remembers and anticipates events.	Makes three- to-four-word sentences. Vocabulary increases rapidly. Comprehends and uses some descriptive and action words. Uses plurals. Gives first and last names. Understands ownership, "mine," "I," "me," "you." Uses past tense. Understands simple temporal relationships: "in	Dresses with supervision. Uses spoon well. Holds cup with one hand. Begins to toilet self. Assertive of self. Explorer, investigator. Difficulty sharing or taking turns. Aggressive with peers. Dominated by older children. Shy with strangers. Loving and affectionate with familiar adults. Rigid,

Table 1. (*continued*)

	Physical/Motor	Cognitive/Learning	Language	Social/Emotional
	strokes. Able to do simple puzzle (two to six pieces).		a minute," "after a while." Asks questions "what's that?" Refusals expressed by "no!"; may say "no!" when he means "yes!" Verbalizes immediate experience. Enjoys short simple stories.	inflexible. Tantrums when frustrated. Extreme likes and dislikes. Enjoys rhythmic music. Begins to understand danger (fear emerges.)
3 to 4 years	Gross—Runs well, changing speed and direction. Hops on one foot. Catches bounced ball. Walks heel to toe within one inch. Balances on one foot for five seconds. Jumps from bottom step (twelve inches). Broad jumps twelve inches. Alternates feet going upstairs. Can climb a vertical ladder. Claps hands and stamps feet simultaneously. Fine—Uses scissors. Strings four beads. Swings. Completes simple puzzles. Copies +. Able to do puzzles (six to twelve pieces).	Egocentric. Attributes life to inanimate objects. Reasons that all objects are created by man. Counts with corresponding pointing to three. Able to sort objects. Sequences events. Classifies by groups. Knows appropriate dress for weather. Recognizes sex of self and others. Notices small details or discrepancies. Anticipates consequences. Deals with abstractions. Puts self in place of another person. Makes interesting associations. Plans and carries out activities. Concentrates on one task while keeping track of another.	Asks "how" questions. Nine-hundred word vocabulary. Ninety percent of speech is intelligible. Comprehends some prepositions. Understands opposites. Tells own age and number of siblings. Recognizes basic colors and shapes. Knows a few rhymes. Differentiates between summer/winter; morning/night. Tells long stories. Learns irregular plurals. Compares two objects. Very expressive verbally.	Feeds self, pours from pitcher. Helps set table. Sometimes refuses to feed self. Dresses with little supervision. Familiar with at least one holiday. Toilets self, rare accidents. Learns to share, takes turns. Plays cooperatively and makes friends. Likes to perform. Self-concept begins to form. Gets and holds adult's attention. Uses adults as resources. Expresses affection and annoyance to adults and peers. Leads and follows peers. Competes with peers. Shows pride in accomplishment.

4 to 5 years	Gross—Balances on one foot ten seconds. Walks backward heel to toe. Descends stairways, alternating feet without holding on. Running broad jump. Broad jumps twenty inches. Leaps over objects ten inches high. Turns somersault. Marches in time. Skips on one foot. Fine—Touches tip of nose with eyes closed. Copies rectangles or triangles. May write some letters.	Concentrates on single outstanding characteristics of object (fails to understand parts and whole). Reasons from particular to particular ("I haven't had my nap so it isn't afternoon"). Confusion between reality and fantasy. Draws simple man, three parts. Draws and recognizes pictures. Builds complicated structures and names them (houses, towers). Can reason things out. Groups according to likeness and differences. Remembers and repeats four-digit sequence. Counts to thirteen. Counts up to nine objects. Matches objects for a one-to-one correspondence.	Defines at least six words. Understands composition of objects. Increases sentence length to four to five words and vocabulary to fifteen hundred words. Ninety-eight percent of speech is intelligible. Asks "why" questions. Demands detailed explanations. Can answer more complicated questions. Uses exclamations ("oh!" "hey!"). Comprehends "funny."	Dresses self, may tie shoes. Buttons up. Zips. Knows front from back. Brushes teeth. Likes to serve self and choose menu. Tells tall tales. Selfish, boasts. Calls attention to own performance. Plays well with peers, shares. Bosses and criticizes others.

lent chance of becoming a competent human being. If experiences are negative, then the prognosis for the child's development is not particularly bright.

Rapid changes take place in gross motor development during infancy. Most children, given enough space and encouragement, will learn to reach, sit, crawl, walk, and run. They will do so because of their own curiosity and desire to explore and their emerging maturation skills. For the most part, infants require little prompting in this area, but they do need a safe environment in which to move freely, a variety of objects to manipulate, and places to explore.

Fine motor skills develop naturally when the child is encouraged and allowed to explore and manipulate. Many objects, ranging from household items to complex manipulative toys, should be placed within the child's reach for investigation. For a 3-month-old, this means placing a rattle in the child's grip and moving her hand into her line of vision so that she can see that she is holding something. For the 6-month-old, it means setting several objects a few inches away but within sight so that she is stimulated to reach and grasp. The 10-month-old needs various spots to explore: a low toy shelf, a box of toys, a cupboard of cooking utensils. Toys and household materials can be placed in various spots around the room within the child's reach. By simply having these items available, children have a better chance of developing fine motor coordination on their own with relatively little prompting from the adult.

Cognitive growth is also more rapid in the first 2 years of a child's life than at any other time. Growth ranges from simple reflexes in the newborn to very complex skills at 24 months. During these 2 years, the child develops into a person who can picture events, try out solutions to problems, and master object permanence; that is, she learns that something exists even when it is not visible.

We can help infants develop cognitive abilities by providing many opportunities that advance their growing awareness of the world and their problem-solving skills. We can help them learn to picture events by encouraging them to think about and remember familiar objects and people in their world. We can encourage the development of object permanence by talking about mother even when she is not present. When, between 9 and 12 months, children become interested in hinged objects, we can provide books so that they can learn to turn the pages. When children begin to look for objects after they have disappeared, we can place these objects out of sight.

Language development is critical for children because much of their cognitive and social development depends heavily on their language abilities. Although babies do not express much language during the first year, they can understand it. Therefore, we should speak to infants from birth. They may not be able to understand our words, but they begin to learn language by listening.

Intonations, facial expressions, volume, gestures, and touch are aspects of communicating with infants. When our communications are responsive and loving, the infant will want to elicit more communication from us. He will do this by maintaining eye contact at first, then smiling, and eventually responding vocally to our words. Once the baby starts responding vocally, we can encourage more vocalizing by rewarding him when he vocalizes, by talking to him, often repeating the same sounds he uses, smiling, touching him, and responding when he calls.

Basically, verbal interactions with infants are of two types. The first is normal adult usage of language in carrying on one-sided conversations. By talking to infants in complete sentences we teach receptive language. Although children cannot say the words or sentences we use, they learn to understand what we say, thereby learning labels for objects and intonation patterns.

The second type of verbal interaction focuses on the child's level of language production that changes as language abilities develop. We speak to infants at their level of production and at a slightly more advanced level so that they are stimulated to learn new words. In this manner, we encourage expressive language by stimulating children to produce or repeat new sounds and words.

At about 2 or 3 months infants begin cooing, or making various vowel sounds. Babies coo at things that interest them, thereby expressing pleasure and interest in the world around them. Babies who grow curious and trusting, and who use oral language, become competent language users later on. We can encourage language growth by tuning in to these early cooing sounds and by taking turns making cooing sounds with the baby.

Around 6 months, children begin to babble and produce simple syllables such as "mama," "dada," "nana." Again, we need to repeat sounds that the baby makes and take language turns. When infants get fairly proficient at babbling, we can initiate simple repetitive words like "bye-bye" and use them in the proper context.

Between 8 and 12 months words appear. These words are simple and most often represent concrete, familiar objects and people to the baby. We should repeat these words often to babies. During this period of time infants also learn pointing, which is a very powerful tool in language learning. When babies point to an object, we should repeat the name of that object. In this way, children learn that objects have names, and that those names can be learned from people.

From 12 to 18 months the vocabulary expands to objects and people. As children begin to make up words for objects, we should read them books that have bright, bold illustrations of familiar things and simple but emphatic sentences. We should discuss the pictures and make the sentences come alive. By about 18 months of age, children begin to recognize pictures in books and enjoy pointing to them. We should encourage pleasure in labeling pictures. We should also encourage infants to play with sounds and words and thus learn language rhythms, rhymes, and cadences.

Toward the end of the second year, two-word sentences appear in children's vocabulary, and gradually their language increases beyond those two words. To encourage language growth at this age, we should expand on the child's words by taking the words he says and making more descriptive, complete sentences.

During the next 3 years language will continue to develop and expand rapidly. As teachers, we need to be available to help children become excellent language users because they profit from the giving and requesting of information. They also profit from being with adults who are responsive to their language needs.

One of the most critical areas of development in infancy is social/emotional. During this period children learn to be cooperative, trusting, independent, and interactive human beings.

During infancy, the development of attachment is of particular interest. Attachment refers to the emotional bond that develops between an infant and a significant person, usually a parent. Many studies have demonstrated that it is extremely important that an infant form an attachment to at least one adult, who is special and responds promptly to her. Normally, this person is one or both parents, but it can also be any person who provides care for the child. Attachment gradually develops during the first 18 months of life. At first, the infant's attention is drawn to people rather than objects. Then, the infant begins to distinguish special people from strangers. Finally, the infant forms a strong emotional bond with those few special people.

Infancy is a period of rapid growth that can be assisted by competent adults who recognize normal developmental patterns and respond appropriately to them. We can help children get off to a good start by understanding their early needs.

The 2- to 3-Year-Old

The onset of age 2 brings with it a whole array of new and interesting challenges for the adult who works with a child of this age. The period of infancy has ended and a new age of independence has arrived.

The child of 2–3 years is just beginning to figure out how the world is organized; he is learning that there are rules, schedules, and order to everyday living. He feels uncomfortable with a lot of change and is most secure if every movement follows a prescribed pattern; thus, he insists upon following schedules, on doing everything exactly the way it was done before. Our understanding and patience with these new patterns addresses the 2-year-old's developmental needs.

Because of the 2-year-old's emerging sense of independence, we may find that he is sometimes difficult. By working with him rather than against him, we can encourage him to be loving, compliant, and eager to please. Although now and then there could be an unavoidable temper tantrum, patience and the ability to stay calm help prevent outbursts. The 2-year-old needs loving firmness and understanding to help him channel energies in a constructive manner.

While the infant grows rapidly by gaining weight and height, the 2-year-old begins to slow down. He continues to grow but at a much slower pace. Gross motor development of the 2-year-old child is best described by constant action. He enjoys movement for its own sake. Stairs are enjoyed for the climbing movement, not necessarily to get to the top. He can tiptoe, jump over a string, stand momentarily on one foot, and run well.

Fine motor skills are also developing quickly. The child now likes to color, unscrew tops, work with clay, and stack four blocks. The 2-year-old will not sit back and watch. He is an explorer with his whole body. We can provide space, materials, and freedom to accomplish these tasks, so that the child has the opportunity to meet these developmental needs.

Changes in the cognitive development of the child also occur when he approaches 2 years of age. While the child younger than 2 needs to experience things in order to learn about them, the 2-year-old develops internal representations—pictures or other images in his mind—about the things in his world and can represent concrete objects and actions through some words. For example, he can call a dog by its name.

The child develops a new method of learning and thinking. What the 2-year-old sees and learns is processed in his brain like information into a computer, where it is analyzed, organized, and filed. This organizational thought process allows him to classify concrete objects such as blocks or buttons by size, shape, or color, as well as to organize thoughts into language. Simple puzzles are not merely a physical challenge but a cognitive challenge as well. Given a puzzle with two pieces, one a square and one a circle, the 2-year-old does not arbitrarily try to fit either shape into the slots. He looks at the shape, creates an image of it in his mind, and then looks for the identical slot.

Although he is now able to solve simple problems in his head, the 2-year-old still learns best with the hands-on approach. For example, if we hide a toy under a cup and rotate the cup, he is not likely to point to the cup and say "that one," but will grab the cup to look underneath.

Another abstract development during this year is understanding time relationships. The 2-year-old can remember what happened earlier in the day and anticipate what will happen later. Routines are very important to him, and he knows that after lunch, nap time happens in the afternoon. If nap time does not occur, then it is not afternoon. Verbalizing anticipated events helps the 2-year-old learn to anticipate what comes next.

Between 2 and 3, most children begin to learn about number and amount. They learn to tell the difference between "one" and "many" and begin to use plurals in their speech. They can identify "one" penny or point to the picture with "lots of" cars. Though many children begin using words like "another," "all," and "big," they may not yet have the capacity to compare objects, such as pointing to the bigger doll. Children of this age begin to learn about things by taking them apart or opening them up. Boxes, stacking toys, toys that unscrew, or toys that come apart and snap back together are all enjoyed by the 2-year-old.

The 2-year-old's maturing thinking abilities permit him to engage in make-believe and role play. Objects often become something else—a stick becomes a horse, a wand, or shovel; and roles are acted out—putting a doll to bed, setting a table. We can facilitate this emerging ability by providing a corner of the room for housekeeping, with dolls and doll-sized beds, table, dishes and stove, ironing boards, dress-up clothes, and hats and shoes. Role playing is important to young children because it helps them to take the point of view of another person and thus develop an important social skill.

Language development in the 2-year-old is the most striking change for this year. It coincides with cognitive development. As the child learns more about the world, his vocabulary increases. As he becomes able to conceptualize thoughts and actions other than physical objects, he learns to verbalize them also, using action and descriptive words like "pretty," "go," "run," and "hungry."

To facilitate language development we can speak to a child in complete adult sentences, and sometimes at the child's speech level or slightly above it. We can talk about what we are doing and why, and put actions into words, such as "Oh! Jane is sliding down the slide. I can tell you really like to slide." Verbalizing actions helps the child to think in words about what she is doing and consequently to learn new words. We can also provide opportunities to talk by asking questions and listening to, and taking an interest in, what the child says by answering her questions.

Books play a primary role in learning language. Through them, the child learns to correlate words with pictures, hears the rhythm of language, becomes familiar with the written language, and learns about sequencing of action. Good books for 2-year-olds have large, clear, distinct pictures or photos and a short narrative of one or two sentences per page with simple words. Appropriate books include topics with which the child is familiar: animals, playgrounds, birthdays, families, cars, trucks, trains, buses, and planes.

The child responds best when we read slowly and distinctly. He becomes involved when we ask questions and have him point to objects: "Joe, do you see the blue bird?" "Can you point to the bus?"

"What is the horse eating?" These kinds of directives help the child learn to use the language.

Social/emotional development of the 2-year-old is marked by independence that grows rapidly during this year. Children like to do things by themselves. They may be slow but their competence and self-concept grow when they are allowed to put on their own socks or coats, pass out paper for art or cups for a snack, and spread their own blankets.

Self-identity is unfolding as children of this age realize their separateness from others. "Mine" becomes a popular word in their vocabulary. We should set aside certain items that belong only to them, such as their own locker, coat hook, or cubby hole, as they learn about possession.

Two-year-olds will play next to their peers and may even become involved in a joint project now and then, but not without their share of arguments and aggression. They like to tell others what to do and how to do it. They also have a habit of becoming intrigued with a toy that another child has, but they will not let another child take their toy away without protesting. In other words, 2-year-olds need to be supervised closely during play. Their social skills are not yet polished, and they need help in learning how to play together and share.

Two-year-olds tend to get lost in the crowd with older preschoolers. This year is often referred to as the "watching stage," for they spend a lot of time watching others. They are busy gathering information. They also do not have the verbal skills to keep up with older children, so they often become dominated or pushed around. Because of this, it is best to have a separate 2-year-old program for most of the day.

Question Starter: How would you plan a program for 2-year-olds to meet their developmental needs? (Responses may include: separate room; 2-year-old space, such as corners of rooms; low staff-child ratio; hands-on activities.)

If a separate room for 2-year-olds is not available, a corner of the room can be used, such as a book corner or a corner with large blocks. During this time, activities designed especially for 2-year-olds, which allow them plenty of time to work at their own pace, can be used. Messy activities such as water play, sand play, and gluing are usually favorites with 2-year-olds, but they also like quieter activities such as reading books with few words and large pictures.

The 3- to 4-Year-Old

Just as 2-year-olds are explorers, 3-year-olds are experimenters. They experiment with materials they have found, enjoy all types of art and science projects, and draw shapes and letters. They experiment with their bodies, pushing themselves to see how far they can jump and how fast they can run. They love to have people watch their great feats. They experiment with language, grammatical rules, and sentence construction. Finally, they experiment with adults.

During the second half of this year, children are frequently in conflict with others. They may be impossible with their parents and totally cooperative at the child care facility. Between 3 and 4, children sometimes become negative, always fighting to get their own way. Many routines, whether bathing, dressing, or eating, become a battle. Children of this age are very capable of doing these tasks, but they do not want to be told what to do. They would rather wait until they make the decision to get dressed or go to bed, and then they want to do it their own way. When we know that 3-year-olds can be negative, it is easy to explain to parents who mention that their child is occasionally unruly that the child is developing normally. The 3 1/2-year-old is actually supposed to be this way.

As with the other difficult stages, it is best to approach the child cautiously, understanding the stage and dealing with it in a matter-of-fact manner. Whenever possible, we should let the child manage things for herself, so that she can be sure they are done her way, as well as give her time to accomplish them. For example, we can remind her that lunch will be ready in ten minutes and she will soon need to wash her hands. Then it is best to let her do it on her own and not aggravate her by looking over her shoulder. Once she has accomplished this task, we should compliment her for doing what we asked. When we want her to do tasks for herself, we can provide options from which to choose. For example, we can ask, "What colors of paint would you like to mix?"

The gross motor development of the 3-year-old consists of expanding skills and refining the already developed ones. The 3-year-old perfects running, jumping, and hopping skills, so that she maneuvers smoothly when running, jumps gracefully, and hops on one foot. She achieves competence in ascending stairs one foot per stair. Now she can incorporate these abilities into games, like Mother May I or Red Light or catch and throw games. She enjoys tricycles, especially if there are paths with signs and obstacles to maneuver.

The 3-year-old is the experimenter when it comes to fine motor development. She loves to manipulate everything in a variety of ways. She enjoys painting with brushes, fingers, potato prints, shaving cream, sponges, and cotton. She likes to cut and glue anything including bottle caps, pasta, string, and crepe paper. For the 3-year-old, it is the means of the art experience that is pursued, not the end. It is not unusual to observe a child of this age creating a picture and then painting over the whole thing in black or cutting it into shreds. Some children show a greater interest in preserving their artwork than others.

The cognitive development of the child continues to advance. Now that she better understands how the world is organized, she enjoys creating her own ordered structures. Blocks, tinker toys, clay, and puzzles help the child learn about the relationship of parts to whole. Puzzles encourage the child to learn rules about putting pieces together by matching colors to form a picture, matching shapes, or working inward from the edges.

The child's understanding of time greatly increases. She understands and uses phrases such as "all the time," and "a long time ago." She knows how old she is, what happens at Christmas, the difference between summer and winter, and morning, afternoon, and evening. She understands sequences of events and appropriate dress for different weather conditions.

The 3-year-old's classification skills improve as she becomes able to classify objects according to groups (fruits, toys, clothing) and to decide whether three given objects or pictures are the same or different. She also increases her understanding of number concepts, including "one," "two," or "many."

Other developing concepts of the 3-year-old are those of weight and material makeup. The child enjoys examining the properties of objects, feeling the weight, weighing on a scale, and studying the look and feel of objects to determine their composition. Through experimentation, the child learns that some objects break, bend, stretch, float, melt, and stick to a magnet.

We can provide materials and equipment for the young scientist, but the child needs to do her own experiments. She will not be content to sit and watch others manipulate the materials. She can, however, be encouraged to put the results of her experiments into words and realizations when questions are asked and new words appropriate to her experiment are introduced.

Children between 3 and 4 are great fantasizers and storytellers. Because their thinking processes are beginning to grow and expand, they enjoy making up stories and playing make-believe games. We should offer many opportuniies to encourage this facet of development.

The 3-year-old pronounces most sounds in the language correctly. She can be understood fairly well by anyone. She still makes mistakes and may even use words incorrectly that she previously used correctly. Prior to this age, the child tends to use irregular plurals, such as "men," correctly by imitation. After she learns the rule of adding *s* to form plurals, she may start saying "mans." This word usage is a normal developmental pattern. She is creating words from her growing internal knowledge of grammar. Rather than correct a child's mistake, we should help her rephrase sentences. For example, if she says, "I not want more milk," our response can be, "Oh, you don't want any more milk?"

The 3-year-old has a love for language at this time. She can say just about anything that she wants to say and can talk with other children rather than to them. She talks constantly, asking endless who, what, when, where, and why questions.

We can help the child develop good language skills by taking an interest in what she asks and answering questions to stimulate her natural curiosity to learn. She also continues to ask questions to which she already knows the answers. She does not do it to annoy anyone, just to recheck her answers. We can patiently answer her repeated questions or redirect them back to her.

During this year, the child learns to use words such as "biggest," "most," and "hardest." We can help her learn comparisons by presenting her with several items of different sizes. Rhyming word games and games that involve listening and comparing the beginning sounds in words are fun for a child of this age. We can use pictures or stories with the same beginning sound to teach the child about rhymes. Sounds that are easy to hear like "m," "b," "d," and "z" should be used first.

While the 2-year-old feels the continual urge to express her independence, the 3-year-old accepts her individuality and even learns to understand the feelings of others. She now makes friends, shares toys, takes turns, and plays cooperatively more frequently. When conflict arises during play, she is more apt to express her anger though words than by grabbing or hitting. We can encourage her to express her feelings to lessen the occurrence of physical fights and to help her identify with the emotions of others.

When appropriate, we should try to mediate arguments between children and encourage them to express their feelings and listen to each other. It is important to provide assistance when they need it: "Shawn, you are mad because you had the toy first and Ricky came and took it away, right? Ricky, can you tell Shawn what you think about that?"

During this year the child enjoys entertaining others by dancing, singing, or doing stunts. Show and Tell provides the child with a chance to be the center of attention for a few minutes. Whether he sings a solo, reads a book, or tells about a family outing, this activity presents a great opporunity for him to practice speaking, to show off, and to build self-confidence at the same time.

Three-year-olds obey not out of fear of punishment, but because rules are known and understood. They are capable of formulating reasonable rules (given a few hints), understand reasons behind rules, and are more respectful of them when they have participated in the rule setting process.

Now that the child has a sense of self separate from others, her self-concept continues to develop. The significance of the self-concept is important because it lasts a lifetime. For a child or an adult to be successful in a career, hobby, or with family and friends, a positive self-image is important. We can help children develop a strong positive sense of self by reinforcing their positive characteristics.

The 4- to 5-Year-Old

The child, as she moves into the fifth year, has matured so much that we hardly recognize her as the same child we knew at 2. She can do so many things now that she is quite independent.

The gross motor development of the 4-year-old involves further improving balance and control. She skips and gallops and enjoys simple dances, rhythm, or marching and swaying to music. Physical education exercises and gymnastics stunts, such as somersaults and leapfrog, can now become part of the curriculum. Favorite games are races, obstacle courses, and any simple organized games involving cooperative play with peers.

The 4-year-old's fine motor skills include careful cutting, pasting, drawing, and coloring. Her drawings become recognizable as people, animals, trees, and houses, and some children at age 4 may be writing letters and numbers.

The cognitive development of the 4-year-old continues to grow. The child begins to understand that the world is organized into parts and wholes. She now spends time trying out rules, changing rules, and making new rules. There are many concepts that she learns to manipulate.

The memory capacity of the 4-year-old expands steadily. Both her long-term and short-term memory improve. She can remember and repeat a four-digit sequence or a sentence with eleven syllables. She can remember and follow three commands in one sentence: "Pick up your book, put your glass in the sink, and come here." Dozens of activities promote this memory growth. Games can be made out of the following playful commands: "Walk to the door, touch the window, and then hop to the record player." The sequence of events in books can be reviewed.

Question Starter: What are some games that can be played to promote memory expansion? (Responses may include: start a message, let each child pass it to another child, and ask the last child to repeat aloud what he heard; hold up a picture for thirty seconds and ask the child to name what she saw.)

The concept of time expands greatly during this year. The 4-year-old knows all the major holidays, recognizes parts of the day and what occurs in each part, uses "yesterday," "today," and "tomorrow" appropriately, plans activities with an adult using a calendar, and understands how long a given task takes. For example, she knows it takes an hour to do the shopping and a whole day to drive to grandma's house.

Other concepts that the 4-year-old is learning are grouping objects according to likenesses and differences; distinguishing "most" from "some" and "half" from "whole"; and recognizing coin names. She is learning to match objects for a one-to-one correspondence. For example, she can put a napkin next to each plate at the table.

There are, however, a number of concepts that she cannot yet understand. A typical child under seven cannot arrange a group of objects from smallest to largest without some mistakes. She cannot see that if one of the two rows of five pennies is bunched up, there is still the same number of pennies in each group. Likewise, if one of two rows of pennies are spread out further, she will say there are more pennies in that row. By the same token, she cannot understand that there is the same amount of clay in a ball when the ball is flattened or rolled into a snake. If two sticks of the same height are held up, one higher than the other, the 4-year-old thinks that the higher one is longer.

A big change occurs in the language growth of the 4-year-old child. She is no longer basically learning to use words but is using words to learn. She continues to increase her vocabulary and knowledge of sentence structure, as well as sentence length, which is now an average of four to five words. She now understands and uses "backwards," "forwards," and many prepositions. She defines nouns by telling how they are used: if asked "What is a hammer?" she will respond, "Something you pound nails with." By the time she is five, her words are almost always in the correct order. She talks endlessly when telling a long detailed story, asks for detailed explanations, and is delightful during a long conversation.

The 4-year-old is usually cooperative and enjoyable. She adjusts easily to change, learns to settle problems with some maturity, and accepts that which cannot be changed. She begins to learn by self-motivation instead of awaiting others' approval. She enjoys her peers and seeks approval from them as much as from adults.

Summary

Our interactions with young children are improved when we understand how they grow and develop. We can be responsive to their emerging needs only when we know what to expect at various touch points of their lives. The success of any program we plan for children is contingent upon our knowledge of how they develop.

Enrichment Activities

1. If possible, select a child from each age group (infancy, 2- to 3-year-old, 3- to 4-year-old, and 4- to 5-year-old) and list the development characteristics of each child in each functional area. Compare and contrast the developmental differences among the age levels.
2. Select one child to observe and describe the behaviors you observe in each of the developmental areas. Develop an enrichment plan to foster the child's optimal growth and development based on the recorded observations.
3. Plan a week-long program that is responsive to the developmental needs of a group of children in one of the age categories. Provide a rationale for the activities you select.
4. Select one age category on the Normal Child Development Guide found in this unit and design activities to foster the development of a child in that age category.

Bibliography

Ames, L. B., Gillespie, C., Haines, J., & Ilg, F. (1979). *The Gesell Institute's child from one to six.* New York: Harper and Row.

Describing the successive stages of development in children, the authors emphasize that behavior development is, to a large extent, dependent on experiences, training, level of development, and individual differences in general. Boys and girls develop differently and at different rates. To some extent the difference is genetic, but environmental factors are also responsible.

Bailey, R. A., & Burton, E. C. (1982). *The dynamic self: Activities to enhance infant development.* St. Louis: C. V. Mosby.

The book stresses the importance of encouraging and reinforcing young children's motor development through new experiences that also develop what the writers call "movement vocabulary." The chief value of this work lies in the provision of a wide variety of activities conducive to the stimulation of child development.

Caplan, T., & Caplan, F. (1983). *The early childhood years: The 2 to 6 year old.* New York: Perigee Books.

Drawing upon the work of researchers and theorists such as Erikson, Freud, Gesell, Goodenough, Havighurst, Mahler, and Piaget, the authors provide an overview of child development in the early years. They discuss the characteristics and behavior of normal children at different stages of development, although it is emphasized that each child is different and should therefore not be expected to develop according to a rigid timetable. Hyperactivity, dyslexia, child abuse, divorce, and many other special problems are also discussed. Sources of help for parents are identified, and phone numbers and addresses are provided.

Charlesworth, R. (1982). *Understanding child development.* Albany, NY: Delmar.

This comprehensive work deals with child development from birth to 5 years of age. Theories on the physical, cognitive, and affective development of children are reviewed, discussed, and applied to educating and guiding young children. Examples and case studies are also presented.

Church, J. (1975). *Understanding your child from birth to three.* New York: Pocket Books.

The book provides practical information on various aspects of the behavior, development, and training of young children. Written primarily for parents, it is useful for teachers as well.

Donaldson, M., Grieve, R., & Pratt, C. (Eds.). (1983). *Early childhood development and education: Readings in psychology.* New York: Guildford Press.

This well-organized and readable book is useful for both parents and teachers. The social, linguistic, and intellectual skills and capabilities of children are dealt with in detail, and research relevant to the development of children between the ages of 3 and 6 is cited. The book is divided into four sections dealing with *(a)* social play, friendship, rules and social language use; *(b)* linguistic skills and communication; *(c)* intellectual development, number comprehension, thinking, reasoning and remembering; and *(d)* the development of self-awareness and self-control.

Erikson, E. (1963). *Childhood and society.* New York: W. W. Norton.

The development of children's ego and psychosocial behavior is discussed. The influence of parent-child relationships is also stressed.

Evans, J., & Ilfeld, E. (1982). *Good beginnings: Parenting in the early years.* Ypsilanti, MI: High/Scope Press.

An informative book about seven general stages of development in infants: heads up, looker, creeper-crawler, cruiser, walker, doer, tester. The authors also provide several useful enrichment activities that parents and caregivers can use with young children.

Fitzgerald, H. E., & McKinney, J. P. (Eds.). (1977). *Developmental psychology: Studies in human development* (rev. ed.). Homewood, IL: Dorsey Press.

A variety of interesting, enlightening, and, on the whole, readable essays. These are divided into two main sections. Under "Attachment," areas dealt with include engrossment, infant communication and crying, sex differences and attachment behaviors, and an interesting study on infants' exploratory separation from their mothers. The section on learning and cognitive-social processes highlights infant conditioning, malnutrition and its effects, arrested development, language acquisition theories, and research on child development.

Flake-Hobson, C., Robinson, B. E., & Skeen, P. (1983). *Child development and relationships.* Reading, MA: Addison-Wesley.

This book emphasizes the empathetic approach to child development. Those interested in child development should not only understand children's growth and relationships but examine their own feelings and reactions to children. Factual information on child development is supplemented by material on adult involvement with children—which is in itself closely related to healthy development. Other important topics involve black English, cross-cultural development, child abuse, divorce, single parent families, and the influence of fathers on their children's development.

Gregg, E., & Knotts, J. (1980). *Growing wisdom, growing wonder.* New York: Macmillan.

A creative and practical resource book for parents and teachers of young children. The theories of Dewey, Piaget, Montessori, and others are used to put into practice and reiterate the fundamental belief that learning develops sequentially, that it occurs through active engagement and experience, and that the relationship between a nurturant adult and the child is central to intellectual development. The writers present an assortment of activities and much useful and fascinating information on the senses, feelings, and relationships. The activities and information are relevant to different developmental levels of early childhood.

Honig, A. S. (1982). Prosocial development in children. *Young Children, 37* (5), 51–62.

An interesting and informative study review for those interested in children's social and moral development. Recent and relevant research is cited on age, sex, and cognitive and moral levels in relation to modeling, situational determinants such as mood, and environmental determinants such as television and the movies. Based on this research, the study recommends ways in which children's prosocial development may be fostered: through meaningful contact with a nurturant adult; through provision of opportunities to identify their own and others' feelings; through a consideration of consequences; through adult modeling; through chances to respond sympathetically to those in distress; and, finally, through encouragement and problem-solving situations.

Infant development program: Birth to 12 months. (1976). Piscataway, NJ: Johnson and Johnson.

This practical guide presents exercises and activities designed to enhance development and learning. Attachment as an important element of the teacher-child relationship is also discussed.

Leach, P. (1981). *Your baby and child: From birth to age five.* New York: Knoff.

A useful and up-to-date resource and guide book on child development and care. Its special feature is that it focuses, in a sensitive yet authoritative way, on the child's point of view.

Leach, P. (1983). *Babyhood* (2nd ed.). St. Paul, MN: Toys 'n Things Press.

The book focuses on relevant research in the field of child development. It also deals with activities accompanying the gradual development of infants.

McDavid, J. W., & Garwood, S. G. (1978). *Understanding children: Promoting human growth.* Lexington, MA: D. C. Heath.

The physical, social, and intellectual development of children is dealt with in depth, and developmental charts, tables, photographs, and drawings are provided to facilitate our understanding of children's growth in these areas. Major developmental ideas and theories, such as those of Freud, Erickson, Piaget, and Kohlberg are explained, and their applications are discussed in a readable and interesting way.

Peterson, C., & McCabe, A. (1983). *Developmental psycholinguistics: Three ways of looking at a child's narrative.* New York: Plenum.

The authors analyze children's discourse and language development after the mastery of complete sentences has taken place. A large assortment of narrative examples are presented for analysis.

Piaget, J. (1952). *The origins of intelligence in children.* New York: International Universities Press.

This important and perceptive book describes in detail the six progressive stages of sensorimotor development. The discussion is based on Piaget's observation of his own children.

Rubin, R. R., Fisher, J. J., III, & Doering, S. C. (1980). *Your toddler.* New York: Macmillan.

Adopting a developmental approach to toddlerhood, the writers examine toddler growth, toddler personality development, toddler play, and parental guidance as discipline. They recommend interesting and valid activities to aid and stimulate growth physically, intellectually, linguistically, and socially. The book is enhanced by delightful photographs that portray the many facets of toddlerhood.

Schickedanz, J., Schickedanz, D., & Forsyth, P. (1982). *Toward understanding children.* Boston: Little, Brown.

The book successfully establishes the rationale for studying and understanding children. Further, it provides an overview of children's physical, cognitive, social, and linguistic development and presents important developmental theories and research. A significant feature is the discussion of problems and issues relating to development, modern family life, and modern life in general.

Skinner, L. (1979). *Motor development in the preschool years.* Springfield, IL: Charles C. Thomas.

This readable book deals specifically with the development in young children of basic movement, muscular strength and relaxation, and sensory motor and language skills. Special emphasis is placed on sensory motor development, which is further divided into nine subareas. Relevant and appropriate activities are recommended for each area of development, along with various suggestions for enrichment and stimulation.

Wachs, T. D., & Gruen, G. E. (1982). *Early experience and human development.* New York: Plenum.

The impact of experience on the cognitive, intellectual, and social development of children is examined, and various research studies are presented and discussed. A useful reference book for educators and researchers.

White, B. L. (1975). *The first three years of life.* Englewood Cliffs, NJ.: Prentice-Hall.

Theories regarding the cognitive development of babies are applied in a practical way to child rearing in the early years. The author also presents and discusses a variety of useful activities, games, and toys that stimulate infant development.

3 Communicating with Children

COMMUNICATION is the key to all interactions between human beings. In our work with children, communication is particularly important. In fact, effective communication is the foundation of our work with children. The better we are at communicating, the more effective we are in working with children. The more we know about appropriate ways of communicating, both verbally and nonverbally, the better able we are to help children develop to their fullest potential.

Objectives

In this chapter we will examine what talk is, why it is important, and how we affect children with what we say. We will identify ineffective talk patterns and discuss why they do not work. We will discuss the importance of listening as a communication skill and demonstrate how we can become more effective listeners. We will identify characteristics of nonverbal communication as they relate to children and adults. Finally, we will describe five effective communication skills and indicate why they are important.

Key Ideas

The primary determinant of the quality of child care programs is the quality of interactions between adults and children in the child care setting. Communication between adults and children can either be effective or ineffective. In our work with children it is essential that we recognize ineffective ways in which we interact with children and understand how these ineffective approaches can lead to communication breakdowns.

To be able to improve our communication skills, it is important that we understand that effective listening is the first and most important skill, because it allows us to hear the child and respond more appropriately. While it is sometimes difficult to listen to a child, there are several ways in which we can improve our listening skills.

Nonverbal communication is another way in which we communicate with children and they communicate with us. As teachers we are better able to respond to children when we can read their nonverbal cues and can, in turn, send supportive nonverbal cues to them.

All of us who care for children need to be able to talk effectively with them. We are better able to engage in positive talk when we are aware of the different modes of effective communication and thus can select the most appropriate kind of talk for different situations.

The Power of Talk

All of us know how to talk. In fact, talk is so automatic that we seldom give it a second thought. To talk is to be powerful. We are especially aware of the power of speech when we compare adult talking skills with the less developed talking skills of young children. Because we have a large vocabulary and understand what words mean, we have the capacity to do things that children cannot do. For example, we can verbalize our needs and try to get what we want. On the other hand, when a toddler approaches the refrigerator and gestures, we may offer her a carrot when in fact she wants something else.

Because we can talk, we can express a variety of different feelings. For the infant and young child, communication is expressed in single words or short sentences and other signals such as laughter, tears, pointing, or silence. Each of us has, at some time, probably observed a toddler sitting on the floor, crying and pointing. What was he trying to say? Did someone take his toy? Who? Why did he want the toy back? Or did he get upset about something but did not want to talk about it?

In addition to being able to identify our needs and express feelings, talk also enables us to ask for information which, in turn, allows us to solve our own problems. Children, on the other hand, are less capable of asking for the information they need, and consequently have more trouble resolving their problems.

Ineffective Talk

Just as effective talk is the foundation of positive work with children, ineffective talk can present roadblocks to working well with children. Ineffective talk occurs when we do not get our messages across. It is like a short circuit. What we intend to say is not what is heard. Instead of understanding, we have confusion and resistance.

Ineffective communication includes talk patterns and habits that, unfortunately, are easy to use with children. We will examine thirteen common ineffective talk patterns that are frequently used with adults and children. In fact, we have all used these talk patterns at one time or another. For instance, we place blame on children when we say, "It's your fault." We make them feel bad when we engage in name calling, such as "You dummy." We use threats when we try to get children to do what we want: "If you dare do that, you'll be sorry." We intimidate children when we use sarcasm, such as "That was really brilliant." We lecture and moralize when we assume that children understand more than they actually do: "Don't you realize how important this is?" We alarm children when we use warnings: "Watch it!" We prophesy when we carry warnings one step further and attach consequences to the action: "Watch what you're doing with those scissors, or you'll cut off your finger." We belittle children when we use comparisons such as "Why can't you be like Susie?" We use bribes when we try short-term methods of getting results from children: "If you'll be quiet right now, I won't tell your parents about this." We place shame on children when we accuse them: "Shame on you. How can you do this to me?" We judge when we imply there is something wrong with a child:

"You're impossible. You'll never learn." Finally, when we explain too elaborately, we cause young children to lose interest before we have finished talking.

Why do we sometimes use these ineffective ways of communicating with children? First, they are habits that we have developed over a period of time. Second, they are natural responses when we feel impatient or angry or are under pressure of some kind. Whatever the reasons, using ineffective talk has a negative effect on the child's self-image. A child who is put down feels immobilized, powerless, and less valued. Self-concept erodes and responses of anger, fear, or indifference become more likely.

Learning Activity: To develop the idea of ineffective talk, divide participants into small groups and assign them several ineffective talk patterns. Ask each group to role play how a child feels when these talk patterns are used. Share responses in the large group.

Effective Listening

Listening is the first and, perhaps, most important communication skill. In fact, careful listening is often the best solution to communication breakdowns. How words are received, how the child feels about them, and what the words mean to the child, often make the difference between effective and ineffective communication.

Learning Activity: To demonstrate how not listening makes the talker feel, divide participants into pairs and assign a speaker and a listener in each pair. Instruct the speaker to take one or two minutes to describe a recent movie or television show while the listener's eyes are closed. Ask them to reverse roles upon completion. Elicit a discussion on how they felt talking to someone whose eyes were closed.

We all know that listening is difficult because it requires patience. The talking skills of children are less sophisticated than ours. Some children talk so slowly, so haltingly, that we lose interest in the middle of the conversation. Some talk nonstop. Others seldom talk at all.

Listening is difficult, too, because it requires our own stillness. In order to listen we have to be still, yet it is difficult to concentrate when there is a lot of activity around us. Finding a quiet place to listen to a child is important when working in a noisy environment. Sometimes taking a long deep breath, holding it for a moment, and exhaling, before plunging into a conversation with a child will provide the composure we need to listen.

We can learn to listen better by employing several strategies. For example, we should establish eye contact with the child when we communicate. Our eyes send messages and enable us to collect and transmit a great deal of information. Eye contact improves communication with a child in a variety of ways. It helps us to hear what the child is saying without his having to repeat a statement. It allows us to assess how important the question is, pause a moment to figure out how we are going to respond and, in that brief moment, teach an important listening skill. Eye contact also shows the speaker that we value what he has said.

When we talk with children, we should establish body attention, which involves eye contact and a relaxed, natural, but alert posture. Body attention communicates interest and caring and shows that we are listening. Have you ever had the experience of talking to someone who was too busy watching someone else to look at you or listen? If you have experienced a situation like this, you know that you felt less than important.

A third skill we need for good listening is verbal attention. It involves paying attention to what the child is saying and letting her know that we hear her. It means inviting the child to say more about the subject, as well as not abruptly changing the subject. Sometimes repeating a message helps us pay attention; it shows the other person that we have listened. It also helps stimulate our own ideas so that we are better able to speak when it is our turn.

There are several benefits to being a good listener. For example, a good listener makes a better talker. The better we listen, the more interesting what we hear becomes. We can test this notion with children. If we are actively listening, children will talk more responsively. We will note changes in their voice, tone, speed of talking, and investment in what they are saying.

Good listening becomes loving listening. As we perfect our listening skills, we learn to hear not just the words, but through to the heart of the child, to unexpressed needs, to the deepest message.

Good listening can also be a source of enjoyment. If we approach a child with the spirit of "I wonder what this child is really trying to say," it is likely that we will be very glad we have listened. This attitude also helps the talker feel more confident about what she is saying.

Effective Nonverbal Communication

Although children have limited vocabularies and sentence structure, they compensate for what they lack in word power with signal power. Adults also communicate with nonverbal language. More important than what we say is how we say it, how we behave, and the feelings we convey. Our vocal tone, facial expressions, gestures and actions are what the child hears. When our words do not match our behavior, we give the child a mixed message, and it is likely that the child will respond to the message behind the words.

Children tune into our silent language. If we do not understand the silent messages we send, we cannot understand children's responses. To improve nonverbal communication, we need to increase our skill at reading children's nonverbal messages and body language, and match our talk with consistent, clear nonverbal cues. By tuning into children's body language and developing a sense of different temperaments, we can help children identify and discuss feelings and reactions.

Question Starter: What kinds of nonverbal cues have you seen infants, toddlers, and preschoolers send? What did these nonverbal cues convey? (Responses may include: crying, smiling, pouting, looking away, pulling away. They conveyed distress, happiness, anger, frustration.)

Infants communicate with us directly. Crying and smiling are part of their basic language. Yet we know that different crying sounds mean different things: If the baby's legs are drawn, or she is pounding with her fists, something more than the discomfort of a wet diaper is occurring. We know that babies smile with pleasure at familiar faces and objects and that, by 8 months, they do not make eye contact when they are angry (Szasz, 1978).

As they grow older, infants and young toddlers use eyebrow language. One lifted eyebrow expresses disbelief, two lifted eyebrows mean surprise, and lowered eyebrows indicate mistrust. An intensely furrowed brow means concentration on fingers or a toy. Other nonverbal cues include pouting and holding the breath (Szasz, 1978).

At 2 and 3 years, children's body language becomes more subtle. They gradually become aware of what is acceptable, can label feelings, and begin to figure out what they should hide. Some children literally cover their mouths in order to keep "bad" words inside. A hand raised to the mouth means surprise or confusion; a hand to the forehead means a child feels overwhelmed. Both hands to the head indicate surprise or confusion (Szasz, 1978).

At 4 or 5 years, children become more aware of their peers, and a careful study of their body language reveals how they are feeling about themselves and others. Walking with downcast eyes, dragging feet, and sagging shoulders means that the child is experiencing some problem. The child may feel vulnerable and powerless. Hands held stiffly as if ready to strike indicate fear and anxiety toward others. By contrast, smiles, an open stance, and relaxed body all reveal a positive, strong attitude. Squared shoulders show determination while one shoulder raised means indifference (Szasz, 1978).

When we take time to pay attention to children's nonverbal signals, it is not too difficult to understand what they are saying to us with body, face, and gestures. Signals become rather easy to decode.

Adults also communicate nonverbally. As adults we have usually learned how to hide feelings—in fact, we are experts at disguising what we mean. We are accomplished at saying one thing and meaning another. Young children are quite capable of reading these signs. Therefore, one of our tasks in working with young children is to recognize the nonverbal messages we send. We can learn to change our behavior to match what we say and what we mean. Often, our attitudes and feelings toward a particular child in a particular situation strongly influence our behavior toward that child, regardless of what our words say.

How do we begin to understand and identify our own nonverbal messages? We begin by looking at common nonverbal patterns that all of us use, by becoming aware of their impact, and by changing them when necessary. For example, we need to know that our negative behavior toward children, and toward each other for that matter, communicates unacceptance, inattentiveness, unhelpfulness, and disapproval. On the other hand, our positive behavior toward children, and toward each other, communicates acceptance, attentiveness, helpfulness, and support.

It is easy to be aware of our verbal messages because we can hear them. It is more difficult to be aware of our nonverbal messages because we cannot see how they look. Yet how we look and what we do with our face, voice, gestures, and body communicate our attitudes to children. To illustrate, consider the teacher who is attempting to get 4- and 5-year-olds ready for a field trip. Children of these ages dress themselves with varying degrees of skill. Some are well coordinated and have little difficulty dressing. Others are less adept, cannot button up or use zippers correctly, and put boots on the wrong feet.

Question Starter: What kinds of negative and positive nonverbal messages could the teacher in this situation send to the children? (Negative responses may include: leaning against wall; hands on hips; scowl on face; twiddling thumbs. Positive responses may include: cheerful help; patting a child's back; efficiently speeding the dressing process; hugging a child who buttons well.)

Learning Activity: Further develop the concept of nonverbal messages by asking participants to role play positive and negative messages we send to children in each of the following ways: facial expression; gesture (hands and feet); body movement and posture; tone of voice; and feelings communicated. Discuss implications of these messages.

To summarize, communication is a lot

more than talk. Negative nonverbal messages convey coldness, low regard, indifference, rejection, anger, tension, stubbornness, judgment, and disgust. Positive nonverbal messages convey warmth, respect, enthusiasm, patience, support, helpfulness, consistency, joy, and caring.

We must remember that when we communicate with children nonverbal messages are worth a thousand words. When we become conscious of a communication breakdown, we should check the nonverbal messages we are sending. First, we should check the tone, speed, and inflection of voice. Second, we should visualize our facial expression. Third, we should check our gestures to see what our hands, feet, and body are saying. Fourth, we should check our movements to see if they are rushed or relaxed, open or closed, welcoming or judging. Fifth, we should check our silence to see if we are being patient, receptive, or hassled and distracted. Sixth, we should be aware of eye contact to see if we are attentive, interested, indifferent or disinterested.

As we look for these nonverbal messages in ourselves, we can also look for similar messages from children. We can be alert to times when children do and do not use eye contact and the circumstances of those situations. We can notice the times of the day when a child is most attentive and most inattentive.

Effective Talk

The primary determinant of the quality of a child care program is the interaction between adults and children, because it sets the tone for all personal contact in the group. The quality of communication among children is also an indicator of the quality of the program, since children model adult behaviors.

Effective talk is a skill that can be learned. We will examine five kinds of talk: questioning, supporting, reflecting, explaining, and directing. Being aware of, and knowing how to use, each of these talk patterns can help us approach a particular situation with confidence. Using the right approach and good listening skills and paying attention to our own and children's nonverbal messages can help us to communicate effectively, even when time, pressure, and chaos are against us.

Questioning talk is used to get information. When a child is crying or is particularly excited about something, we may want to find out why. Whatever the situation, when we ask for more information, we engage in questioning talk. The intent of this kind of talk is to clarify, discuss, or develop a point. We should ask questions only when more information is needed to keep a conversation going. It is best not to ask too many questions at one time, since doing so can sometimes lead to more silence. It is wise to pose questions that make it easy for the child to give the information we request. Open-ended and friendly questions should be asked. For example, instead of asking, "Did you enjoy the birthday party?" the question could be phrased, "What did you like best about the birthday party?" The first question is a closed question. Closed questions can be answered with only one word. Open-ended questions cannot be answered with only one word, and encourage further discussion (Della-Piana, 1973).

It is important to ask questions only when the answer is not known. Asking a question when the answer is known poses a difficult moral dilemma for the child. Should she lie? Should she use her own nonverbal skills and pretend she did not hear? If she knows she will be scolded, it is unlikely that she will admit to inappropriate or negative behavior (Della-Piana, 1973).

Finally, we should not ask questions that threaten punishment, for they usually result in the child responding very cautiously or not at all. For example, if a child spills a glass of juice, and we already know who spilled the juice, it is pointless to ask who did it.

Learning Activity: To check the participants' understanding of questioning talk, divide them into small groups. Ask half of the groups to write a friendly, nonscolding question and the other half to write an unfriendly, scolding question in response to the following situation: Several children are playing in the art area and have left it messy. Have representatives from the groups rôle play their responses and discuss the following: (*a*) what each response communicated with words; (*b*) what the nonverbal message communicated; and (*c*) how the children felt.

Sometimes children are so upset about something that even the friendliest question will not generate more information. At such times it is useful to switch to *supporting talk.* This type of communication shows children that we understand, and that events will work out even though it may not seem so at the time. For example, if an upset child reports that he got paint all over himself, we can respond by offering to help him wash off the paint. Sometimes we may want to let a child know that things are not as bad as they seem at the time. For instance, when a crying child reports that other children will not play with her, we can guide the child to someone who will play with her (Della-Piana, 1973).

Supporting talk is often the appropriate response to an emotional situation. A child who expresses strong feeling either verbally, by shouting or crying, or nonverbally, by hiding, sulking, or looking fearful, needs help to get out of the situation (Della-Piana, 1973).

Learning Activity: To develop the concept of supporting talk, ask half of the groups to write a supportive talk response, and the other half to write an unsupportive talk response to the following situation: Eric emphatically screams that he will not take his nap. Each group should report or role play its response and discuss why each response is or is not supportive talk.

Another type of talk is *reflecting talk,* which functions somewhat like a mirror. When we use reflecting talk, we reflect the child's feelings. Our role is to describe or feed back these feelings, so that the child is able to identify her reactions and respond better to the situation (Della-Piana, 1973).

Reflecting talk combines many of the talking skills we have already identified. We have seen that it is necessary to try to accurately identify the emotions a child is communicating. Emotions sometimes overlap, and a child may be feeling several things at once. Our job is to help the child sort out these emotions and understand the main problem. To illustrate, a child struggles to stack a pile of colored blocks, knocks them over, and then cries, "I try and try but it never works! I wanted to put them all together to show you but they keep falling over." The child could be feeling guilty, angry, or frustrated. We can help him try to sort out these feelings. Is it primarily guilt? Probably not. After all, he is trying, and guilt usually comes with having given up or not having tried at all. What about anger? Anger is a strong emotion. James is not having a tantrum or lashing out. What really seems to be happening is that James has set a goal for himself—to stack the blocks—but has failed and feels frustrated.

Once the problem has been identified, we need to reflect the feelings back to the child and help solve the problem. We could say, "Trying to stack all these blocks is a tough job. It is frustrating when they fall down. Maybe we can do it together. May I help?"

Good reflecting talk restates what the child said without adding to or changing the subject. It indicates that we understand what the child said, and what he is feeling. Moreover, such talk helps the child understand his own feelings and leads him toward problem solving (Della-Piana, 1973).

Another type of talk is *explaining talk,* which can be thought of as talk involving facts. There are many occasions when all that a child needs is a fact or an opinion about how or why something is done. We can tell that a child is ready for an explanation when we observe that she is seeking an answer to a question or problem but is not upset or fearful at the time (Della-Piana, 1973).

Reflecting talk is used when a child is upset. Explaining talk, on the other hand, is not emotionally charged. For example, a child may be trying to get the lid off a box by pulling from one end. We can explain that it is easier to get the lid off when we hold both ends and lift straight up. The child is encouraged to succeed when we take the time to give a simple, useful explanation.

The most effective explaining talk is brief, simple, direct, and to the point. Long explanations are boring and they do not get the job done. The job of effective communication is to keep things moving through a process of dialogue, give-and-take, and action. Preaching, on the other hand, blocks the action and effective communication comes to a screeching halt, even if the speech is well said (Della-Piana, 1973).

Many situations in a child care facility call for giving directions, demonstrating, or practicing something. We are confronted with trying to get a child to do a particular thing or behave in a particular way. At such times it is necessary to use *directing talk.*

Every time we introduce a new game or activity we are using directing talk. Directing talk has consequences. After we have finished with directing talk, we expect something to happen. But, as is the case with all that we have said about communication, the quality of thought and care that goes into directing talk determines what will happen when it is time for the listeners to act on what we have said (Della-Piana, 1973).

Directing talk is not limited to activities. Sometimes we have to help children know exactly what to say when they are unable to provide the words. Thus, directing talk is useful when we ask children to act on a specific interacting behavior. To illustrate, a child says, "Billy won't stop teasing me. I punched him but he still won't stop." The child is frustrated because his solution—punching—did not work. He cannot think of any other alternatives, so he has asked for help in a specific situation. An appropriate response to the child would be, "Maybe Billy is bored. Let's ask him if he wants to help put the chairs around the table for snack time."

Directing talk is simple and clear. It should lead to appropriate action. It takes knowledge, awareness, and work to be able to use directing talk effectively.

Summary

In this chapter we have focused on the power of talk and nonverbal communication and recognized the role that effective communication plays in a quality child care program. We have identified several ineffective talk patterns that we all use and the effects that they have on children. We have examined the important role listening plays in effective communication and the benefits it provides to quality adult-child interactions. We have recognized that at times we all have trouble listening, but that we can incorporate certain skills that make listening easier and more enjoyable. We have also explored the ways in which adults and children use nonverbal communication and discussed strategies that can be used to improve our skills in this area. Finally, we have examined some very specific ways in which we can learn to talk more effectively with children.

Effective communication is the foundation of all the positive work we do with children. In order to be effective in other aspects of the child care program, we must first learn to communicate appropriately with children. Communication is a complicated process involving speaking, listening, interpreting language, facial expressions and body movements, and paying attention. The development of each of these skills is dependent on our early efforts to help the child become an effective communicator.

Enrichment Activities

1. Encourage children to listen more effectively by playing games that foster good listening skills. For example, play games that require children to follow directions correctly. Reward them with praise and encouragement when they succeed.
2. Learn to recognize good and poor listening behaviors by observing listening behavior in yourself and others, including eye contact, body attention, and verbal attention. Record at least one listening incident that you observe and describe the behavior of the speaker and the listener.
3. Increase your awareness of children's nonverbal behavior by selecting one child to observe for at least one day. Record exactly what you see. Later, identify the kinds and ranges of feelings the child expressed throughout the day.
4. Observe children as they arrive at your child care facility. Record as many different kinds of behavior as you see, such as clinging to parents, running to a teacher or other children, lowering the head, crying, hiding the face, skipping, dragging feet, displaying sadness or joy. Try to describe exactly how each child feels based on the nonverbal messages that the child sends.

Bibliography

Bos, B. (1983). *Before the basics: Creating conversations with children.* Roseville, CA: Turn the Page Press.

All talk and interactions with children can be beneficial. Even repetitions and interruptions can enhance language skills and understanding. A variety of activities are offered.

Brooks, J. B. (1981). *The process of parenting.* Palo Alto, CA: Mayfield Publishing Company.

While providing parents with a knowledge of child development and behavior, the book deals with a variety of parenting strategies and techniques. Three of these are concerned with establishing firm adult-child relationships and with the communication of feeling. Two behaviorist strategies stress changing child behavior.

Busch, R. E. (1984). A red marble! Guidelines for speaking to young children. *Young Children, 39* (5), 64–66.

A veteran speaker observes that speaking to children entails a knowledge of their developmental level and abilities. It requires careful planning, a positive and friendly attitude, and a lively presentation. Appropriate choice of materials is extremely important. Children should, of course, be encouraged to ask and answer questions.

Cazden, C. B. (1981). *Language in early childhood education.* Washington, DC: National Association for the Education of Young Children.

This book clearly explains how language and reading are related. It details how adults can promote language development when children learn English either as a first or second language.

Center Accreditation Project 4. (1983). Four components of high quality early childhood programs: Staff-child interaction, child-child interaction, curriculum and evaluation. *Young Children, 38* (6), 46–52.

Two of the important components dealt with here are concerned with interactions in child care programs. The tone and quality of adult-child interactions, both verbal and nonverbal, have an immense impact on a program's quality. An understanding of children's interactions with each other is also essential for those who work with children.

Della-Piana, G. (1973). *How to talk with children (and other people).* New York: John Wiley & Sons.

This book is useful for both parents and teachers as a guide to effective talk with and management of children. Talk, it is stressed, leads to better understanding and communication. Various styles of talking to children are illustrated and analyzed: scolding, questioning, supporting, accepting, explaining, directing, shaping. Alternatives to punishment are suggested. Self-tests and exercises are also provided to determine the method or combination of methods that works best for each person.

Faber, A., & Mazlish, E. (1980). *How to talk so kids will listen and listen so kids will talk.* New York: Avon.

The writers give evidence of sensitivity and insight into the problems involved in child rearing and child care. They present, in a humorous and interesting way, ideas on feelings and emotions of both adults and children, reinforcement and praise, discipline, self-esteem, autonomy, communication, and the growth of respect and understanding between adults and children.

Galloway, C. (1976). *Silent language in the classroom.* Bloomington: Phi Delta Kappa Educational Foundation.

The book stresses the importance of nonverbal behavior in communication, especially in the classroom, where nonverbal communication can affect relationships, learning, and achievement. Children learn quite early to interpret nonverbal signals, gestures, and facial expressions; they learn to send messages; they assume certain stances that are signs for the discerning adult. It is suggested that teachers be aware of and examine their own nonverbal behavior to discover whether it inhibits or encourages students. Models for checking and analyzing are provided, along with characteristics of positive and negative behaviors. Strategies for creating a positive environment are also given.

Garvey, C. (1984). *Children's talk.* Cambridge, MA: Harvard University Press.

The author makes a detailed study of children's language usage and skills. Discussions include the ways in which children exchange messages, manage conversations, learn social speech usage and identity, and think aloud.

Genishi, G., & Cyson, A. H. (1984, Winter). Ways of talking: Respecting differences. *Beginnings,* pp. 7–10.

Using examples and comment, the authors present an interesting discussion about characteristics of good language programs where standard and nonstandard English differences are respected. In the ideal language program, talk is activity-oriented and meaning-oriented. As a tool, talk helps children understand and integrate with the world and others around them. Moreover, teachers can learn a lot about children from their talk. A quality program should promote talk through various activities.

Gordon, T., & Busch, N. (1974). *T.E.T.: Teacher effectiveness training.* New York: Peter H. Wyden.

The book deals in detail with how teachers can establish effective relationships with students, open up channels of communication, modify the classroom environment, and handle conflict. Sections 3 through 5 are specifically related to the problem of communication—or the lack of it. Various ineffective techniques are contrasted with effective ones, such as active listening, responsiveness, an inviting attitude, and the "I-message" strategy.

Honig, A. S. (1982). Language environments for young children. *Young Children, 38* (1), 56–67.

The author details research on language as a powerful means of communication that humans learn early in life. Topics include: early language learning; the effect of parental language style; the influence of socioeconomic status and differences in language interactions, learning motivation, and success in school; cultural differences, language environments, and group care; teacher talk; and differences between home and group care language environments. It is stressed that teachers should be aware of the language environment and experiences they provide and should strive to help children develop and acquire the powerful and important tool called language.

Honig, A. S. (1984, Winter). Why talk to babies? *Beginnings,* pp.3–6.

The author stresses the need for parents and teachers to talk to children and to pay attention to their early sounds and expressions. Adults can contribute to language development by reading to infants and young children, by playing with sounds, by matching their own language skills to those of children, and by modeling good speech and language for children.

Martin, N., Williams, P., Wilding, J., Hemmings, S., & Medway, P. (1976). *Understanding children talking.* New York: Penguin Books.

While adults at home and at school often initiate and determine the pattern of children's talk, children do, in the absence of adult direction, explore what interests them through talk. The authors present transcriptions of children's conversation among themselves, or in informal situations with adults, on a variety of subjects. The result is a fascinating revelation of children's thinking and, to some extent, their linguistic and cognitive development. Good talk needs special situations and relationships. Can teachers and parents effectively provide these? Or does their presence prove an inhibiting factor? Do some children, in fact, lose the skills of talking as they grow older because of certain inhibitions? These questions are examined and, finally, it is suggested that if children's self-confidence is kept intact and encouraged, and if they do not feel threatened, progress in talking skills will take place.

Maxin, G. W. (1985). *The very young: Guiding children from infancy through the early years* (2nd ed.). Belmont, CA: Wadsworth.

The chapter on language discusses language internalization and growth from infancy onward. Parents are given useful suggestions on how to stimulate this development. The importance of the teacher's role is stressed in encouraging interaction through questioning, listening, stimulating, and reinforcing. Strategies and enrichment activities for the classroom are also presented and described.

McCartney, K. (1984, Winter). Caregivers talk to children. *Beginnings,* pp. 11–13.
The author reports on a study carried out in Bermuda on language skill acquisition and language interaction of children with adults outside the home in child care settings. The researchers found that children's language skills are, indeed, enhanced by meaningful interactions with caregivers. Although children learn a lot through exploration and peer interaction, they benefit greatly from adult guidance. Children's language skills, self-esteem, and response to the environment are affected by both the quality and quantity of adult-child interactions. Thus, it is essential that teachers talk well with children.

McDonald, P. (1979). How you say it counts. *Day Care and Early Education, 6* (3), 12–13.
The writer describes some practical ways of getting positive responses by communicating more effectively. One's choice of words is extremely important, as is eye contact, and helping children explore and express their feelings. Seeing things from the child's point of view also aids adult understanding of children's responses.

Miller, P. W. (1981). *Nonverbal communication.* Washington, DC: National Education Association.
Teachers need to be aware that actions speak louder than words. Understanding nonverbal behavior can make teachers better receivers of children's messages and allow them to send positive messages as reinforcement to children. Facial expressions, vocal intonation, physical contact, posture, movement, proxemics, even dress, are part of nonverbal communication. However, nonverbal behavior can differ among individuals and certainly among cultures—another factor today's teachers should keep in mind.

Packer, A. B., Lamme, L. L., & Roberts, D. P. (1984, Winter). All the ways to talk: The world of adult-child conversations. *Beginnings,* pp. 224–26.
The preschool years are an important period for language skills acquisition. Parents, teachers, and families can use various means to encourage language development. These include having extended conversations with children, encouraging pretend play, story making, storytelling, story taking or writing down children's dictated stories, and chanting and singing.

Patterson, C. J. (1978, April/May). Teaching children to listen. *Today's Education,* pp. 52–53.
The writer reports on a study, carried out on preschoolers to fourth graders, that explores children's reactions when they fail to understand something said to them. The study showed that while few young children asked questions to have ambiguous statements clarified, they usually learned better once they were taught to ask questions. Thus, asking questions is very important, but it is pointed out that teachers' attitudes and responses to questioning can also make a difference.

Rowen, B. (1975). *Tuning in to your child: Awareness training for parents.* Atlanta: Humanics Associates.
The book describes ways in which parents can train themselves to be more aware of children's growth, development, experiences, and problems. Awareness establishes more effective communication and interaction. Included are a variety of games, activ-

ities, observation techniques, and strategies to encourage adult awareness, children's self-expression and skill development, and to help cope with various emotional and developmental problems.

Rubin, D. (1974). Listen to me! *Children Today, 3* (5), 7–9.

The article deals with the development of listening skills in children as a critical step toward effective communication with others. Activities that aid interpretive, creative, and critical listening are described.

Szasz, S. (1978). *The body language of children.* New York: W. W. Norton.

Body language is a powerful indicator of children's feelings, moods, emotions, and desires. The book captures the numerous facets of children's nonverbal communication through a wide variety of photographs. The commentary accompanying the photographs explains how to read the signals a child sends through facial expressions, gestures, and posture, and provides information about children's developmental stages as well as about normal emotional reactions to certain situations.

Weir, M. K., & Eggelston, P. J. (1975). Teacher's first words. *Day Care and Early Education, 3* (2), 17–21.

Daily conversation is the best way to stimulate language development, and the article gives a variety of suggestions on how to get children to communicate verbally on any typical preschool day. Every situation can be exploited: entering school, eating, playing, using the bathroom, washing, settling down to nap, and going home.

4 Creating a Positive Environment for Children

MANAGING children's behavior in a child care setting is one of the primary concerns of preschool teachers. In fact, one of the most challenging aspects of child care work involves guiding children's behavior and helping them learn to manage their own behavior. Effective management requires skills in guiding children toward behavior that reflects the best interests of the child, the group, the family, and the staff.

Instead of focusing on handling problems with children once they have occurred, the overall goal is to plan so that potentially conflicting situations are minimized. In other words, we are more successful when we are able to anticipate where and when problems have the greatest potential to occur. The more astute we are in recognizing problem areas and planning to minimize them, the more opportunities we have to work successfully with children.

Objectives

The overall purpose of this chapter is to identify ways to prevent the need for discipline in a child care setting. We will describe ways to design a child care environment that minimizes conflicts. We will study other influences on the management situation, including how a child's self-esteem and a careprovider's self-discipline influence children's behavior. We will examine ways to strengthen a child's self-concept. We will also analyze how stress management influences our work with children.

Key Ideas

Management practices in a child care environment directly affect children's behavior. Thoughtful planning of the environment, schedule, and program can reduce the need for discipline. Well-defined responsibilities of adults and children can also minimize conflict and decrease the need for discipline.

Factors that influence the positive development of behavior include the attitudes of both children and careproviders. Children who feel good about themselves, and have high self-esteem, are more likely to behave in a positive manner. We can help children learn to manage their own feelings and behaviors by recognizing and providing for these and other developmental needs.

Finally, management of stress in the child care setting is an integral part of child care work. Effective stress management is an essential skill needed by adults and children to ensure a well-managed environment.

Characteristics of a Well-Managed Environment

Question Starter: Can you list some of the factors that contribute to a well-managed child care environment? (Responses may include: well-designed environment and schedule; age-appropriate activities; clear child and adult responsibilities.)

A well-managed child care environment offers a number of excellent opportunities to minimize conflicts. Good management is probably the first and foremost ingredient in determining whether there are few or many problems that arise between and among children. We are all aware that when we have things in order, the whole day goes more smoothly. In general, thoughtful planning of the environment and schedule, designing activities that are interesting and age-appropriate, and specifying well-defined responsibilities of adults and children will minimize the occurrence of conflicts and reduce the need for discipline. Adequate and well-arranged space where supervision is easily managed can help promote positive relationships among children, and enable them to work and play together with a minimum amount of conflict.

Question Starter: If you had the opportunity to design a child care environment that would minimize the need for discipline, what features would you include? (Responses may include: interest centers; quiet areas separate from active areas; well-defined play areas; accessible traffic flow; ready and responsive adults; furnishings and equipment reflecting children's changing needs.)

In a well-designed child care environment, children and adults can move easily from one area to another without running into each other and disturbing others in the room. Quiet play areas are separated from busier ones that generate more noise and activity. For example, the reading corner is separated from the large wheel toy area. Boundaries are well-defined, so that children are clear about where they can and cannot play. Boundaries can be defined in a number of ways. For example, lines made with masking tape or cabinets can be used as dividers.

An environment that minimizes the need for discipline is designed so that adults have easy access and exposure to all children, and problems can be spotted before they become uncontrollable. Space is organized so that younger children have a separate area set aside for themselves. Two-year-olds particularly need the security of a space for themselves that can help to minimize unnecessary conflicts with older children. Finally, the physical environment is changed to meet the evolving needs of individuals and the group. For example, older children have different space needs than younger children, and the physical room arrangement should reflect these age and stage needs.

Sheenan and Day (1975) discussed space as a factor that influences children's behavior. They refer to the concept of closed space, which suggests a combination of large and small areas as opposed to one large area. This arrangement takes into account that sometimes children need a place to do a quiet activity or find solitude, while at other times they seek a busier, noisier activity. The closed space concept caters to these differences by providing environmental alternatives. The arrangement also prevents children from racing across the room, thus avoiding potential accidents and conflicts. Moreover, ample play spaces in and between each area, with rugs, tables and chairs out of the flow of traffic, provide plenty of room for movement.

A closed space environment can be created in a number of ways even within a single large room. Semipermanent or movable walls can be constructed by using 2 x 4's as frames with insulation or cork as sound buffers. Burlap, tapestries, or draperies can be hung by using a clothesline or wire to give the illusion of a wall. Canopies or banners can also be hung over small areas to reinforce the concept of a room within a room.

Another dimension of the closed space environment is the private hideaway to which children can retreat for a brief period of time. A private hideaway can be a small tent, a cubby constructed from plywood, an old packing crate, a loft, or a large cardboard box. Almost anything will work that gives the illusion of privacy.

When closed spaced is incorporated, we should always take into account the need for adult supervision. The environment should be designed so that adults have eye contact with all children in the room at all times.

Potential conflicts can be avoided by creating interest centers to provide variety for children. Creating small areas that feature some aspect of children's learning processes is an excellent way to break up one large room, and designing interest centers is an ideal way to highlight various ingredients of the program. Four interest centers with one that changes periodically can challenge the child's interest. Additional materials that are organized and changed periodically keep interest centers absorbing and productive for children. Interest centers can also be arranged to promote independent use by children. Convenient open shelves, labeled with words and pictures that children can learn to identify, encourage independence and the growth of self-esteem—two factors that help eliminate problems.

Learning Activity: Divide participants into small groups. Using a blank piece of paper, ask them to design a floor plan incorporating the following items in one large room: science area; reading area; four tables, each for six children; art area; low shelves; activity tables; large wheel toy area; blanket and cot storage area; dress-up area; manipulative toy area; cubbies; and block area. When completed, have participants share their floor plans with the larger group and tell how the placement of these items would contribute to minimizing problems and conflicts. The floor plans should reflect interest areas, easy traffic flow, and quiet areas separated from busier areas. Figure 1 can be reproduced and used to illustrate a floor plan that would incorporate these qualities.

Another factor in a well-managed environment that minimizes problems is the planning of a daily schedule reflecting sensitivity to children's needs and capabilities.

Learning Activity: Reproduce the daily schedule in table 2. Ask participants to analyze the poorly planned daily schedule and predict problems inherent in this schedule. (Responses may include: imbalance of busier and quieter activities and lack of continuity between activities.) Discuss potential effects of this schedule on children. (Responses may include: boredom, rowdiness, tiredness.)

A poorly planned schedule does not allow for enough variety or continuity at appropriate times and provides too much activity in a short amount of time. The result is that children become bored, tired, or too rowdy.

Learning Activity: Ask participants to analyze the well-planned daily schedule

1. Science
2. Reading area
3. 4 Tables for 6
4. Art area
5. Cabinets
6. Low shelves
7. Activity tables
8. Large wheel toys
9. Blanket/cot storage
10. Dress-up
11. Manipulative toys
12. Cubbies
13. Block area

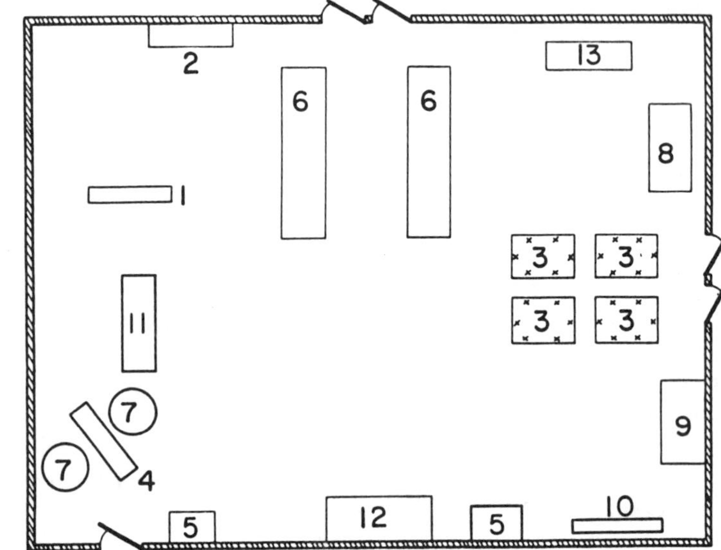

Figure 1. *Model floor plan*

Table 2. Daily Schedules

Well-Planned		Poorly Planned	
7:30	Arrival and free-choice activity	7:30	Arrival and large group activity
8:30	Breakfast	8:30	Breakfast
9:00	Outdoor activity	9:00	Free choice
9:30	Indoor self-selected small group activity	10:30	Snack
10:15	Snack	10:45	Large group activity
10:30	Self-selected small group	11:45	Lunch
11:15	Free play—indoor/outdoor	12:30	Large group competition
11:45	Lunch	1:15	Nap time
12:30	Outdoor play	3:30	Small group activity
1:15	Nap time		
2:30	Flexible small group activity		
3:15	Snack		
3:30	Self-selected small group		
4:15	Self-selected indoor/outdoor activity		

and identify characteristics that make it desirable for increasing the efficiency of the program. (Responses may include: provides continuity; varied activities; reasonable time allocations; smooth transitions.) Discuss the effects of this schedule on children. (Responses may include: lower stress levels; fewer conflicts.)

The well-planned schedule includes characteristics that ensure a smoother day. It consists of activities that are varied and allows for smooth transitions. Quiet activities are interspersed with busier ones throughout the day. Time spans for each activity are appropriate, thereby reducing the amount of stress caused by long activities. Free play is interspersed with more structured events.

In addition to these characteristics, a well-planned schedule is flexible enough to meet the needs of children: it is always open to change if something not originally planned seems appropriate at the time. Although a flexible schedule requires some skill and cooperative effort on the part of teachers, individual interests and needs of children are more likely to be met.

In summary, a carefully conceived schedule allows for flexibility, little waiting on the part of children, and many and varied activities. Moreover, an effective schedule reduces the need for discipline, since it also encourages children to take more responsibility for their own behavior.

Another way to reduce conflicts is to keep groups small, thereby giving each child an opportunity for individual assistance and attention. The number of children in a subgroup should be about the same as the age of the children. That is, there should be about three children in a group when 3-year-olds are present.

Well-planned activities that are interesting and varied can also help reduce conflicts. When children are doing activities they enjoy and find stimulating, they are less likely to become involved in conflicts with each other. Therefore, when planning alternative activities for children, there should be about twice as many options as there are children. Activities that are interesting to children are those that are appropriate to their developmental needs. When activities are either too advanced or too easy, children are much more likely to become bored or frustrated and ready to engage in conflicts.

Well-defined activities also help to minimize unnecessary problems. That is, when children are clear about directions and know what they are supposed to do, they are more likely to take responsibility for their own behavior. In addition, well-defined routines of eating, toileting, napping, dressing, and making transitions limit confusion and help children move easily from one activity to another. It is useful to give children advance notice of an activity by creating songs or rhymes about it, by playing silent games, or by using other challenging techniques. Generally, if we make something interesting, children will respond.

Well-defined responsibilities for children and adults also contribute to a child care environment which functions smoothly. Again, when children know what is expected of them, confusion and the frequency of conflicts are usually reduced. Clear rules and limitations help children set boundaries for themselves. These guidelines also help adults carry out their responsibilities in guiding children.

No matter how well planned the environment is, some conflicts will always arise. Therefore, a well-defined set of policies and procedures for managing children should be written, posted, and discussed so that staff and parents are aware of them, and children know what to expect. Unclear discipline policies create confusion and lack of consistency and often lead to bigger problems. On the other hand, when policies are clear and are followed, children are better able to assume responsibility for their behavior, since they can anticipate what to expect if they fail to cooperate. Items that can be included in a discipline policy are: center philosophy; state laws regarding discipline; procedures that will be used if conflicts arise; center policies that reduce the need for discipline.

Influences on Children's Behavior

Problems often result because children seek attention in unacceptable ways. The attention-seeking child may become aggressive or display other annoying behavior toward adults and peers. The child usually does these things to gain attention. The competent child, or the child who is more sure of himself, is likely to seek attention in more socially acceptable ways.

Self-esteem is a key ingredient in the way all of us behave. Children respond in ways that reflect their own self-concepts. If they feel good about themselves, they are more likely to respond in positive ways.

White (1975) has identified a number of social characteristics of children who seem to function well in situations with other people. Children who have developed a sense of self-esteem know how to get and hold the attention of adults in socially acceptable ways. They use adults as resources after deciding that something is too difficult for them and express affection and moderate annoyance to adults. These children lead and follow their peers, express affection and mild annoyance to their peers, and compete with them. They show pride in their accomplishments and engage in role-play and make-believe activities. In general, the child who displays these characteristics has a positive view of himself.

We, as teachers, are in an excellent position to encourage the development of these characteristics in children. We can help them to develop self-control and behave responsibly as they grow into competent human beings. For example, to help a child learn to get and hold the attention of adults in an acceptable manner, we should be alert to ways in which the child tries to hold on to our attention. We can help her learn how to ask for attention, and respond positively when her request is appropriately made. Again, to help a child learn to use adults as resources, we can encourage her to seek help without encouraging overindulgence. We can let her know we will help, but at the same time guide her toward developing her own problem-solving skills, and give her attention and some assistance as she works to achieve this goal.

We can also help a child learn to express affection and moderate annoyance to adults. When a child spontaneously shows affection, we should respond and enjoy it. If he is angry, we can pause to think about it, and perhaps give some leeway. On the other hand, we must firmly handle serious hostile behavior. Although the expression of negative feelings is a natural part of growing up, we must set firm limits and explore the possible causes for the behavior so that we can deal with it.

Since children need to learn to lead and follow, we can provide opportunities for them to do both. We can arrange for regular experiences with peers in pleasant and supervised circumstances. We should never leave young children unsupervised in a larger group, especially where older children are involved. As stated before, it is best to keep subgroups small so that they will have opportunities to lead and follow in fairly nonthreatening situations.

Children can also be helped to express affection and mild annoyance to peers in much the same way as they learn to lead and follow peers. Small subgroups that are as nonthreatening as possible contribute to the development of this skill. We can also provide positive examples by showing affection to children and by letting them know when we are unhappy with their behavior.

Children can be encouraged to develop a reasonable spirit of competition. In this sense, a competitive person is very much interested in achieving, in doing well, and in having his products compare favorably with others. It is in this healthy sense that children should be encouraged to be competitive. We can stimulate healthy competitiveness by paying attention to the child's achievements, by appropriately expressing pride, by providing assistance to help him develop his skills and, in general, become a more capable person.

We can also help a child learn to show pride in personal accomplishments. By age 3, children begin to seek approval for activities or products they have successfully achieved. They become interested in being praised for their achievements. We can foster this feeling of personal achievement by letting the child know how much we appreciate what he has done. However, we should probably avoid praise of things considerably below his real ability level, since he could begin to develop inappropriate aspiration levels.

Between 2 and 4 years of age children enjoy role-play or make-believe activities that contribute to the development of their overall feelings of self-esteem. We can encourage this developmental need by providing opportunities for engaging in such activities. Activity centers that feature dress-up materials and directed make-believe activities are excellent ways to foster this development.

White (1975) has also identified a number of nonsocial characteristics that seem to be particularly important to the development of self-esteem in children. They include: good language ability; the ability to notice small details or discrepancies; the ability to anticipate consequences; the ability to deal with abstractions; the ability to put oneself in the place of another; the ability to make interesting associations; the ability to plan and carry out multistep activities; and the ability to use resources effectively.

Good language development is one of the key elements in the growth of a child's self-esteem. Language use is basic to the way all of us feel about ourselves, as well as how others respond to us. Language provides the mechanism that all of us use to relate to each other. The key to good language teaching lies in identifying what the child is really interested in at the moment. Once we know what interests the child, we can increase opportunities for talk and interaction and thus help her develop good language skills.

We can also play a part in helping the child learn to notice small details or discrepancies. For example, when a child is interested in a picture of a house it is an excellent time to point out the small details of the house, such as the panes in windows, the number of steps in the porch, or features of the roof.

There are usually many opportunities when working with children to help them learn to anticipate what comes next, thereby building the ability to anticipate consequences. We can help the child learn the habit of thinking ahead by frequently pointing out what has happened and what is about to happen next.

Helping a child learn to deal with abstractions is a little more difficult, since this cognitive ability is not well developed in young children. However, we can talk about objects in terms of their use and makeup and thus begin fostering the development of abstract thinking.

We also want to help children learn to develop the ability of putting themselves in the place of other people. Although young children essentially see the world from their own point of view, we can use opportunities to point out what the world looks like to someone else. Aggressive or hostile behavior provides some opportunities for discussions of this nature. We would, of course, want to help children develop this capability when they are not angry or displeased.

We can help children develop interesting associations by praising efforts at original thinking and by providing experiences that will help them increase their creative powers and problem-solving abilities. We can also encourage them to notice similarities, differences, opposites, consequences and cause-and-effect relationships. The assorted activities related to learning should, moreover, be enjoyable and challenging for each child, so that the association between interest and learning is positive.

To help children develop the ability to plan and carry out activities we can provide opportunities to actually organize and follow through with them. We can describe activities as we do them, so that children learn to pay attention to the ways in which things are done. We can set up episodes that encourage children to plan and carry out the events step by step.

Finally, we can help children learn to use resources effectively by explaining ways to accomplish something. For example, we can explain that a variety of materials may be used to build a house. Or, we can demonstrate how to make candy or cookies, displaying each separate ingredient, explaining why it is essential, and showing how everything is mixed together, then cooked until the desired result is attained.

In summary, the development of self-esteem in children is a result of the interaction of many factors. As teachers, we can make a significant contribution to the growth of social and nonsocial abilities by being aware of them and by following a few relatively commonsense practices in our work with children. Since self-esteem contributes so significantly to the way in which children behave, it is worth committing time and energy to help each child develop a positive self-concept.

Self-Discipline

The fact that the word "discipline" derives from the word "disciple" suggests an important element in self-control. Since children want to be like adults, what we do and how we behave are important. We can provide either a positive or a negative model. For instance, when we manage our feelings well, we provide a positive example. When we speak in a calm, steady voice, we demonstrate that we are managing our feelings effectively. If we handle the child with firmness and understanding, we are demonstrating that we are trustworthy. In turn, the child learns that there are limits for behavior and ways to channel behavior in a constructive manner.

Every person has to cope with stress and strain at times. Certainly, as preschool teachers we have a fair share of stress and strain, which probably means that we do not handle every situation with the calmness and steadiness that we know is best. When this happens, it is a time to model ways to accept responsibility for our own actions and apologize when appropriate. Children are remarkably resilient, and such behavior provides them with another example of ways in which they can deal with their own feelings.

The process of modeling acceptable behavior helps us teach children appropriate ways of managing their own behavior. We are in excellent positions to provide them with ways of becoming responsible for their behavior. The foundations for personal management of behavior are established in the early years of life and we can play an integral part in helping children get a good start.

Managing Stress

Stress is an ongoing part of life. As teachers of young children, we are often under a great deal of stress. We are always dealing with problems and are constantly faced with making decisions that affect the lives of children.

Stress basically originates from two sources: the stress of physical activity and the stress of mental/emotional activity. Certainly, in child care jobs we experience both, with the mental/emotional activity probably creating the most tension. Stress in general does not have to be harmful. Distress, on the other hand, is harmful. Distress is continual stress that demands constant readjustment or adaptation. For example, when we really do not enjoy working with children, we are constantly frustrated, and frustration is distressful. Distress can also occur if we are unable to effectively help a child learn to manage her own behavior. The process is somewhat cyclical, but if we can effectively deal with our own stress, we are in a better position to help children learn to manage their behavior. Consequently, stress management can positively affect the way in which we work with children.

Given that stress is a natural part of life, there are certain ways in which the body reacts, cuing us that distress is, in fact, setting in. When we are aware of these signs, we are better able to deal with stress.

Seyle (1978) has identified three stages of reaction that the body makes to stress: alarm, resistance, and exhaustion. In the alarm stage, the body recognizes stress and prepares for fight or flight, releasing hormones from the endocrine glands that cause an increase in energy. The body then chooses either fight or flight. In the resistance stage, the body repairs any damage caused by stress. If the stress does not go away, the body cannot repair the damage. In the exhaustion stage, migraine headaches, heart irregularity, or even mental illness may result. Continued exhaustion causes the body to become depleted of energy.

Because stress is inevitable, we must develop ways to cope if we are to avoid job dissatisfaction and physical illness. One of the first steps in controlling stress is to recognize the signs of its presence. Rapid breathing, a pounding heart, or butterflies in the stomach are all stress reactions (Kuczen, 1984).

The second step toward coping with stress is to gain mastery over the situation. Stress control can be accomplished in a number of different ways. We can use a deep breathing technique or practice progressive relaxation in which we learn to tense and relax muscles on command (Kuczen, 1984). We can also work off stress by taking a walk or getting some exercise. We can talk about our concerns with colleagues. Getting sufficient sleep and rest and a proper diet can reduce stress. We can learn to balance work and recreation. We can try doing something for someone else. We can learn to take one thing at a time, accept the things we cannot change, and avoid tackling all tasks at once. We can learn to give in occasionally instead of fighting. Finally, we can make ourselves available instead of withdrawing and feeling sorry for ourselves.

We should also remember that most problems eventually disappear. When a problem arises that involves a child or an adult, the first thing we should do is find out what occurred to cause the problem. In the process, we may find that the problem disappears or resolves itself. Even when problems are not resolved, they become clearer when defined, and are therefore more easily managed.

To define a problem we should describe it as specifically as possible. We should write down everything we can recall about a situation: how it began, who said and did what, what happened after each person said or did something, and how it all turned out. To illustrate, if we were to say, "Charles is always hitting other children," we would be providing a general description. However, a specific description would be more helpful in solving the problem. A specific description would be: "Jon accidentally brushed Charles' arm while they were painting. Charles turned around and hit Jon. Jon started crying and ran to me. I asked him what happened. He told me."

In essence, many problems disappear or can be managed when we are able to describe specifically what bothers us. When this effort does not work, we can use some of the other strategies we have described for coping with the stress that we inevitably feel at times.

Children, like adults, often suffer from stress and we can help them cope. Since stress-stamina, or the ability to cope with stress, is tied to a child's self-esteem, we can help children feel loved, respected, and unique. We can learn to recognize the signals of stress in children and then help children analyze the effectiveness of their coping behaviors. Sudden behavioral changes that are evident in several areas, and that continue, can signal danger. According to Kuczen (1984), some of the stress warning signs are attention-seeking, headaches, hair pulling, frequent urination or diarrhea, defiance, explosive crying, unusual shyness, and hyperactivity.

Children can be taught to deal with stress. They can be taught to practice progressive relaxation, to use imagery to picture pleasant thoughts, to laugh, and to otherwise gain rather than lose control of a difficult situation. Kuczen emphasizes the need for children to be able to make informed decisions and solve problems. As teachers of young children, we should teach them how to pinpoint the source of stress and deal with it. Once the stress is identified, it can be managed. Kuczen suggests an effective way of teaching children to use problem solving. The steps she recommends are: get the facts; verbally express the exact nature of the stress; develop a plan; suggest alternative approaches; try out the plan; discuss progress frequently; evaluate the original plan; and make changes as needed.

Stress is a fact of life. When we can help young children learn to cope with stress, we help to create a situation that minimizes the need to discipline children.

Summary

There are many factors that influence how successful we are in guiding children so that they grow into responsible individuals. Managing the environment, both physical and otherwise, can contribute to this goal. Of utmost importance is the need to help children develop a positive self-image that is influenced by our behavior and self-discipline. Self-esteem is the foundation upon which children can learn to cope with the many variables in their lives. We can help children learn to manage their behavior and actions and by so doing create an environment where very little discipline is needed. Guiding children's behavior is comprehensive and complex. It involves a number of factors, working in combination with each other to provide the setting for increasing optimal behavior.

Enrichment Activities

1. Design a daily schedule that can be used in your child care setting. Be sure the schedule reflects those characteristics that encourage positive behavior in children and are conducive to children's level of development.

2. Using your child care facility as the setting, design a floor plan that incorporates the principles of a well-managed environment.
3. If your child care center does not have a discipline policy, write one reflecting the philosophy and practices of your center.
4. Using the components of a well-managed child care environment, identify specific strategies that you can use to improve your child care facility in each area: adequate and well-arranged space; well-planned schedule; small subgroups; well-planned and age appropriate activities; well-defined responsibilities of children and adults. If no improvement is needed in one or more areas, explain why.
5. Select one child to observe and analyze according to the characteristics of a competent child as specified by White. Identify specific ways in which you can help the child improve or maintain each behavior.
6. Select one child in your child care facility and describe three situations in which she did something you would like her to stop doing. Be very specific by taking into consideration what happened before the incident, what occurred during the incident, and what followed the incident. Use this method to analyze why conflicts arise and steps that can be taken to avoid them.
7. Develop a personal plan for reducing the stress in your own life. Learn to recognize the signs of stress and devise strategies for managing stressful situations.
8. Identify specific ways in which you can help children in your child care facility cope with stress. Write a plan and regularly evaluate its success by analyzing stress reduction in children with whom you work.

Bibliography

Barman, A. (1980). *Pressures on children.* New York: Public Affairs Pamphlets.

While reasonable amounts of internal pressure may motivate children to learn, too much pressure can be destructive by creating stress and strain. Children need to develop at their own pace, and teachers and parents are advised to offer encouragement and support without exerting stress-producing pressures.

Blom, G. E., Cheney, B. D., and Snoddy, I. E. (1985). *Stress in childhood.* Hagerstown, MD: Teachers College Press.

A book designed to assist teachers in applying a stress intervention model without becoming therapists. The book is informal and covers such areas as stress intervention and identification, as well as common stressful situations in childhood.

Cherry, C. (1981). *Think of something quiet: A guide for achieving serenity in early childhood classrooms.* Belmont, CA: Pitman Learning.

An interesting and challenging book for early childhood teachers. The author believes that sensitive and caring adults can help young children reduce and manage their own stress through a variety of simple relaxation techniques and games. Various strategies, designed to help teachers maintain serene environments and effectively respond to tensions in children, are presented.

Cherry, C. (1984). *Parents, please don't sit on your kids.* Belmont, CA: David S. Lake.

Nondiscipline discipline is firmly advocated as an alternative to punishment in dealing with children's discipline problems. Why children misbehave and why they irritate adults are questions reconsidered here. The child's point of view and that of parents is also examined. Cherry offers a variety of suggestions for adult alternative action. These include anticipating problems, providing humor, offering choices, praising and encouraging, ignoring provocation, pointing out logical consequences, reminding, distracting, and discussing.

Clarke-Stewart, K. A., VanderStoep, L. P., & Killian, G. A. (1979). Analysis and replication of mother-child relations at two years of age. *Child Development, 50,* 777–93.

An interesting study of mother-child interactions that relates the positive responsiveness of young children to their mother's behavior during play.

Clemes, H., & Bean, R. (1980). *How to teach children responsibility.* Sunnyvale, CA: Enrich, Division of Ohaus.

The difficult question of helping children become responsible and make effective choices is explored in this perceptive handbook. Parents and teachers are offered a variety of alternative methods and strategies, along with suggestions on curriculum, procedures, effective utilization and handling of situations, choices, rules and limits, and consequences of actions and decisions.

Kuczen, B. S. (1982). *Childhood stress: Don't let your child be a victim.* New York: Delacorte Press.

An excellent book that emphasizes the need for helping children in today's society manage stress and related problems. Techniques are suggested for recognizing stress and stressors and building defenses against them. Strategies for making family lifestyles more relaxed are also discussed. A book parents and teachers should read.

Kuczen, B. S. (1984). A.C.T.—A program for stress management. *Early Years K-8,* pp. 26–27.

An informative article on stress and stress management in children. Stress affects even children in the modern world, and the author emphasizes the need for adults to help children cope. This can be done by (1) encouraging awareness of self, of stress signals, and of one's individual coping patterns; (2) teaching children how to maintain control by following a healthful daily routine of eating, resting, exercising and relaxing, and by using certain mental techniques to counteract strain; and (3) training children to identify stressors and use problem-solving strategies to deal with difficulties.

Leonetti, R. (1980). *Self-concept and the school child: How to enhance self-confidence and self-esteem.* New York: Philosophical Library.

This valuable book deals with the role of the teacher in encouraging the growth of healthy self-concepts in children. Relevant theories are reviewed, and teachers are urged to renew their own self-esteem to create supportive environments for children.

Marshell, H. H. (1972). *Positive discipline and classroom interaction: A part of the teaching-learning process.* Springfield, IL: Charles C. Thomas.

The need for mutual respect and trust between teachers and students is emphasized. Interaction is reinforced by efficient planning and the setting of limits. By viewing these three factors together in a positive and constructive way, the teacher can avert many discipline problems before they occur.

McNamee, A. S. (1982). *Children and stress: Helping children cope.* Washington DC: Association for Childhood Education International.

This is a useful resource book for both parents and teachers. Stress in children can be caused by internal factors such as learning disabilities and poor self-concept or by external factors such as child abuse or neglect, disease, death, and everyday life experiences. Suggestions are given on recognizing signs of stress and on helping children cope.

Miller, C. S. (1984). Building self-control: Discipline for young children. *Young Children, 40,* 15–19.

Distinguishing between punishment and discipline, the author discusses the prevention of behavior problems. Parents and teachers should examine their interaction styles and toleration levels, the environment from a child's point of view, schedules that might contribute to problems, and types of expectations. Problems may be averted by making children aware of consequences, encouraging problem solving, using redirection and time-out, applying gentle restraint, and ignoring inappropriate behavior. It is stressed, however, that if these strategies are utilized, they must be used with care and skill.

Miller, M. S. (1982). *Childstress.* Garden City, NY: Doubleday.

An authoritative work on stress as experienced by children in today's world. The author identifies stresses in the home, in society, and at school, and discusses five possible responses children employ to cope with stress: aggression, apathy, escape, "playing the game," and self-destruction. Suggestions are offered on means of avoiding unnecessary stress, recognizing stress, and helping children deal with stress when it arises.

Samuels, S. C. (1977). *Enhancing self-concept in early childhood.* New York: Human Sciences Press.

The book offers practical and theoretical information about the recognition, development, and enhancement of self-concept in young children. Important research is presented and reviewed, and various techniques for enhancing self-concept are provided.

Seyle, H., & Cherry, L. (1978, March). On the real benefits of stress. *Psychology Today,* pp. 69–70.

Stress can have negative results but can also be beneficial. Individuals should understand their normal reaction to stress and learn to monitor their behavior accordingly. By choosing one's own goals, by looking outside oneself, and by seeking one's own stress level one may find an antidote to stress.

Setting limits and explaining rules clearly can help children know where they stand and help avoid discipline problems that occur because of confusing expectations and lack of clear guidelines.

Stone, J. G. (1978). *A guide to discipline* (rev. ed.). Washington, DC: National Association for the Education of Young Children.

Teachers and parents are provided with useful information about how to avoid and manage behavior problems, how to communicate with children, and how to deal with various crises.

Warren, Rita A. (1977). *Caring: Supporting children's growth.* Washington, DC: National Association for the Education of Young Children.

This concise book examines the importance of respecting children's intelligence and integrity. It demonstrates how to become self-disciplined, caring people in the child care arena, and it encourages readers to avoid gimmicks and share strengths with children.

Youngs, B. B. (1979). *Stress within students: Do educators cause and/or prolong it?* San

Diego, CA: San Diego State University. (ERIC Document Reproduction Service No. ED 195 862)
The author analyses and discusses anxiety and stress in children from infancy through adolescence. Stressors, signs, and symptoms are identified, and various ways in which teachers can help children cope with stress are described.

5

Guiding Children

ADULTS who work with young children have an excellent opportunity to establish the type of adult-child relationships that can promote social cooperation. Babies are born with built-in mechanisms for learning to comply (Honig, 1985a). They clearly demonstrate that they are capable of empathetic responses to others (Honig, 1985b). They comply with simple requests and imitate kind, helpful adult behavior.

By the age of 2 or 3, the foundations for social cooperation and compliant behavior have already been established. We, as teachers of young children, can help them learn to master compliance and cooperation in a variety of settings. We are best equipped to help children develop prosocial behavior when we understand why they behave as they do and consider specific ways in which we can foster cooperative behavior.

Objectives

In this chapter we will examine the development of social cooperation in young children and ways in which we can build adult-child relationships which encourage this behavior. We will distinguish between punishment and discipline and examine why effective discipline works and punishment does not. We will analyze specific discipline techniques that promote the development of cooperative behavior in young children. We will specify ways children can be helped to develop self-control, responsibility, cooperation, consideration, and helpfulness. We will identify ways in which we can assess our own behavior in an effort to improve our responses to children.

Key Ideas

Compliant behavior comprises an immediate, appropriate response by a child to an adult's request (Honig, 1985a). Noncompliant behavior, in contrast, is an inappropriate response by a child to an adult's request. The adult can promote the development of compliant behavior in a number of ways.

Punishment and discipline are two separate entities. Punishment is any act that causes a child to suffer physically or emotionally. Discipline, on the other hand, is any action taken by an adult to guide a child's actions. Effective discipline leads to permanency in the development of a child's self-control, sense of responsibility and behavior, while punishment produces no long-term effects. Several adult behaviors, when used correctly, can increase cooperative behavior. Explanations, directions, redirection, anticipation and prevention of potential problems, time-out (or sit and watch), and recognition and encouragement of approprate behavior are effective strategies that can be used to prevent inappropriate behaviors and help children learn more appropriate ways to handle conflicts.

Guiding children's behaviors helps them to develop into competent human beings. The behaviors of adults strongly influence the behaviors of children. Praise and encouragement increase desirable behavior and motivate children to learn how to act appropriately in relationships with other people.

Developing Compliant Behavior

In order to understand how children develop compliant behavior it is necessary to understand the meaning of compliance, which includes immediate, appropriate responses to adult requests. From birth, babies have the capacity to comply, but the extent to which cooperation in fact occurs is dependent upon adult-infant interactions. Compliance is an early appearing social skill that children between the ages of 4 and 5 1/2 can understand and demonstrate (Honig, 1985a).

Noncompliant behavior is frequently a result of the struggle for autonomy and independence. It is a normal facet of a child's development. Children need to learn how to successfully negotiate independent behavior. Our goal is to help them develop a balance between autonomy and cooperation by providing opportunities for independence that incorporate social demands (Haswell, Hock, & Wenar, 1982).

As preschool teachers we can help children master autonomy and independence in a variety of ways. We can make transitions between activities by gradually shifting children's attention and forecasting changes that will be occurring. We can make requests of children in the form of suggestions rather than commands and allow time for them to comply (Haswell, Hock, & Wenar, 1982).

Question Starter: How can we help children develop compliant behavior? (Responses may include: build children's self-esteem; provide praise and encouragement; encourage mutual respect; model appropriate behavior; suggest alternatives.)

There are a number of ways in which children can be taught to develop cooperative behavior. Nondirective speech, positive interactions with children, and responsiveness to their social expressions have all been associated with the development of compliant behavior (Clarke-Stewart, VanderStoep, & Killian, 1979). Adult helpfulness and explanations also influence a child's willingness to cooperate.

We can foster compliant behavior by helping children feel good about themselves and feel rewarded when they behave in positive ways. We should praise them—verbally or nonverbally—when they act appropriately. We all know how good it feels when others compliment us about something we have done that they appreciate. Children respond in the same way. They are much more likely to repeat a behavior if they are praised for it. It also makes them feel good about themselves, and after all, feeling good about oneself tends to increase self-esteem. Praise sets up the conditions for more positive behavior. It also serves to remind all children present about the kind of behavior that is desired.

Our reinforcement of positive behavior should be purposeful. We can hug or verbally praise a child after he has done something we want him to do. We can rephrase statements in a positive manner rather than use negative ones. For example, we can say, "Seymour, you played so well with Billy today," instead of saying "Seymour, why didn't you put those blocks away again today?"

Another way we can build positive behaviors in children is to encourage them. When we encourage children we stress recognition of the effort rather than the accomplishment. We place value on children as they are, not as they could be. We emphasize appreciation for their contributions and demonstrate that we have faith in the child as a useful and capable person.

We can develop the language of encouragement. Some statements that can encourage children are: "I appreciate what you did"; "It looks like you really worked hard on that"; "Thanks, that helped a lot"; "I liked the way you handled that"; "It looks like you really thought that out"; "That's a rough one, but I'm sure you'll work it out"; and "I really enjoyed today, thanks."

We can help children develop positive interactions in a number of ways. We can promote decision-making skills by offering choices and encouragement. We can believe in and respect children, encourage independence and mutual respect, and recognize that no one is perfect and therefore set realistic standards and focus on children's strengths.

Honig (1985a) has identified a number of ways in which we can help children become ego-resilient, self-disciplined people. Because we serve as primary examples for children, we should model consideration, patience, courtesy, and helpfulness. We can use hugs, cheerful smiles, and a loving voice to instill in children the idea that adults are helpful people. We can clearly convey that hurting others is not acceptable, but that having and expressing angry feelings appropriately is acceptable. We can, moreover, help children learn to think of alternatives to unacceptable behaviors and consider consequences of inappropriate behavior. Children are more likely to comply when they fully understand the results of their actions.

Sometimes we may have to physically hold a child who is out of control or find a place where a child can be angry. It may be necessary to refocus some children away from inappropriate or aimless activities to appropriate, constructive ones.

Punishment and Discipline

"That's bad!" "That's stupid!" "Gosh, why don't you watch what you are doing?" "That isn't the way to do it." These statements all fit into the category of scolding or punishment. So does spanking a child.

Any action taken by an adult to change a child's behavior by making him suffer physically or emotionally is punishment (Della-Piana, 1973). Punishment includes spanking, scolding, and intimidating a child. Punishment has probably been used by most people at one time or another and will undoubtedly continue to be used, since it occurs rather naturally. It is easier to scream at a child than to try other approaches to change behavior.

When punishment is used, the child is affected in a number of ways. If the young child is unclear about why he is being punished, he may also be unclear about what is acceptable behavior. Consequently, when punished, he may become angry, resentful, or guilty. He is less able to see clearly what is expected of him and, consequently, is less ready to assume responsibility or self-control.

If punishment is used regularly, there are several negative results that make it difficult to change behavior more permanently (Della-Piana, 1973). First, punishment is only temporarily effective. It is effective only as long as the threat of punishment is there. Once the threat is removed, long-term change of behavior is less likely. Second, the child will do whatever it takes to avoid being punished. For example, if the child is being threatened to tell why she spilled paint all over the carpet, she is more likely to lie about it to avoid punishment than to explain what actually happened. Consequently, the chances for long-term change of behavior are minimized. Third, when punishment is threatened or used, the child learns to react emotionally to the situation in which the punishment occurred. For example, if a child is scolded for crying when his mother leaves him at the child care facility, he is likely to become more anxious in that situation and cry even harder.

In essence, punishment is difficult to implement effectively, and does not result in long-term positive changes of behavior. The major outcome of punishment is learning to avoid and escape from those who punish. Some of the avoidance and escape procedures we teach children are: cheating or avoiding the consequences that go with being wrong; running away, or escaping the many punishments that can be used; lying, or avoiding the punishment that follows doing something wrong; and hiding, or avoiding being caught.

Discipline, on the other hand, refers to those actions that adults take to change a child's behavior in a positive manner (Della-Piana, 1973). When discipline is used instead of punishment, the adult helps the child to identify acceptable behavior and to understand the possible consequences of her actions. Discipline can mean stopping a child and helping her take responsibility for her behavior. With a toddler, it can mean a simple "no" or redirection toward another activity. In other instances, it can mean giving a simple explanation of why something should be done.

Under any circumstances, discipline, when used effectively, can change behavior permanently rather than temporarily. It can also help children learn to develop self-control and responsibility, which in the long run is everyone's goal. In fact, the overall goal of disciplining rather than punishing children is to help them develop self-control and eventually be able to accept the responsibility of self-discipline. Through effective discipline we can guide children in this direction.

Observing an adult effectively redirecting another child is less humiliating and less threatening than observing an adult scold or spank another child. Thus, effective disipline can also serve as a positive model for other children in the group. Again, the overall goal is to change behavior over the long term in positive ways.

Learning Activity: To further clarify the differences between punishment and discipline, divide participants into small groups. Ask half of the groups to resolve the following problems by using punishment and the other half to use discipline techniques in role-play situations: Two 3-year-old children are painting on an easel; one child takes the other child's paintbrush and paints on her sheet, which initiates an argument. After each role-play situation, have participants discuss how each approach affects children differently.

In summary, effective discipline tends to create positive feelings that ultimately lead to higher levels of self-esteem. Punishment more often leads to embarrassment, frustration, and repetition of inappropriate behavior. Discipline has the potential of producing long-term effects, while punishment does not. An understanding of this concept can save hours of unnecessary and unsuccessful attempts to stop negative behavior.

Effective Discipline

Our overall goal as teachers of young children is to guide their behavior in creative, positive ways. However, at times we may need to use a variety of discipline approaches to prevent inappropriate behaviors and help children learn more appropriate ways to handle conflict. As children become more accomplished in managing their behavior, we can move from being directive to democratic (Honig, 1985a).

Question Starter: What are effective strategies that you have used to reduce discipline problems? (Responses may include: explaining and directing talk; ignoring certain behaviors; eliminating problems; time-out; and distractions.)

Effective discipline is a way of helping children develop appropriate behaviors and is used when other efforts to guide a child have not been successful. The exact approach that is used with children depends on the child, the circumstances, and other factors influencing the situation. Being aware of the alternatives prepares us to help children learn appropriate behaviors.

Effective communication techniques are useful when trying to change children's behavior. They are direct, easy to use, and quite natural. In addition, children learn to be responsive to these techniques when they are used correctly.

Explaining and directing talk are two communication techniques particularly effective when trying to redirect behavior (Della-Piana, 1973). Redirecting noncompliant behavior may be as simple as explaining to a child that what she is doing is harmful or disruptive to other children. A simple explanation may stop the negative behavior.

Explaining talk works best when the problem is fairly clear, and the child and the adult are not too tense. It may not work, however, when anxiety or negative feelings exist. If explaining talk does not work, we can provide more explicit directions. Sometimes the child needs simple, clear directions about how to resolve the conflict.

When explanations and directions are not successful, ignoring the situation may be another approach to eliminating undesirable behavior (Della-Piana, 1973). Ignoring means that we do not acknowledge or give importance to the negative behavior, and we can sometimes get a child to stop doing something by simply not paying attention to her actions. Ignoring works best when the child is doing something to get attention because, by ignoring such behavior, we may be able to get the child to stop seeking attention and to become interested in doing other things.

Ignoring undesirable behavior is not always easy, however, because it requires patience and time. Moreover, it is not always an appropriate means of guidance. For example, we cannot ignore behavior that endangers the child, other children, or property, or that is too disturbing to others.

There are other reasons why ignoring behavior does not always work. It is less likely to work when we are very upset or when the child needs some emotional support. It is also less effective when the undesirable behavior has been occurring for a long period of time and the behavior pattern is firmly established. Ignoring as a way of redirecting behavior, however, is worth considering under the right circumstances.

Eliminating the source of the conflict can be an effective way of changing behavior (Della-Piana, 1973). Some problems can be solved by simply removing the cause, especially if the cause is a desirable object or situation. At other times, the problem may arise from another kind of motivator, such as the look on someone's face, which may either disturb the child or be misunderstood by him. Whatever the particular cause of the problem, if removing it helps and is convenient, then it is a worthwhile solution. For instance, if we have only two pieces of clay and we know that six children want to use them, we should consider not putting out the clay until we have enough for everyone to share.

Elimination of some problems may necessitate room rearrangement. For example, when children run indoors after we have repeatedly reminded them not to run, rearranging the physical environment in such a way that it is not possible to run may eliminate the problem.

Removing the cause of the problem works well with very young children because their memory span is somewhat limited. They are less likely to remember what they are not allowed to do from one time to the next. Therefore, removing the cause of the problem can temporarily get rid of an undesirable behavior. For example, when a 2-year-old continues to tear pages from a book and does not respond to an explanation about why it is not acceptable to do so, it may be necessary to take the book away from the child.

Another effective approach to discipline is distraction, which is used to elicit from the child a behavior different from the one causing the problem (Della-Piana, 1973). Distraction can be accomplished in a variety of ways: telling a joke, directing the child to another activity, questioning, or explaining. Although distraction is a temporary solution to a problem, it sets up the circumstances for teaching new ways of behaving. Whenever the distraction is enjoyable, the chances of further changing the behavior are enhanced.

Distraction works best with younger children because their memory spans are more limited. They quickly forget earlier directives explaining why they should not do something. Distraction also works best when a child is not unhappy or angry. Using humor or setting up another situation may not work when the child is too upset to deal with it. However, making a child laugh or finding something else for her to do can sometimes be effective and can be used to set up the conditions for further changing the child's behavior in a positive manner. If the distractions are satisfying enough to the child she learns other ways of adjusting to problems.

When an act cannot be ignored, explanations do not work, distraction is unsuccessful, and eliminating the conflict source is not practical, it may be necessary to temporarily remove the child from the situation. This approach is called time-out, or sit and watch when it is used with very young children. When a child is removed from a situation, it is not the removal itself that makes a difference, but what happens during the time away from the situation.

Time-out, or sit and watch, is the removal of a child from a situation where a problem exists. It involves removing a child who is being very disruptive or aggressive and is used when other attempts to encourage compliant behavior have not been effective. The child is taken to a place in the environment where he can sit and watch, or observe, what other children are doing. This is not a place of isolation, such as another room; it is a place in close proximity to the other children where the child can observe other children who are playing cooperatively without being disruptive.

When using time-out, several guidelines identified in table 3 should be followed if this technique is to be successful.

First, time-out should be used immediately after a disruption. Children need to learn that certain behaviors may lead to

Table 3. Guidelines for Using Time-Out (Sit and Watch)

Remove child immediately after disruption.
Be consistent.
Explain to child reason for removal.
Be calm and talk gently.
Have child sit and watch nearby.
Praise cooperative children playing nearby.
Invite child to return after a few seconds or minutes.
Wait for child's response.
Praise child for cooperative play.

removal from the situation. If reactions are delayed, the child may feel confused about which behavior is the wrong one.

Second, time-out should be used consistently. Children find that it is difficult to learn proper behaviors if they are not consistently enforced. Time-out should last only a short period (a few seconds or minutes).

When using time-out, we should be gentle and explain aloud to the child what we are doing. Children need the opportunity to learn what is inappropriate about their behaviors. Explaining what was wrong can educate the child and other children about what is acceptable and unacceptable behavior.

Success with time-out depends not only on what we do but also on how we go about doing it. Our attitude toward the child who is upset or has misbehaved may come through in words and tone of voice and can make a big difference in whether the child learns to act appropriately or becomes more upset, angry, and resentful.

When using time-out, we should be calm and talk gently to a child who misbehaves. Using harsh words or scolding only draws attention to the child. Even though it is hard to resist saying, "Sam, I've told you a million times . . ." or "Sam, won't you ever learn?" such statements attack the child rather than the behavior we want to prevent. In addition, when we become angry, we present the child with a model of the very behavior we want to control.

Most important of all, at each step of time-out it is necessary to explain aloud to the child what is happening. The child learns how to behave when we explain what he did inappropriately and what could have been done differently in the situation. Explaining aloud lets other children and the teachers know what has occurred and helps them to understand what is happening.

During time-out, we should have the child sit and watch. Since the child needs to know what to watch for while sitting on the side and observing other children, we should praise other children while the child is observing. We can use specific compliments for children who are playing acceptably. For example, "We never see Jeff hit anyone" is more specific than "Look how nicely Susan plays."

We should then invite the child to return by establishing eye contact and asking if he is ready to return. We should be specific about what we expect and should wait for an answer—even very young children can at least nod or smile. A positive response from the child is crucial for the procedure to be effective. We should guide the child back to the same play group or give him the same kind of toy. As soon as he is busy, we should praise him and give him a hug or pat to show we are glad to have him back.

Recognizing when to use time-out and knowing how to explain to a child why he is being placed in time-out are equally important. The effectiveness of this approach is only successful if the child is able to comprehend the implications of

Table 4. When to Use Time-Out

When a Child:	Suggest:
Shows physical or verbal aggression (hitting, name calling, biting)	Touch gently or talk nicely
Takes a toy from another	Ask for a toy
Goes into "off-limits" area	Play in an area where there are toys
Acts dangerously or destructively toward furnishings	Use the furniture correctly

the situation and its effects on others. Examples of when to use time-out and suggestions for what to say to the child are provided in table 4.

Learning Activity: Demonstrate how to use time-out by having participants role play the following situation: Three children are playing when one child pulls a toy away from another child. The adult intervenes and uses time-out to resolve the conflict. To correctly implement time-out, each step should be followed correctly.

The variety of approaches that we have discussed to effectively guide children's behavior will work with some children, under certain circumstances, and with certain teachers. Responding effectively is an individual matter, and what works at one time may not work at another. The important point is that when we have a number of different approaches at our fingertips, we have a better chance of selecting one that does work.

In addition to guiding children's behavior, it is important to examine our own manner of dealing with problems. We can all recall situations where we have consistently become upset because of a particular child. For instance, suppose we have a child who seems to be purposely misbehaving just to irritate us. We even think that if we did not have to deal with this one child all of our problems would be solved. When this type of situation exists, we should stand back and observe our reactions to see if the child's behavior is less of a problem than we thought initially. We may even be able to change our ability to handle the problem by observing our own responses to it.

If we want to try to change our own behavior, we should first identify the problem and the behavior we want to change. Then we should record in some manner the number of undesirable ways we respond on a given day. We should keep a record of this for one or more weeks to see if in fact we are able to change our behavior. A record of our own behavior pattern provides a way to analyze whether our responses are encouraging a child's negative behavior.

Summary

Effective guidance of children in the child care setting is possible when a number of factors work together to create a favorable environment. We have reviewed various approaches to discipline and ways in which we can guide children toward positive behavior. We have also examined ways in which we can provide encouragement and instill in children the desire to respond appropriately.

Enrichment Activities

1. Identify a behavior you want to change. Describe the behavior and for one week keep a record of the occurrences of this behavior. At the end of the week, count the occurrences and see if the behavior diminishes. If so, describe the result.
2. Select one day and describe the conflicts that arise in the child care setting and the specific ways in which you respond. Analyze the results of your responses and try to determine if they were successful or unsuccessful. Were there better ways to handle these conflicts? If so, what were they?
3. Select one day and record every positive response/statement you make to children. Describe the effects on you and the children. Did the children exhibit more compliant behavior because of your actions?
4. Write a self-improvement plan for handling the management of children's behavior. Try implementing the plan for one week. Evaluate the results at the end of the week.

Bibliography

Della-Piana, G. (1973). *How to talk with children and other people.* New York: John Wiley and Sons.

This book is useful for both parents and teachers as a guide to effective talk with, and management of, children. Talk, it is stressed, leads to better understanding and communication. Various styles of talking to children are illustrated and analyzed: scolding, questioning, supporting, accepting, explaining, directing, shaping. Alternatives to punishment are suggested. Self-tests and exercises are also provided to determine the method or combination of methods that work best for each person.

Dreikurs, R., & Goldman, M. *The ABC's of guiding the child.* Chicago: North Side Unit of Family Education Association.

A useful booklet for parents (but good for teachers, too). The authors, stating that rewards and punishment are out of date, propose alternative, more effective techniques to guide children. These are: natural and logical consequences; acting instead of talking; withdrawal as counter action; taking time for training; avoiding overprotection; encouraging independence; understanding the child's goals of misbehavior; having family councils; showing sympathy but not pity; and having fun together.

Gilstrap, R. (Ed.). (1981). *Towards self-discipline.* Washington, DC: Association for Childhood Education International.

This compilation deals with an important aspect of discipline: the child's movement toward self-control, purpose, and responsible social behavior. Contributors emphasize that self-discipline cannot develop out of control by others. Techniques are presented to teach self-direction and self-discipline, and it is stressed that there is a need for meaningful interactions that take into account children's emotions, feelings, and understanding. This book will be appreciated by teachers and parents who have a serious concern for both children and society as a whole.

Haswell, K. L., Hock, E., & Wenar, C. (1982). Techniques for dealing with oppositional behavior in preschool children. *Young Children, 37* (3), 13–18.

The negativistic period between approximately 18 months to 5 or 6 years of age is part of the child's search for autonomy. However, children need to achieve a balance between independence and dependence, and certain techniques can help deal with oppositional behavior while still providing opportunities to develop autonomy. For example, during transitions from one activity to another, adults should be flexible, give verbal alerts, offer choices, and allow time for compliance. Moreover, adults should be positive in their own behavior. Time-out as an effective means of controlling oppositional behavior is also discussed.

Hildebrand, V. (1980). *Guiding young children.* New York: Macmillan.

Working with young children involves a commitment to guiding them in their physical, social, and emotional development. This book provides useful information for caregivers on how to play with, care for, talk to, and disipline children.

Honig, A. S. (1985a). Compliance, control, and discipline. *Young Children, 40* (2), 50–58.

Young children are born with built-in biological skills for learning to comply. Adult-child interactions, adult language, and child-rearing styles influence compliance and disobedience. Another crucial factor is attachment. Research shows that children with a secure attachment to an adult are more likely to be resourceful, flexible, and competent in problem-solving situations. Attachment has also been found to relate to self-control. Timing and setting may have much to do with children's compliance. To substantiate this assertion, Honig reports research on compliance in laboratory playrooms, in the supermarket, and in the home. Adult behaviors in all these places have some effect also.

Honig, A. S. (1985b). Compliance, control, and discipline. *Young Children, 40* (3), 47–52.

Honig reviews research dealing with the effects of child care on compliance. She discusses peer aggression in day care, compliance with parents among day care children, and the relationship of a child's sex to compliance in general and in child care in particular. The goal of compliance is not to instill slavish obedience but to develop self-control and self-regulation among children. Various helpful suggestions toward this end, such as catching the child in good behavior and expressing appropriate pleasure, conclude the review.

Kamii, C. (1984). Obedience is not enough. *Young Children, 39* (4), 11–14.

A thought-provoking article based on Piaget's belief that children can behave with integrity and responsibility if adults interact appropriately with them. Different types of interactions produce different results. The author discusses reward and punishment, kinds of morality, the necessity of exchanging points of view with children and allowing them to make their own decisions. Moving toward autonomy and self-regulation at an early age is stressed.

McDaniel, T. R. (1981). Identifying discipline problems: A self-evaluation exercise. *Childhood Education, 57,* 224–25.

A variety of discipline problems faced by teachers in average classrooms are identified. A ladder leading from least severe to most severe problems reveals that different teachers rate behavior differently, according to their own personality and tolerance levels. Thus, teachers need to learn to evaluate themselves in regard to their attitudes. Reasons for children's problem behavior are briefly outlined, and some general suggestions are given on ways of reducing or at least meeting these openly. Finally, the writer reminds us that each child must be taken on his/her own terms and helped to develop into a mature and healthy individual.

Osborn, D. K., & Osborn, J. D. (1977). *Discipline and classroom management.* Athens, GA: Education Associates.

A practical book that presents research findings and applies them to classroom management. There are helpful discussions on topics such as self-analysis in teachers and the necessity of observing children in order to understand problems that may lead to lack of discipline in the classroom.

Stone, J. B. (1978). *A guide to discipline* (rev. ed.). Washington, DC: National Association for the Education of Young Children.

Teachers and parents are provided with useful information about how to avoid and manage behavior problems, how to communicate with children, and how to deal with various crises.

6

Observing Children

AS teachers of young children, we need to develop skills as observers. We need to be able to see as accurately and objectively as possible into individual situations (Read & Patterson, 1980). We need to become observers of young children so that we can better interpret the messages that children convey.

Observing children and being able to accurately interpret that observation is a skill that is learned. It is more than looking—it is seeing and feeling what is observed. As an observer, the teacher is involved, is interested in the meaning behind a behavior, and is able to be objective without being influenced by value judgments (Read & Patterson, 1980).

The experienced teacher usually becomes a good observer because of years spent watching children. Recognizing the importance of knowing children, she may even have developed a system for readily recording notes about children's behaviors. The teacher sets aside regular times to do more sustained observing, especially when there are specific purposes for finding out more about a child's behavior.

An astute teacher will take the time to observe, make records, and use these records to increase her knowledge and understanding of children. She will use the information to become better acquainted with children's interactions with material, equipment, and people. She will make interpretations based on objective observations and try to apply this information to the ways in which she works with children.

Objectives

In this chapter we will specify why it is important to record observations of children in a child care setting. We will identify what it means to be a skillful observer and interpreter of observations. We will identify and analyze various methods of observing children. We will examine the need to develop a systematic plan for observing children and ways in which this goal can be accomplished.

Key Ideas

Observation of children is a learned skill that all teachers of young children need. Skillful observation should provide support for the following: development of sensitivity to the uniqueness of a child; the identification of a child's needs that might otherwise be overlooked; and the provision of information for planning activities and interactions for a particular child.

Accurate records of observations of children are objective and free of value judgment. They document what is seen, not what is felt or believed. They describe an event, scene, or behavior in such a manner that someone who was not present can identify with the situation and visualize what had occurred.

Various methods of observing children can be used, including narrative, sampling, and rating. Selection of an observation method is dependent on the purposes of the observation and the resources available. A systematic plan for observing children provides the framework for achieving the goal of observation.

Rationale for Observing Children

Question Starter: Why should we observe children? (Responses may include: understanding children; identifying needs; seeing children's viewpoints; planning activities; assisting in adult-child interaction.)

Successful work with children implies that the teacher has skills in observing and interpreting children's behavior. By contributing to our knowledge of children in general and a child in particular, observation helps us correct the biases and distortions we make about children (Phinney, 1982).

Observation provides the raw material from which our understanding of children can grow. It allows us to describe more accurately what a child is able to do and to gather information that is not necessarily apparent. For example, close observation of a child may reveal that he is hesitant to attempt new tasks, which could be a sign of lack of self-confidence.

Skillful observation of children can also help us identify needs that might otherwise be overlooked. For example, observing a child who is irritable and uncooperative day after day can prompt us to check more closely into his physical health.

Skillful observation of children allows us to understand a child's point of view. It can provide clues about what a particular activity means to a child or how the child actually experiences a particular incident. For instance, if we regularly observe that a child does not want to use scissors, we may find that he needs direction and more opportunities to practice this fine motor skill.

Through observation, we can identify the learning needs of a child. We may discover, for example, that Sue can count to ten but does not understand what four means if she is asked to put four blocks in a row. This information helps us plan for Sue's next learning step.

Skillful observation provides a basis for planning for each child each day. The information obtained from observations helps us make decisions about what types of activities we plan for a particular child. If we are aware that a child is having difficulty using scissors, we can help her learn to use scissors if she is developmentally ready by implementing a step-by-step process.

Observation can also improve our interactions with a child, as well as help us to understand the child's interactions with other children. For example, even though we may be aware that Mary usually plays alone, through observation we might learn that she plays alone because other children tease her when she tries to interact with them. By being aware of this problem, we can take steps to help her feel comfortable when playing with other children.

Observation records provide the raw material for interacting with parents about their children. The information can also be useful in guiding parents to interact better with their children and in providing new staff with up-to-date and continuous information about children.

In summary, a skillful observer develops sensitivity to the uniqueness of personality and becomes increasingly able to interpret the language of behavior. The ability to fix attention on one child at a time makes it possible to look more deeply into that child's behavior for clues to understanding the significance of his actions, gestures, facial expressions, spoken words, and the tempo of his day-to-day behavior.

Skillful Observations

Question Starter: What skills are needed to become a good observer of children? (Responses may include: objectivity; clarity; unbiased interpretion of observations; knowledge about child development.)

One of the goals of observation is to describe an event, scene, or behavior in such a manner that someone who was not present at the time could either understand what the person had observed or could visualize what had occurred. In order to accomplish this goal, observations must be objective. For example, the phrase "in a rage" is ambiguous: it could mean shouting, pushing, crying, fighting, or any number of other behaviors. Objective language, on the other hand, is specific and describes precisely what the child is doing.

Objectivity is a very difficult but essential skill. We are all aware of what is called the eye-witness report. At the scene of any accident, law officers are eager to have firsthand reports from all who witnessed the incident. And without exception, each person's report differs. Each person saw the incident from his or her own point of view and interpreted it with individual feelings, biases, and ideas. We naturally draw conclusions and make interpretations that reflect our personal opinions. What often gets lost in the shuffle of opinions are the facts, the evidence, regarding what actually occurred.

In our work with children, it is easy to conclude that some children are aggressive. In this generalization of children, we may categorize them and thus prevent ourselves from dealing effectively with their behavior. If we have not carefully and objectively observed children, we are less able to identify the specific situations that seem to aggravate aggressiveness, the specific children or adults who upset them the most, or the activities which seem to interest them. Lacking an actual record of specific behaviors prevents us from knowing how to plan for children.

Objectivity means simply to record what is observed so that another person can interpret the recording exactly as it is stated. For example, we do not actually see anger, happiness, insecurity, or feelings of rejection. These statements are judgments based on many observations—not on one observation only.

Objectively describing an event or behavior does not mean that there is no place for subjective interpretation. Personal feelings and ideas can be applied after an accurate record of facts and direct evidence has been documented. We can then ask how the information helps in understanding and planning for a particular child or an aspect of the child care program. What is important is that we are clear about what is objective and what is subjective.

Learning Activity: To provide practice in writing objective statements, ask participants to rewrite the following statements so that they are stated objectively: (*a*) Joan was glad to see her mother; (*b*) Susan is tired in the morning; and (*c*) Peter does not want to go outside. Examples of objective statements are: (*a*)

Joan jumped up and down and laughed when her mother came in; (*b*) Susan yawns and sits at the table without touching the crayons, rubs her eyes, and places her head on the table; and (*c*)Peter holds the doorknob and says, "No, I'm not going!" when the adult asks him to go outside to play.

To become a skillful observer, it is important to practice observing a child and to write down exactly what is happening. It is necessary to use language precisely. For example, if a child runs to another side of the room, we should use the word "run" instead of "moves." Other information that should be recorded on the observation form is: date, time, setting, children involved, age, and a brief description of the child.

Skillful observation involves recording only what we see, not what we feel, think, or believe. There is a tendency to conclude that the person we are viewing thinks or feels the way we would if we were in the same situation. Consider the statement, "Jennifer threw herself on the floor in a rage." This statement, which appears obvious enough, actually makes an assumption about her feelings that cannot be verified scientifically. "Jennifer threw herself on the floor screaming and kicking her feet" is better because it describes overt behavior and could be verified by another observer.

When observing children, it is best to be as inconspicuous as possible. Observations should last no more than 10 to 20 minutes, but should be done at various times so that it is possible to obtain a more comprehensive picture of the child.

Skillful observation means making a clear distinction between what is actually seen or heard and the conclusions drawn from it. Facts should be clearly separated from interpretations. Interpretations should be made from what is observed, using the child's point of view rather than our own perceptions. Any conclusions should be based only on the actual observation. Exact words and behaviors, including body language, should be recorded. Individual feelings or opinions should not influence the observation (Irwin & Bushnell, 1980).

Skilled observers are involved in the child's world and use their senses to observe its various dimensions. They accept the child's actions and are able to differentiate between subjective and objective thought. They keep short accurate notes while observing and write up the observations as soon after observing as possible.

Skillful observation means that we observe not only what the child does but how he does what he does. We strive to capture the quality of his behavior, including the most exact expression of his feelings. This necessitates noting on paper not only the actual words the child says or the obvious actions he performs but the subtle characteristics of facial and postural expression by which he reveals his pleasure, dissatisfaction, fear, and other emotions. When making observations about the quality of a child's behavior, it is still necessary to record observations as objectively as possible. This is a skill that is learned with some practice. At the end of the observation record, a note should be made of exactly what the child is engaged in doing, to provide clarity about what he was doing when the observation ended.

Each person brings to the observation situation certain information about child development. Every effort should be made to apply sound child development knowledge to the situation. The more accurate information we have, the better able we are to objectively assess the developmental status of the child. For example, when we know that the motor or language skills a child possesses are appropriate or inappropriate for her age, we are in a better position to plan for her needs.

It is obvious that objectivity is a difficult skill to develop. But, once we have mastered the skills of observation, we can gather a wealth of evidence to help understand and plan for the individual child. Skillful observation provides the tools that are needed to address the physical, cognitive, and social needs of every child within our care.

Learning Activity: To sensitize participants to the skills of objective observation, engage them in the following role-play situation. Select four persons to leave the room, and four to role play this scene: An adult is reading a book to two children when two other children standing nearby begin to push each other. The observers remaining in the room should record exactly what they see. When the four persons who have been outside the room return, ask several people who have observed the role play to describe it to those who returned to the room. Based on the verbal description, have them reenact the role play for the group. Subsequent discussion questions are: How accurate were the observations? How much difficulty did the group who returned have in understanding the scene? How could the observation be improved?

Interpreting Observations

Once we become proficient in observing children, we are better able to interpret the information recorded on our observations so that the needs of individual children can be addressed. The observations provide information about the children's developmental status, including physical, language, cognitive, social, and emotional development. Knowledge about child development in general provides the clues that allow us to interpret the information about the individual child. For example, when a child has been observed over a period of time and it is noted that she seldom interacts with other children, the teacher can purposefully encourage her to play with another child who is sensitive to other children's needs.

In addition, through observation we may notice that a particular child is really advanced in manipulative skills. In such a case, more advanced activities can be planned for this child. The observations could also reveal that another child needs more help with the development of age-level motor skills. Whatever the needs of children, they will become more obvious when systematic observations are implemented.

Interpretations should never include assumptions beyond the obvious information. Interpretations should not include value judgments, because what bothers one person does not bother another, and what is acceptable in one group of people is not acceptable in another. Thus, instead of saying, "Mary is shy," we can say, "Mary often does not interact with other people."

Methods of Child Observation

There are many methods of observation that are useful for different purposes. Each method requires the skills that we have reviewed. Observation methods fall into three categories: narrative, sampling, and rating (Irwin & Bushnell, 1980). Selection of the type of observation method that will be used is dependent on the goals of the observer, time, and resources.

Narrative methods reproduce the information in much the manner in which it occurs. One example of the narrative approach is the keeping of anecdotal records. Anecdotal recording, or event sampling, is used to record behaviors that tend to be recurrent. Brief records are made of a series of separate episodes that focus only on the events of interest. Little writing is required, but since several separate recordings are made, a cohesive picture is provided of the child's behavior pattern. Anecdotal records focus on causes, effects of intervention, and after-effects (Phinney, 1982).

Another example of the narrative method is the diary description, which includes recording observations at regular daily intervals. Diary descriptions focus on developmental changes as they occur and provide a narrative summary of growth changes over a period of time (Irwin & Bushnell, 1980). Some specific developmental tasks that we might observe and record are: riding a tricycle; swinging; throwing and catching a ball; matching forms; stringing beads; copying forms; cutting with scissors; initiating activities; accepting limits and routines; and showing curiosity.

Running records, or specimen description, is the method most commonly used by teachers of young children. Continuous behavior sequences, or everything the child does, are recorded for a specified period of time. The setting, behavior of the child, and the behavior of others who interact with the child are recorded. Each event is reported in a separate sentence in chronological order. Only the child's actions are recorded, and interpretive comments are avoided, separated by parentheses, or placed in a column (Phinney, 1982).

Another approach to observation consists of sampling methods. One such method is time sampling, which is generally used for research purposes. When time sampling is used, the total observation time is divided into 30- or 60-second blocks, and one check or comment is made for each occurrence of a behavior being observed. Within each time block what the child did or said and who initiated the conversation or activity is recorded. Time samplings collected over a period of time provide information from which interpretations can be drawn. This method is useful in observing the type of material and equipment the child chooses, peer patterns, and adult interactions (Phinney, 1982).

Event sampling is similar to time sampling except that specific events are observed. That is, the observer is interested in observing only certain events or behaviors. The primary problem with event sampling is that much time can be absorbed by waiting for a behavior to occur. Some time can be saved by using on-the-spot coding or narration.

Checklists are sampling methods that incorporate a selected list of behaviors of interest that are precisely defined and can be indicated with a check. They can be used to identify frequency or patterns of children's behaviors. Checklists are more useful when they include operational definitions to describe the specific behaviors that are identified (Phinney, 1982).

Rating scales are other tools for observing children. They permit observation of selected aspects of behavior or situations. Ratings are based on cumulative direct observation of children. They are easy to develop and use and provide fairly objective means of evaluating children's developmental growth (Irwin & Bushnell, 1980).

Finally, informal interviews can be used to gather information about children. They can be implemented as opportunities arise and are used to gain an understanding of a child's strengths and weaknesses. Interviews should be simple and in the form of interesting and enjoyable games or activities. As children converse and perform, their language, cognitive, and motor skills can be assessed.

Each method of observation provides its own advantages and disadvantages. Selection should be based on the purposes for making observations and the results which are desired. A combination of approaches can perhaps meet the qualitative and quantitative needs that each teacher considers to be necessary. The important consideration is to have a plan that addresses the concerns of all children and the program.

Implementing Observation Recording

One example of observation recording is a combination of time sampling and narration. The recording sheet provided in figure 2 is a mechanism for recording observations. It includes a place for the child's name, age, sex, and the date and time of

Observation Form

Name of child: Age: Sex:
Date and time observed:
Setting:
Names of others present:

Minute 1

Activity:

Language:

Task:

Social:

Minute 2

Activity:

Language:

Task:

Social:

***Figure 2.** Blank observation form*

observation, which, of course, should be noted on all observations. Each minute of observation is subdivided into four categories: activity, language, task, and social.

As the observations are recorded, what the child does minute by minute is written under the activity section. What should be recorded is what happens without adding any interpretation. Also, the activity and materials and whether other children or adults are present should be noted.

In the language section, what the child says and what other children or adults say to him during each minute should be recorded. Although it may not be possible to write down the exact words a child speaks, the list of comments should be noted as extensively as time allows. Abbreviations, such as initials for children or adults, and symbols can be used. A quick glance at the language section signals the extent of the child's conversation with other children and adults and reveals whether he initiated talk or mainly responded to others.

In the task section, the general category of activity the child is doing such as pretend, art, or manipulation, as well as nonplay behavior such as watching or cruising, should be recorded. This section provides a clue about the type of activities that a child selects over a period of time.

With whom the child is playing or interacting is described in the social section. A glance at this section identifies whether the child was alone or with others during each interaction. A review of the social section provides minute-by-minute information about the child's interactions over a period of time. A completed observation form is shown in figure 3 to illustrate the type of information which can be included.

Question Starter: What does the completed observation form tell you about the child named Beth? (Responses should in-

Observation Form

Name of child: Beth Age: 35 mo Sex: F
Date and time observed: June 30, 1986, 3:00 p.m.
Setting: Clay activity around a small table
Names of others present: Ted, Rod, Mary, and Shala

Minute 1

Activity: Scratches face, handles clay, pats clay, shows clay to teacher, and hands clay to teacher.

Language: Beth to Shala: *Me making strawberry cake.*
Shala to Beth: Strawberry cake.
Beth to Shala: *Pretend to eat.*
Shala to Beth: Pretend to eat. It's dirty.

Task: Manipulative

Social: Small group

Minute 2

Activity: Watches others; handles clay; pretends to eat; responds to teacher.

Language: Beth to Shala: *I make a bottle.*
Shala to Beth: A bottle?
Beth to Shala: *Yeah*

Task: Manipulative

Social: Small group

Figure 3. *Filled-in observation form*

clude: The observed child is a 35-month-old female and is enrolled in a child care program for 2 1/2- to 3 1/2-year-olds. The teacher's name is Shala. The child is involved in a clay activity with three other children and the teacher. They are sitting around a small table.

The clay activity is described as a manipulative activity in the task section. In the social section, the child is described as playing in a small group. In the activity section, physical actions are described in each of the three minutes, and the language section includes a record of what the child and the adult said. The child's language is underlined.

Although in reality we could observe the child for a longer period and at various times, this brief observation reveals a number of important clues about this child. Her hearing is good: In response to the loud banging, she said "Ouch" and put her hand to her ear. She seems anxious to please the teacher—her attention is primarily focused on what the teacher says and does. She is a watcher, and is interested in what goes on around her, but is inclined to be somewhat easily distracted. She is cooperative with the teacher and other children. While she does not evidence a great deal of interaction with the other children (typical of her age), she also does not disrupt them. She seeks attention in age-appropriate ways by showing the teacher what she has made and waiting for her approval. She evidences some creativity and enjoys make-believe as shown by her identification of the clay as a strawberry cake, which is less common than a chocolate cake. She is a good listener. She responds to the teacher's remarks and requests. Her language skills are age-appropriate, while her ability to identify the clay as a strawberry cake reveals that she has the cognitive skill of creating something that does not really exist.

Based on our observation of this child's skills and style of play, there are a number of activities that we could plan for her. Because she is easily distracted, we could plan activities that require longer periods of concentration. To increase her leadership skills, we could give her specific tasks to perform, such as handing out napkins at snack time.

This brief observation shows us that the child does enjoy watching and following. We can help her balance these interests by giving her a manageable opportunity to take the initiative and complete a task on her own. We could encourage her to interact with other children in activities designed to help her overcome some of her natural shyness and to feel more comfortable as an active participant in the group. By asking her specific questions and setting up small interactive opportunities, we could encourage her to interact. The observed child may need particular assistance in integrating into activities with older children. Her behavior is a good illustration of why children under 3 benefit greatly from the opportunity to play in small groups with children of similar age in a space set aside especially for them.

The method of observation we have analyzed is only one approach but it illustrates the need to organize in a systematic way the manner in which observations will be recorded. There are other systems that can be implemented to provide the assurance that observations will become a natural part of the routine in a child care center.

Systematic Planning of Observations

Having information about observation methods and knowing how to use them is not enough. We must be able to implement observations of children in a systematic way. Implementation requires that we devise a plan for looking at and recording behavior to provide the assurance that we actually do observe children systematically.

We should follow several steps when implementing a systematic plan for observing children. First, we should decide exactly what we want to accomplish through our observations. To identify what we want to do, we should begin by specifying our objectives and how we want the end product to help us in working with children.

Once we have identified our objectives and have a clear picture of what we want to accomplish, we are able to make decisions about what types of instruments we need to use. Criteria for making these decisions should include, in addition to our objectives, the time and resources that are available. We may decide to use standard instruments, or we may need to develop our own tools. Whatever decisions we make, they should reflect our needs, time, and resources.

We also need to plan specific times for making observations. If we fail to consider this step, all of our good intentions can be wasted. As we become more proficient at making observations, less time will be required. To begin the process of observing children, it is wise to set aside a certain amount of time each week as observation time. This time should be clarified to other staff so that they understand what is occurring. Even though established times are identified, other opportunities for observation recording should not be overlooked, especially when an incident occurs that is particularly pertinent to understanding a child.

Once needs, systems, and time factors are identified, we should examine all available resources that can provide support for accomplishing our goals. Resources include staff, parents, volunteers, and anyone who can assist in either providing relief time or ways to keep track of the information that is collected. Recordkeeping is a large task that requires preplanning but is clearly beneficial.

The process of observation is most beneficial when all of these steps are followed. It is not enough to simply decide to do observations. Much thought and planning must go into the endeavor.

Summary

Skilled observation of children plays a vital role in the quality of the entire child care program. It enables the teacher to address physical and developmental needs in a professional manner and plan programs and activities that are of maximum benefit to children. Observation records provide important information for parents and significant others, such as social workers, who have an interest in and contact with a particular child. Observation records are also useful when preparing for conferences with a parent and in recognizing the progress and changes made by a child. Finally, observation records are useful when individual staff change. Reviewing materials in a child's folder can provide a quick and accurate introduction of children to new staff members.

Enrichment Activities

1. To improve your skills at making narrative observations, observe one child who is playing alone. Describe the place, time, and materials or equipment in use. Write a running account of what the child says and does. Record all the steps of an action in the order in which they occur. Ask someone else to read and review the observation and describe it to you. Rewrite the sections that were unclear.
2. Survey the literature on other types of observation forms, such as rating scales and checklists. Using these samples, develop your own form, making sure that it addresses the ages and needs of children with whom you work. Use the revised form to record information and keep track of children in your care. Or use the checklists and rating scales as they are to record information about your children.
3. Develop a systematic plan for regularly observing children in your care. Identify your purposes for observation, what you hope to accomplish, and how you plan to use the information. Select observation tools to meet your objectives. Identify times when you can observe children and note any resources that are available to assist you. Implement the plan as soon as you can.
4. Using the observation recording system described in this unit, select a child to observe. Make the observations and, utilizing the information, develop a specific educational program for that child.

Bibliography

Boehm, A. E., & Weinberg, R. A. (1977). *The classroom observer: A guide for developing observation skills.* New York: Teachers College Press.

Here is a book for both researchers and teachers. Its chief value for teachers is that it can help them understand and choose appropriate observational methods, techniques, instruments, and equipment for their daily interaction with, and observation of, children.

Chan, I. (1978). Observing young children, a science working with them, an art. *Young Children, 33* (2), 54–63.

The author compares child rearing and child care in China and the United States. Two observational research studies carried out in children's natural environment are described. Children's interactions, language, and innate curiosity were observed, and the benefits of group settings to stimulate these are advocated.

Cliatt, M. J. (1980). Play: The window into a child's life. A checklist for observing children's play. *Childhood Education, 56,* 218–20.

A valuable article to help those who observe children's activities to learn and understand more about children and their needs. Play frees children to express themselves: it therefore provides a natural means for teachers to listen, observe, and evaluate language skills, social behaviors, and emotional development. A useful checklist is provided to assist observation. The checklist consists of searching questions, which are themselves based on sound developmental ideas.

Cohen, D. H., & Stern, V. (1978). *Observing and recording the behavior of young children* (2nd ed.). New York: Teachers College Press.

As an in-depth account of observing and recording, this book will be very helpful for teachers. The writers go into detail about every aspect of children's activity that can be observed, including general behavior, use of materials, socializing, role playing, relationship with adults, cognitive functioning, individual style, thinking, and language development. Suggestions on how to synthesize, summarize, and interpret observations are also offered.

Irwin, D. M., & Bushnell, M. M. (1980). *Observational strategies for child study.* New York: Holt, Rinehart and Winston.

The authors trace and describe the history and background of various important strategies for observing children. Some of the techniques dealt with are narrative description, sampling methods, rating scales, and observational systems. Checklists and rating scales such as the Flanders' Interaction System, Caldwell and Honig's APPROACH System, and Stalling's SRI System are discussed.

Lasky, L. R. (1978). Personalizing teaching: Action research in action. *Young Children, 33* (3), 58–64.

A teacher describes how she observed children's responses and behavior in an art class episode. Her observations led to action research in which further observation and inquiry revealed specific patterns of responses to given situations with children. It was found that alternating classroom arrangements could suit and modify individual behavior styles and stimulate student creativity.

Lindberg, L., & Swedlow, R. (1976). *Early childhood education: A guide for observation and participation.* Boston: Allyn and Bacon.

This useful book is based on the rationale that systematic observation helps teachers and others understand children's interactions with different types of materials and people, thus making it possible to know how different children learn. Observation should be an ongoing, well-organized, thorough, and objective process. Moreover, to form an accurate picture of children's behaviors, observation should extend over a wide range of materials and subject matter. Hence, several early childhood curriculum components are covered in this book. Workshops to aid detailed and systematic observation are also provided.

Mowbray, J., & Salisburg, H. H. (1975). *Diagnosing individual needs for early childhood education.* Columbus, OH: Charles E. Merrill.

The book stresses the individuality of each child and looks at development as an integrated process. Procedures and strategies are described for observing and learning about children on an individual basis.

Phinney, J. S. (1982). Observing children: Ideas for teachers. *Young Children, 37* (5), 16–24.

Understanding children through observing their behavior is, according to the author, an art as well as a necessity. A variety of observation techniques are described, and the advantage of each is pointed out. Tables are provided to illustrate these methods, which include running records, checklists, time sampling, and informal interviews.

Read, K., & Patterson, J. (1980). *The nursery school and kindergarten: Human relationships and learning* (7th ed.). New York: Holt, Rinehart and Winston.

A useful handbook for teachers. The section on observing children gives practical advice and examples on how to observe and understand the behavior of children, and how to keep records, make informal notes, comment on and interpret what has been observed.

Touliatos, J., & Compton, N. H. (1983). *Approaches to child study.* Minneapolis: Burgess Publishing.

This comprehensive and useful book deals in detail with ways to collect, organize, synthesize, and interpret information about children. Topics include a review of various theories, methods, and approaches applied to child study, direct observation of children, techniques of observation, observational aids, testing and other measurement strategies, interviews, questionnaires, projective techniques, family background and characteristics, case studies, and ethical guidelines for studying children.

7 Assessing Children

DEVELOPMENTAL assessment of preschool children is a relatively new concern for early childhood teachers. The roots of the interest in assessing young children originate from the belief that the earlier developmental deficiencies are identified, the more opportunity there is to address potential problems.

While preschool teachers cannot be expected to provide complete evaluations of children's developmental levels, they can participate in screening processes that could in turn lead to referrals for evaluations. Astute teachers, by their very nature, already engage in informal screenings of children when they make observations and keep accurate, up-to-date observational recordings of behaviors and interactions. Their task becomes one of formalizing their observations and utilizing the information to help children.

Developmental screening is a process used to identify children who should be evaluated more extensively (Meisels, 1985). Formal screening instruments are available for this purpose. We need to be aware of these instruments and learn to use them to gain additional information about children's development. In this chapter we will focus on screening instruments and other devices that are available to assess children.

As teachers of young children we are in an excellent position to screen children for physical, emotional, and mental behavior that may indicate serious emerging problems. We have the advantage of seeing children of similar ages and backgrounds over long periods of time. Therefore, we can observe and assess children and identify difficulties earlier, so that potential handicaps and undesirable habits and emotional reactions can be addressed. We may be the first to notice hyperactivity or hearing or visual problems. Early diagnosis sometimes means that a problem can be ameliorated or reduced.

Objectives

In this chapter we will identify the purposes for assessing young children. We will examine in some detail the Denver Developmental Screening Test, since it is frequently used. We will analyze other instruments for screening preschool children and their environment, including the Developmental Profile, the McCarthy Screening Test, the Minneapolis Preschool Screening Test, the Early Screening Inventory, and the Home Observation for Measurement of the Environment. We will examine the procedures used for assessment purposes. Finally, we will specify ways in which results of assessments can be used to assist the optimal development of children.

Key Ideas

As teachers, we can play a key role in observing and screening children to determine their developmental status. Accurate assessments of children enable us to identify deviations from normal developmental patterns and can be used to guide us in planning individual programs for young children.

Screening is a limited procedure that can only indicate that a child either is developing normally or may have a problem needing further examination. Screening instruments are used to identify children who may have a condition that could affect their potential for learning (Meisels, 1980). The Denver Developmental Screening Test, the Developmental Profile, the McCarthy Screening Test, The Minneapolis Preschool Screening Test, and the Early Screening Inventory are screening instruments commonly used by preschool teachers and other professionals and paraprofessionals. The Home Observation for Measurement of the Environment is used to assess the animate and inanimate home environment.

The results obtained from screening can be used to plan activities to enhance a child's development. The results can also be used to furnish parents with specific information about their child's developmental status and to provide a rationale for referrals for further evaluation and intervention services.

Purposes of Assessment

Assessment is part of an overall process that is used to determine the developmental status of a child and to plan subsequent action based on the results. It is the starting point in a dynamic, ongoing process that takes the guesswork out of understanding how a child is growing and developing. It involves a series of steps that include systematic observation, documentation, analysis, and application of information. Assessment is most useful when it includes a variety of measures collected at several different times during the growing years (Erickson, 1976).

As early childhood teachers, we are not responsible for diagnosing and labeling children's conditions. We are, on the other hand, responsible for screening for developmental delays and for taking steps to correct delays at an early age. We are also responsible for informing parents about the results of screening so that children can be referred to specialists for further testing, if needed.

Question Starter: Why should we assume responsibility for assessing children? (Responses may include: early detection of delays; referrals; program planning; parent conferences; basis for understanding and interacting with children.)

A primary purpose for assessing young children is to detect delays in development so that early intervention can occur. Standardized instruments provide a formal means of assessing behaviors without fear of overlooking some areas. Recognition of potential problems early in the child's life can be the most successful preventive measure to the perpetuation of developmental delays. We should look for patterns of behaviors that seem to indicate that further attention is needed to establish the presence or absence of a problem (Erickson, 1976).

Formal assessments provide the data for making decisions about whether or not a child should be referred to a specialist for a comprehensive evaluation and, if necessary, for intervention services. Early detection is one of the keys to helping children before delays become more pronounced.

Assessment instruments provide narrative descriptions that are useful in planning for the child's developmental needs. They provide base-line data for meeting the needs of the whole child during the critical early years. Since children change quickly during these years, we are in a better position to assist them when we know more about their overall development.

Information obtained from assessments can be used to plan activities based on the needs of individual children. When we have a better idea about how children are developing, we can determine more precisely what they should be doing next. Thus, we can plan activities that encourage the onset of new and emerging skills.

We should also look for strengths and assets of children. Having information about a child's special strengths can prompt us to encourage emerging capabilities and remind us that all developmental tasks will not unfold automatically. Child assessments can be used to detect developmental advances or gifted children as well. When we know that some children are ready for more advanced learning activities, we can plan enrichment opportunities for them.

Results of assessments provide the information we need to discuss the developmental status of children with their parents. We should always inform parents of the results of assessment and only make recommendations for referrals when needed. Discussions with parents about their child's development is an excellent way of keeping parents involved and aware of their child's developmental needs.

We can also use the information we get from parents to more effectively interpret the results of screening tests. Such an alliance helps to create and strengthen a partnership between the home and the child care facility.

Because the basic foundations for a child's development are established early in life, the more we know about an individual child the better able we are to plan for his optimal growth. Accurate assessments of a child's developmental status can provide the information that is needed to guide him as he grows.

Criteria for Selecting Screening Instruments

The decisions regarding selection of screening instruments should take into consideration several criteria identified by Meisels (1980). First, we should consider who is going to be using the instruments and how much background in child development the instrument requires. The degree of experience and knowledge of the person administering the test should guide us in our selection. Second, we should consider the reliability and validity of the instrument. This type of information is usually included with the instrument. Third, we should find out if normative scores are available on a similar population so that cutoff scores can be established for referrals. Fourth, screening instruments should take no longer than 20 to 30 minutes to administer. Fifth, a desirable screening instrument should cover the age range of the children with whom we work. Sixth, if we plan to assess children who have been raised in different cultures, the instrument should not be culture-biased. Seventh, we should select an instrument that sufficiently covers all the developmental areas, including visual-motor coordination, language, cognition, verbal reasoning, auditory memory, gross motor ability, and body awareness.

Other considerations should be taken into account. The instrument should be enjoyable, interesting, and easily understood by children. Since parents know the child better than anyone else, it is desirable that the instrument include a parent questionnaire that will elicit medical and developmental information. Since preschool teachers do not normally have a great deal of excess time, administering the instrument should be easy to learn. The cost and efficiency of the instrument should also be considered. Finally, the results of the screening should be usable by the examiner if it is to be worthwhile.

On the whole, selection of a screening instrument should reflect what we hope to accomplish by gathering the information. Since no single approach to assessment will accomplish everything we want, we should use a variety of tools to assess different aspects of a child's development. The most reliable tools allow us to observe children under similar conditions.

Learning Activity: Using small groups, ask participants to specify the criteria for selecting a screening instrument that would be most important to them. Each group should consider the criteria identified by Meisels.

Screening Instruments

In recent years a number of screening instruments have been developed for assessing young children. No one instrument meets all the criteria we would desire; however, there are a number of instruments that are available and suitable. We should be aware of the options we have in selecting appropriate screening instruments.

The Denver Developmental Screening Test

The Denver Developmental Screening Test (DDST) is a simple method of screening young children from birth to 6 years of age for the purpose of determining whether or not they are developing appropriately for their age. The test provides a developmental profile in four areas: gross motor, language, fine motor-adaptive, and personal-social skills. It is designed to alert professionals if the need for a more in-depth evaluation of a child is needed.

It is equally important to recognize what the DDST is not. It is not a diagnostic test because it does not reveal causes for delays or advances in development. Nor is it an intelligence test. It is simply a screening test used to detect normal development, as well as delays or advances in development. For example, the DDST may reveal that a child needs further testing to determine whether she has difficulty in hearing or perhaps has some other problem that needs attention.

The DDST is a good test for screening children because it is quick and easy to use and also inexpensive. It requires about 20 minutes to administer. It can be used by almost anyone who receives the training, studies the manual, and follows the manual closely. In addition, the DDST is reliable and accurate. It provides a valid, concrete method for measuring a child's performance against a standardized sample. It also provides a one-page profile of a child's progress during the preschool years.

The DDST consists of a kit of inexpensive materials, a score sheet, and a reference manual. The reference manual is the most important ingredient in administering the test. It contains instructions for calculating the child's age and for making necessary adjustments for prematurity. It provides instructions for administration and interpretation of each item, and explains the formula for interpreting the test results. It contains a self-checklist to help the examiner ensure that correct procedures have been followed.

The DDST is available from LADOCA Publishing Foundation, East 51st Avenue at Lincoln Street, Denver, CO 80216.

Developmental Profile

The Developmental Profile is a standardized test that objectively measures a child's level of functioning. It relies largely on verbal responses from a parent or someone else familiar with the child. It can be used with children from birth through 12 years of age. It assesses children in five areas and is accordingly arranged in five scales: physical age, self-help age, social age, academic age, and communication age. The physical age scale assesses the child's large and small muscle coordination, strength, stamina, and flexibility. The self-help age scale assesses the child's abilities to perform independent self-care activities. The social age scale assesses the child's capabilities to interact and relate with others. The academic age scale assesses the child's intellectual abilities. The communication age scale assesses the child's expressive and receptive language skills.

Use of the Developmental Profile is an excellent way to involve parents in the assessment process. It provides a mechanism for facilitating communication between the teacher and parents. It permits the teacher to listen to what the parent is saying and to discuss concerns that may lead the parent to more realistic expectations of the child (Erickson, 1976).

The Developmental Profile has other advantages. It can be used with children who are ill. It provides information that can be used to plan activities for the child. It also provides a valid reference for discussing the child's strengths with the parents (Erickson, 1976).

Inquiries about use of the Developmental Profile can be addressed to: Dr. Gerald Alpern, P.O. Box 3198, Aspen, CO 81611.

Early Screening Inventory

The Early Screening Inventory (ESI) is a brief screening instrument that samples the developmental achievement of children 4 to 6 years of age. It assesses three general areas of development: visual motor-adaptive functioning, language and cognition, and gross motor and body awareness.

The ESI is easy to learn; it is also reliable, valid, inexpensive, and takes 15 to 20 minutes to administer. It has a moderate to excellent accuracy rate in predictive value through the first grade. The ESI is particularly useful in predicting children at risk for learning problems or handicapping conditions (Meisels, 1985). The results of the ESI can be used to determine if a child is developing normally, needs rescreening, or should be referred.

The ESI is available from Teachers College Press, P.O. Box 1540, Hagerstown, MD 21740.

The McCarthy Screening Test

The McCarthy Screening Test (MST) is used with children 4 to 6 1/2 years of age. It screens for right-left orientation, verbal memory, draw-a-design, numerical memory, conceptual grouping, and leg coordination. The MST may be more discriminating for academically and developmentally advanced children but should be used with caution in regard to its predictability value (Meisels, 1985).

The MST is available from Psychological Corporation, 757 Third Avenue, New York, NY 10017.

Minneapolis Preschool Screening Instrument

The Minneapolis Preschool Screening Instrument (MPSI) is used with children aged 3 years, 7 months to 5 years, 4 months. It includes subtests in eleven areas: building, copying shapes, providing information, matching shapes, completing sentences, hopping and balancing, naming colors, counting, using prepositions, identifying body parts, and repeating sentences. The MPSI includes a large number of classroom readiness tasks and is reliable, valid, and inexpensive. It takes 15 minutes to administer, and is relatively easy to use. It has a good predictive value for detecting learning problems for at least a one-year period (Meisels, 1985).

The MPSI is available from Prescriptive Instruction Center, Minneapolis Public Schools, 254 Upton Avenue, S., Minneapolis, MN 55405.

Procedures for Assessment

Results obtained from administering assessment instruments are beneficial only when they are administered properly. It is essential that whoever administers the tests be well versed in using them. Achieving this competency requires careful study of the test and instructions and experience in using the instruments.

Screening should only be done when children are ready to be tested. Occasionally we encounter children who are either unusually shy, active, or uncooperative. These types of behaviors can usually be modified if we approach the screening situation in a playful though serious manner. Since children tend to respond to games, we may get better results when we approach the test situation as if it was a game or fun activity. Sometimes it may be necessary to reschedule the test at another time.

Our orientation to the child and the test situation influences the child's responses. We must learn to read the child's cues and make the situation as comfortable as possible. Such factors as the time of day, activities that have preceded the testing, and who is doing the testing can influence how cooperative the child is.

There are a number of ways in which we can increase the cooperative nature of children throughout the testing session. First, our explanations should be geared to a child's level of understanding. If they are too advanced for the child, he is less likely to respond. Second, we should always obtain the child's visual and listening attention and maintain it for each task. Third, we should consistently use a format that the child understands. Finally, we should be prepared to repeat instructions, as the test allows, if the child does not respond or acts confused or in doubt.

The testing situation will be as beneficial as we make it. Attention to accurate instructions and sensitivity to the child and testing situation should increase the overall success of the screening process.

Learning Activity: Ask volunteers to role play a situation in which a child is crying during a testing situation. Have them demonstrate appropriate and inappropriate ways to respond to the child. Discuss the implications of each approach.

Home Observation for Measurement of the Environment

Just as important as assessing the child's developmental status is the need to assess the environment in which she spends most of the time. The Home Observation for Measurement of the Environment (HOME) is an instrument that can be used to assess the animate and inanimate environment of the child. It recognizes that a child's growth and development are not isolated but depend heavily upon the child's environment.

The HOME can be used to assess the home environment of children from birth to 3 years and from 3 to 6 years. It provides a profile of the kinds and amounts of stimulation a child may need; the consistency or inconsistency of stimuli presented to a child; the persons who assist the child; activities a child can expect; and the positive and negative aspects of the environment (Erickson, 1976).

HOME (birth to 3) measures six areas: emotional and verbal responsibility of the mother; avoidance of restriction and punishment; organization of the physical and temporal environment; provision of appropriate play materials; maternal involvement with the child; and opportunities for variety in daily stimulation (Erickson, 1976). HOME (3 to 6) measures: provision of stimulation though equipment, toys and experiences; stimulation of mature behavior; provision of a stimulating physical and language environment; avoidance of restriction and punishment; pride, affection, and thoughtfulness; masculine stimulation; and independence from parental control (Erickson, 1976).

A systematic assessment of a child's home environment is an excellent way of identifying the subtle occurrences in a child's life. This type of assessment provides a reference for supplying feedback to parents, who are encouraged to discuss the strengths and deficits of their environment. Furthermore, it is an excellent feedback system for strengthening the bond between the home and the child care facility.

Additional Assessment Formats

We can also assess a child's developmental progress by keeping anecdotal records about her interactions. We can record this developmental information on file cards or in log books and periodically summarize the recordings so that developmental changes are noted.

Another method for obtaining information about children is the checklist. We can use checklists that have already been developed, or we can design checklists that document what we want to assess.

Rating scales are similar to checklists except that they allow a qualitative judgment about the child's development. Rating scales are efficient to use because they permit a quick checking of a child's strengths and weaknesses even when the child is not present. A rating scale is similar to a checklist except that it uses numbers to qualify behavior.

We can use videotape as a means of collecting information about children. Videotape permits us to assess children with no interruptions. Although this method has its limitations, it does provide an excellent way to carefully scrutinize children's behavior.

Using Assessment Results

Assessing children is of value only if the results are used to intervene and help children develop optimally. We should analyze the information we collect and determine the most effective ways in which it can be used to benefit children. **Question Starter:** In what ways can you use the results of screening tests? (Responses may include: program planning for individuals and groups; interactions with individual children; parent interactions.)

Assessment results can be used in a variety of ways. They provide a basis for identifying a child's strengths and weaknesses. Once these are identified, we can design activities to encourage continual positive development of the child's strengths and growth in areas in which he needs assistance. For example, if after assessing a child we discover that he does not understand prepositions such as "under" and "over," we can plan activities that encourage him to use prepositions.

Studying the collective results of a group of children provides data for identifying concepts in which that group needs assistance. For example, if we discover that many of the children in our facility cannot recognize colors, we can plan activities that emphasize colors.

Assessment results can also be used to

reinforce the cooperative relationship between home and the child care facility. The information obtained should always be shared with parents. We should explain the purposes of the test, the results of the test, interpretation of test results, and ways in which the information can be used to help the child. We should encourage parents to assist in planning and implementing activities that foster their child's development in any area. Sharing assessment results offers an opportunity to be supportive and to understand what parents are thinking, discussing, and planning.

Informing parents of a possible delay in their child's development can be touchy. Parents do not want to hear that their child is delayed in any way. However, being candid and having regular conferences with parents make discussing the child's problems easier. In the long run, parents usually appreciate learning about their child's problems even if it is not what they want to hear.

Whenever we are discussing a child, we should put the parents at ease before addressing any problem. We should begin by discussing the child's positive points, as well as the developmental areas in which she is prospering. We should stress that our role is to help the child. If a delay in development has been discovered, we should explain what we are planning to do to help the child and offer assistance in helping parents plan activities to assist their child.

An important consideration when talking with parents is to listen carefully to what they are saying, because they may be verbalizing their concerns but in a different way. We should try to voice our concerns gradually, because it takes parents time to adjust to the notion that their child could have a problem. We should be prepared to provide reasons why we think the child needs special help. We should also make clear that we are not diagnosing the child's problem, only signaling the concern (Hendrick, 1980).

If it is determined that a child should be referred for a comprehensive evaluation, we should offer our assistance in making the arrangements. We should keep a list of names and telephone numbers of people and agencies which can help.

Learning Activity: Ask volunteers to role play a meeting with parents to discuss the results of a screening test and other assessments that indicate their child may be delayed in some area. Be sure to discuss referrals.

Decisions about referrals for further evaluation depend on a number of factors. Decisions are based on normative data, provided by the standardized screening instrument that is used. If the child has been tested several times and consistently appears to be delayed in some area, the parents should be informed and referrals should be recommended. Decisions about referrals are also based on our knowledge of child development in general, and our knowledge of the child's developmental status in particular. Our own observations in these areas can be very beneficial, although they should be substantiated by standardized assessments. Our knowledge of the child's home environment can also contribute to our overall assessment of the child's need for further testing.

We should keep records of any referrals we make and records of any visits the child makes. A recordkeeping system can include such information as: child's name; dates of successful and unsuccessful visit attempts; summary and comments on the screening; and dates of any actions which are taken, including admittance to a program, rescreening results, referrals to named agency, and whether or not further action is necessary. The person who

Referral Screening

Child's name: ______________________________

Child's birthdate: ______________________________

Reason for referral: ______________________________

Dates of Visit Attempts:

Successful ______________________________

Unsuccessful ______________________________

Summary and Comments on Screenings:

Successful ______________________________

Unsuccessful ______________________________

Action: Date Action Taken

Admit to program ______________________________

Rescreen, results questionable ______________________________

Rescreen, not eligible presently ______________________________

Refer to other agency (include agency name) ______________________________

No further action necessary ______________________________

____

Staff Member

Figure 4. *Referral screening form*

records the information should always be identified. A sample of a recordkeeping system for referrals is provided in figure 4.

Management of Assessment

Assessment of children's behaviors and development is most likely to occur when we develop a system of planning and implementing screening and observation. We should determine exactly what information we want to collect, and design a multifaceted system for gathering these data about children.

Before we begin assessing children, we should obtain prior permission from parents. We can design a permission form that becomes part of the regular recordkeeping system. The permission form should include the following information: child's name; parents' name; date; a statement of understanding that grants permission for the teacher to assess the child; and the parent's signature.

Once the decision to assess children has been made, we should determine exactly how much time will be needed to accomplish this goal and how many resources, including people, are available. We should then establish a timetable for systematically assessing each child's progress. In general, screening should occur when a child is first admitted to the program and at regular intervals during the year. If we wait until the end of the year, the test results are less beneficial in terms of our being able to use them to help the child. Whatever methods we are using will dictate to some extent how frequently we do the evaluations. For example, if we use the DDST, we would probably administer it twice a year to each child. Other instruments, such as observation tools, may be used more frequently.

The next step is to decide ways in which follow-up will be accomplished. Follow-up procedures should take into account conferences with parents regarding assessment results, keeping track of referral information, and ways in which we can redesign the program to meet a particular child's needs.

Summarizing developmental information about children on an annual basis provides a focused way of considering the child's program. All of the information collected about a child during the year can be summarized in an annual report of her progress. An annual report should include a composite picture of the child's test results and teacher observation records. An example of an annual report of a child's development is shown in figure 5.

Child's Development Record Annual Report

Child's name: ______________________________

Birthdate: ______________________________

Parents: ______________________________

Teacher: ______________________________

Child care facility: ______________________________

Period: ______________________________

Summary of test results ______________________________

____

Motor Skills

Gross Motor

1. Established ______________________________
2. Emerging ______________________________

Fine Motor

1. Established ______________________________
2. Emerging ______________________________

Cognitive

1. Established ______________________________
2. Emerging ______________________________

Language

1. Established ______________________________
2. Emerging ______________________________

Self-Help

1. Established ______________________________
2. Emerging ______________________________

Socialization

1. Established ______________________________
2. Emerging ______________________________

Recommendations: ______________________________

Comments: ______________________________

Figure 5. *Form for annual reporting of child's development record*

Whatever decisions are made, a systematic approach to assessment should be incorporated into a child care program. Dates for screening and follow-up, including parent conferences, should be placed on the annual calendar. A recordkeeping system should be designed, and someone should be given responsibility for keeping track of this information. All of these steps help to assure that a systematic approach to observing children occurs.

Summary

In this unit we have approached the assessment of children as a total process. It is the first step in systematically identifying strengths and weaknesses that can lead to corrective measures for children. We have established reasons why we assess children and have seen how assessment results can be used to help children. We have identified several assessment instruments that can be used by professionals to obtain an overall picture of a child's development. We have examined ways in which assessment information can be used to help children. Finally, we have recognized the need to design ways to systematically manage the assessment process.

As teachers of young children, we are in the best position to recognize potential problems related to a child's development. We are also in a primary position to help children obtain the services they need to correct or reduce problems early in life.

Enrichment Activities

1. Select one of the screening instruments available to you. Study the instrument carefully and then administer the test to children until you feel comfortable using it. Be sure to obtain permission from parents.
2. Design a form to be completed by parents giving permission for screening. Ask some parents to review the form.
3. Write a letter to parents explaining why you assess children in your child care facility. Make your rationale clear and convincing and explain exactly what instruments you intend to use and why.
4. Establish a committee, composed of parents, staff, and professionals, to develop an assessment program for your child care facility.
5. Design an annual plan for assessing children in your child care facility. Include rationale (goals) for assessing children, methods to be used, dates for administering tests, recordkeeping systems, and follow-up procedures. Ask for input from other staff members.
6. Develop a form, to be completed by parents, for obtaining significant information about a child's behaviors and interactions. State how the information would be used.

Bibliography

Barnes, K. E. (1982). *Preschool screening: The measurement and prediction of children at-risk.* Springfield, IL: Charles C. Thomas.

Methods are surveyed for screening preschool children for sight and hearing, speech and language, readiness skills, and general development.

Caballero, J., & Whordley, D. (1981). *Orientation to infant-toddler assessment: A user's guide for the child development assessment form.* Atlanta: Humanics.

This manual deals with the assessment of young children from birth to 3 years of age.

Unit 1 is especially designed to help parents and teachers use the Child Development Assessment Form (CDAF) and to understand what they are assessing. Unit 2 describes the instrument in detail and explains how it relates to emotional, language, cognitive, and motor skills development. Goals and objectives to help children develop in specific areas are formulated.

Coley, I. L. (1978). *Pediatric assessment of self-care activities.* St. Louis: C.V. Mosby.

Self-care independence depends on children's physiological, motor, cognitive, and socioemotional development. The book describes how to systematically record and assess these areas through the daily activities of the child, using observation and a daily living assessment form.

Coordinating Office for Regional Resource Centers (CORRC). (1976). *Preschool test matrix: Individual test descriptions.* Lexington: University of Kentucky.

This useful reference guide gives information on the selection of screening and assessment instruments to be used with young children.

Devoid, R. R., Hodson, W. A., & Schubert, A. (1975). *Screening preschool children: Design and implementation.* Battleboro, VT: Winston Prouty Center for Child Development.

The rationale for early screening is presented, along with a useful model based on "stations" where evaluations are carried out. The authors describe a longitudinal study on the results of this screening model.

Erickson, M. L. (1976). *Assessment and management of developmental changes in children.* St. Louis: C. V. Mosby.

Information about various developmental and screening instruments is provided. Tools that detect and prevent problems of development and predict future outcomes are described. Methods of assessing children's home environment are also explained.

Frankenburg, W. K. (1973). Increasing the lead time for the preschool aged handicapped child. In J. B. Jordan & R. F. Dailey (Eds.), *Not all little wagons are red: The exceptional child's early years* (pp. 24–33). Reston, VA: Council for Exceptional Children.

The author discusses the rationale for screening in early childhood and provides information on selecting tests.

Frankenberg, W. K., Dodds, J. B., Fanda, A., Kazuk, E., & Cohrs, M. (1975). *The Denver developmental screening test (Manual)* (rev. ed.). Denver: Lodoca Project Publishing Foundation.

The authors describe the DDST, which is a comprehensive test widely used by pediatricians in many countries. Items are given for testing the personal/social, fine motor-adaptive, language, and gross motor development of children from birth to 6 years of age.

Goodwin, W. L., & Driscoll, L. A. (1980). *Handbook for measurement and evaluation.* San Francisco: Jossey-Bass.

An excellent resource book for teachers and parents. The authors ask penetrating questions about the necessity of testing young children, the appropriateness of testing instruments, and whether adults working with children should be measured and evaluated. Distinctions are made between formal and informal evaluation. Tests are clearly described, and ways of evaluating individual performance and programs themselves are discussed. At each stage of the discussion, various examples and suggestions clarify and enhance the ideas presented.

Hale, F., & Juster, D. (1977). *A first look: How to plan and implement preschool screening.* Cumberland, ME: Project Maine Stream.

The authors describe ways in which to implement preschool screening programs. Follow-through educational procedures are also discussed.

Harms, T., & Clifford, R. M. (1980). *Early childhood environment rating scale.* Hagerstown, MD: Teachers College Press.

An easy-to-use evaluation instrument that responds to questions about the adequacy of early childhood settings. Areas addressed are: personal care routines of children; furnishings and displays for children; language-reasoning experiences; fine and gross motor activities; creative activities; social development; and adult needs. Each book also contains a scoring sheet.

Hendrick, J. (1980). *The whole child: New trends in early education* (2nd ed.). St. Louis: C. V. Mosby.

Based on the assumption that education must care for the development of the whole child, this comprehensive book examines five aspects of the child's being: physical, emotional, social, creative, and cognitive-analytical. Topics discussed include stress in modern life, cross-cultural education, language skills, needs of mothers, working with exceptional children, screening, and recent educational trends.

Illingworth, R. (1982). *Basic developmental screening 0–4 years.* St. Louis: C. V. Mosby.

Simple tests that do not require sophisticated instruments are defined. Teachers (and parents) are given tips on when to seek expert advice.

Johnson, H. W. (1979). *Preschool test descriptions: Test matrix and correlated test descriptors.* Springfield, IL: Charles C. Thomas.

This reference guide for teachers, counselors, and parents gives basic information about ways of efficiently evaluating the physical, intellectual, emotional, and sociological development of young children. Various tests are described, and guidelines are provided for making accurate test choices.

Karnes, F. A., & Collins, E. C. (1981). *Assessment in gifted education.* Springfield, IL: Charles C. Thomas.

Means and instruments for assessing gifted children are described. Ways of evaluating programs for such children are also explained.

Kitano, M. (1982). Young gifted children: Strategies for preschool teachers. *Young Children, 37* (4), 14–24.

Identifying gifted children may be difficult in some programs because of lack of funds and diagnostic personnel. But preschool teachers can, with training, learn to recognize and assess behaviors and traits of gifted children. A synthesis of some checklists is given, along with recommended instructional methods and specific techniques that can be used to enhance creativity and cognitive processes once identification has occurred.

Meisels, S. J. (1978). *Developmental screening in early childhood.* Washington, DC: National Association for the Education of Young Children.

Administrators, teachers, and parents will find this a useful guide to the developmental screening of young children. Topics include: the nature of developmental screening and how it differs from other types of measurement; the components of early childhood screening programs; reliability and validity; selecton of a screening instrument; follow-up and programmatic decisions; parent involvement; and costs and limitations. Attachments provide information on screening instruments, sample questionnaires and letters, vision and hearing screening, and laws and regulations regarding screening. An annotated bibliography is also provided.

Meisels, S. J. (1985). *Developmental screening in early childhood: A guide.* Washington, DC: National Association for the Education of Young Children.

This book offers a practical, comprehensive, and ethical approach to organizing and conducting an exemplary early childhood screening program. It includes samples and forms to assist in planning and selecting an appropriate screening instrument.

Powell, M. L. (1981). *Assessment and management of developmental changes in children* (2nd ed.). St. Louis: C.V. Mosby.

A variety of assessment tools that can detect and prevent developmental problems in children are presented. Instruments for predicting the future outcomes of children are also described. Means of assessing and managing interactions of infants, their temperament, home environment, and readiness skills are outlined and discussed. Parent-child-professional interactions are stressed.

Southworth, L. E., Burr, R. L., & Cox, A. E. (1981). *Screening and evaluating the young child: A handbook on instruments to use from infants to six years.* Springfield, IL: Charles C. Thomas.

The authors present a large variety of tests to assess the general development of children, as well as their cognitive, linguistic, and motor skills and socioemotional development. Tests specifically relating to speech, hearing, and vision are also described.

Striefel, S., & Cadez, M. J. (1983). *The program assessment and planning guide for developmentally disabled and preschool children.* Springfield, IL: Charles C. Thomas.

Techniques for assessing the functional level of children, monitoring their progress, training staff, and developing relevant programs are discussed in this useful guide. A large number of behavioral goals and skills are also surveyed.

8 Planning Learning Environments

THE influence of the environment on human beings is important at all times but is especially so in child care settings where much depends on children's early acquisition of the ability to adjust, develop, and learn in the surroundings provided for them. As preschool teachers we need to be actively aware of, and responsible for, the learning environments we create. We need to understand what constitutes stimulating and safe environments, both indoors and outdoors, and how these surroundings affect the mood, behavior, and development of children in our facilities.

Objectives

In this chapter we will, first of all, define the learning environment as it pertains to child care. We will analyze the importance of the learning environment to the child's behavior and development. We will identify characteristics of well-designed indoor and outdoor learning environments and apply these concepts by designing ideal settings.

Key Ideas

The child care learning environment can be defined as all the indoor and outdoor space within which children move and interact while at the facility. Children respond to the physical environment and to the behavior of people in it. Thus, to a great extent we can influence children's behavior by designing challenging, cheerful, and secure environments that meet the various needs children have at different times.

The physical features of all indoor and outdoor space should be designed to optimize development and safety. Arrangement and examination of furnishings, equipment, and displays are important indoor considerations. Safety checks, design, and playground equipment are important outdoor considerations. A good learning environment is one that integrates both the outdoors and indoors to provide maximum learning opportunities.

Defining the Learning Environment

Since children are constantly learning wherever they are, the learning environment encompasses much more than can be discussed in this unit. For our purposes we will limit the scope of the child's learning environment to the child care facility. The learning environment in the child care facility encompasses all of the space, both indoors and outdoors, in which a child interacts while in attendance.

The indoor learning environment includes the environment specifically designed for learning activities, as well as areas such as the bathroom, eating area, entry/exit area, and storage areas. Open space and walkways between areas are also part of the learning environment and can be utilized to make the surroundings as inviting, warm, and interesting as possible for children.

We can examine our own facilities to determine what components comprise the outdoor learning environment for young children. Is the space clearly defined? What are the boundaries of this space? Do they include a fence, a row of trees, bushes, street or alley? Or do they include a combination of these items? In addition to space, the outdoor environment includes play equipment and toys, some of which can be moved with ease, while other items cannot. All natural and artificial objects and structures (slopes, rises in the ground, and so on) are part of the child's learning environment and should be incorporated into a myriad of learning experiences unless, of course, they are safety hazards.

Influence of the Physical Environment

Question Starter: In what specific ways does the physical environment affect children? (Responses may include: behaviors; aspects of development; sense of adventure.)

The physical environment has an effect on the way people act and interact. It can influence the way people behave and can set the tone and mood of individual and group encounters and interactions (Bender, 1978). The environment can either increase or decrease positive behavior. For example, large, open indoor areas invite children to run. Indoor running can usually be limited by rearranging play equipment and materials. On the other hand, if space and equipment are designed for too limited a range or function, children may indulge in rough play or horseplay out of sheer boredom (Frost, 1985). Imaginative designing is thus essential.

In addition to the physical or structural surroundings, we must always keep in mind that we, ourselves, are an extremely important part of the children's environment. Through our behavior and actions we create and project the kind of environment in which children are involved (Kinsman & Berk, 1979).

The physical environment also has an effect on the development of the child. A well-planned, child-oriented physical environment can facilitate growth and development. On the other hand, one that is not developmentally oriented can make little contribution to the child's overall growth and development. When designing the physical environment, special attention should be given to addressing the child's physical/motor, cognitive, language, and social/emotional development, as well as to satisfying his curiosity needs.

Toys and equipment in child care facilities promote gross motor and fine motor development. Slides, swings, riding toys, balance beams, climbing equipment, giant steps, air mattresses, and rocky boats are fun and contribute to the gross motor development of children. Puzzles, blocks, and other manipulative toys enhance the development of fine motor skills.

The physical environment also affects the cognitive development of the child. An environment that is rich in variety and complexity of toys and equipment can stimulate the child's curiosity and desire to learn. The manner in which equipment is presented is also important. For example, rather than simply provide a sandbox in which to play, we can add measuring cups so that the child has the opportunity to learn about size and increase depth perception.

The complexity of play items can easily be increased to foster cognitive development. Increasing the complexity of various play objects stimulates the child's curiosity to use them and helps to expand her repertoire of experiences. For example, buttons, toothpicks, and small pieces of vegetables add interest to clay and increase the child's awareness and utilization of various objects. We should, of course, always supervise children as they play with these objects—especially small objects that can be swallowed easily.

The environment has a powerful effect on the language development of the child. A child care facility that is language-oriented will have many books and other items that stimulate language development and serve as a catalyst for the enjoyment of both indoor and outdoor play (Alexander, 1985). It will also feature quiet areas where children can read, be alone, or converse with each other. It will have materials displayed at the eye level of children to encourage talk about them. It will have toys, such as telephones, which stimulate conversation and are greatly enjoyed by children.

The environment strongly affects children's social and emotional development. An environment that has soft areas, open and closed areas, and quiet places as well as mobile areas meets many different needs and moods of individual children at various times. A child care facility that is oriented to the social and emotional needs of children is well organized, with a broad range of interesting items geared to individual needs so that children can feel competent and comfortable (Kinsman & Berk, 1979).

The environment can either stimulate or inhibit the child's curiosity. An environment that is rich in a variety of materials and contains materials and equipment that are complex and challenging, provides opportunities for the development of curiosity. Inherent in such an environment is the provision of many opportunities for the child to move freely through the environment and discover new features about materials that are provided.

Needs of Children

Question Starter: In what ways does the physical environment influence the needs of children? (Responses may include: children's needs for movement, space, comfort, privacy, variety, organization.)

The physical environment plays an important role in meeting the basic needs of children. For example, a well-planned environment takes into account the child's need for movement. Children need space for low mobility and high mobility. They need low-mobility space for quiet time, as well as for activities such as art. Children need space, situations, and equipment for exploratory and challenging movement, as well as for relaxed, gentle movement.

Children also need to feel comfortable. Soft spaces with rugs, pillows, and foam chairs provide this comfort. Although hard spaces are needed for many activities, a well-planned environment will feature places where children can relax and be comfortable. Cheerful surroundings further add to a child's sense of comfort. Moreover, if the child care environment is made to reflect the individual child's community and home environment in some way, the child will feel more comfortable and at home (Loughlin & Suina, 1983).

Children need variety and richness in their environment. Thus they need simple play materials, as well as more complex items that provide problem-solving opportunities. They need space for both privacy and active play, and equipment for both quiet and energetic activities.

Finally, children need a well-organized environment that is manageable, understandable, and responsive to their needs. Organization helps children learn to manage their behavior and relationships with others. It provides the security they need to learn self-control.

Indoor Learning Environment

An indoor learning environment that is safe and enriches the lives of children can be designed from available space. Since child care facilities often have limited space, careful planning is needed to create a well-organized, stimulating learning environment that takes into account children's perceptions, preferences, recall, and spatial understandings (Baird & Lutkas, 1982).

Before arranging available space, it is helpful to remove all movable objects from the room either physically or psychologically. Once the objects are removed, there are several considerations to keep in mind.

Activity Areas

All the activities and projects in which children will be engaged, as well as all the materials they will need, should be identified. Areas for the following types of activities should be included: quiet, calm activities; structured and free activities; craft and discovery activities; dramatic play activities; and large motor activities. Each type of activity has different requirements that should be considered when designing the space.

Once the various activity areas are specified, the best physical locations and boundaries for each area should be identified. Boundaries should be well-defined either by fixed objects in the room or by masking tape, cabinets, or suitable furniture. Space for activity areas should be maximized by creating a path through the room, but unprotected exposed space should be minimized.

The room should be planned so that compatible activity areas are next to each other. For example, exposed areas where activities such as art occur should be separated from protected areas where reading and similar activities happen. Messy activity areas should not be next to neat activity areas. Quiet areas should be separated from noisy ones. Activity areas that require a good deal of space should not be next to more contained areas.

Whenever possible, activities such as reading, art, and writing, which require plenty of light, should be close to windows which provide natural light. Activities needing electricity should be near outlets. Those requiring water should be near the kitchen, bathroom, or convenient sinks.

When careful consideration is given to the physical arrangement of the room, opportunities for positive growth and development are enhanced. Activity areas can be rotated frequently, but the layout of the room should be fairly consistent, since young children need consistency and stability in their lives. However, the layout of the room can change perceptually when floor levels are altered by adding platforms and other shaped designs to the activity areas.

Work Surfaces

Much thought should be given to the surfaces on which children do activities. Table space should be limited and small in size. In general, there should only be four to six children per table. When there are too many children, it is easy to lose eye contact and interaction with those at the other end of the table.

Round tables provide more opportunities for interaction. Stacking or folding tables conserve space. Low tables suited to children's sizes increase their ability to work and help keep the noise down. Floor space and other permanent surfaces can also be used to work on.

Furnishings

Furnishings should be child-sized, suited to children's stages of development, and arranged attractively. Furnishings scaled to children's sizes contribute to overall safety and aid them in moving comfortably through the environment.

Different types of furniture for seating can be used. Stools are preferable to chairs, since they offer greater versatility and ease of movement. However, foam chairs and rocking chairs offer variety, and children enjoy using them.

It is much easier to plan a stimulating, effective program if the equipment and furnishings are all mobile. Movable furnishings provide greater variety in the total environment by offering endless possibilities for space rearrangement. They also offer children an opportunity to participate in the rearrangement of space. Rearrangements can be made for specific activities, and occasionally the whole environment can be altered. Adding castors to immobile equipment is a simple way to provide some mobility.

Wall Space

Appropriate utilization of wall space contributes to a well-designed physical environment. A bulletin board placed at a child's eye level is an excellent place for displays of artwork, themes, pictures of interest, seasonal changes, and holidays. When materials are at eye level, children are better able to notice and attend to them.

Children's displays should be changed regularly to sustain interest. They should also be kept uncluttered and generally look better when placed on bulletin boards than just anywhere on the walls.

Blank wall space can sometimes be used for a mural or picture made of rug scraps. Such a picture has the additional advantage of serving as a sound buffer and acting as an insulator. Window and wall quilts stretched over frames add color and warmth to winter environments. Individual blocks of the quilt can be made by different children and stitched together by a teacher or a parent.

Storage and Display

The physical environment should be as clean and organized as possible. Cluttered environments invite chaotic responses from children, such as "Why bother to sort and put away the lotto game and the stringing beads? Things are such a mess anyway, they won't even be noticed." Even if we never actually hear young children say these words, we may have seen them push toys or games onto a shelf haphazardly.

We should make it relatively easy for children to help care for the environment. Having a specific place for each item helps children feel secure and allows them to assume responsibility for returning items to their assigned space. For example, it is much easier for children to sort blocks if they know that square ones go on the top shelf and round ones go on the bottom. Likewise, it is easy for children to put balls away when there is a special place where these items are kept.

Question Starter: How can we teach children to learn where different materials belong? (Responses may include: pictures of items pasted on the shelf; color-coded spaces.)

In addition to having a regular, identifiable place where toys and equipment are kept, it is important to keep items where children can see what is available. Rather than hiding materials in covered storage, we should make them visible and easily obtainable.

The variety of materials should be moderate: there should be neither too much nor too little from which to choose. Too many choices confuse children and introduce an element of chaos. Too few choices do not provide enough stimulation and may encourage arguments among children who fight over a limited number of supplies.

Mood

Designers of child care facilities sometimes overlook the notion of mood. Color, texture, and the addition of flowers and plants help create mood in the environment. In general, warm, soft-textured spaces should be used in areas of low activity, such as the reading corner. Harder textures and cooler colors should be used in more active areas, such as the wheeled toy area. The addition of flowers and plants creates a mood of warmth and acceptance. Plants are especially welcome in reading and dramatic play areas.

Color

Use of color is especially important in planning the physical environment. Color helps to create the mood and spirit of the environment. In general, color should be added to work surfaces rather than to walls but can also be achieved through wall displays and colorful storage units.

Safety

It goes without saying that safety should be a primary consideration in planning the physical environment. A few simple precautions can help prevent possible accidents. We can prevent many accidents by paying attention to electrical cords and outlets, poisonous substances in the environment, room arrangement, and equipment and materials.

Electrical outlets not in use should be covered with plastic plug caps. Electrical cords should not be accessible to young children. Outlets and cords can be made inaccessible to young children by arranging the furnishings so that cords and outlets are not exposed and by anchoring cords with heavy tape or placing them under a rug. In addition, cords and plugs should be checked periodically to ensure that there are no exposed wires.

All poisonous, controlled, or otherwise hazardous substances should be locked away and placed completely out of children's reach. This includes all medicines, cleaning solutions, detergents and other cleaning powders, insect and rodent poisons in any form, bleach, ammonia, and any other substance that might be dangerous. Many common house plants are also poisonous and should be avoided. Information concerning poison safety can be obtained from hospitals or poison control centers.

The way in which the room is arranged can contribute to accidents. For example, large open path areas invite children to run even when they are consistently warned not to do so. Rearranging the room so that children cannot run can help prevent some accidents. Freestanding light objects that are easily overturned should be placed in areas of low activity and secured if at all possible. Stairways should be protected by railings and rubber slip guards if possible.

Finally, equipment and materials can contribute to accidents. Baby equipment, high chairs, and cribs should be varnished or sealed with nontoxic substances. Paints, crayons, and other supplies should be nontoxic. Only toys with proven safety features should be purchased. All toys and equipment should be in good repair or taken out of circulation until they are repaired.

Placement of Toys and Equipment

Having lots of the right kinds of toys and equipment will be useless unless they are placed correctly in the learning environment. The materials should be within sight and reach. Ample lighting and space should be provided near shelves to create an inviting play atmosphere. Activity tables should be next to storage areas for ease of use.

Careful consideration should be given to location of activity areas that utilize compatible toys and equipment (Kinsman & Berk, 1979). For example, blocks and trucks go well together. The housekeeping and dress-up corners are compatible; block and book areas usually are not. The different areas should be stationed so that each type of material has its own section.

Items for special projects requiring adult supervision should be stored out of children's reach and sight. For example, small jars of tempera paint can be kept on an easel tray, but large containers of tempera paint should be stored in places where only adults have access to them. However, children can manage many art projects on their own. Crayons, paper, safety scissors, paste, and items for cutting and pasting can be placed on a convenient shelf near a table for individual projects.

The principle of organizing the environment so that children can assume responsibility is applicable to toileting, sleeping, and eating routines. Provisions can be made for children to be as responsible as possible in these routines. For example, towels and soap should be accessible to children in the toilet areas. Children can engage in small chores such as setting the table, clearing their own plates, helping arrange cots for nap time, and so on. Even infants and toddlers can assume responsibility for some routines. They can place bibs and washcloths in a laundry basket and put blocks in a container. These activities provide them with experience in being helpful and responsible.

Learning Activity: Divide participants into small groups, and instruct each group to design an indoor environment that reflects all aspects of a carefully planned indoor learning environment.

Outdoor Learning Environment

The outdoor learning environment can do much to satisfy children, as well as teach them to experience the physical part of themselves and observe themselves in relation to natural surroundings (Farrell, 1985). Therefore, the design of the outdoor environment should be taken as seriously as that of the indoor environment. It should reflect an appropriate understanding of the developmental needs, differences, and limitations of young children. A well-designed outdoor environment can help children meet physical challenges, achieve a sense of accomplishment and control, explore movement, and enjoy pretending.

Developmental needs of young children are a primary consideration when designing the outdoor environment. The play of young children is free, active, spontaneous, creative, and discovery-oriented; it is the mechanism through which children learn about themselves (Almy, 1984). Children need and enjoy the experience of involving their bodies in the forceful movement of their muscles. They also need and enjoy the sensory stimulation provided by the outdoor environment. The physical activity provided by rolling, crawling, climbing, walking, jumping, running, and sliding is necessary to the overall development of the child.

The outdoor environment should be designed to reflect the individual needs of young children. It should accommodate children at varying levels of development. That is, it should be appropriate for the young child with limited capabilities as well as the older child with increased capacities. The design should also accommodate the physically or mentally handicapped child who is delayed in development. Therefore, we should make sure that play spaces and equipment are accessible to all children. Accessibility means that equipment is designed for children to act on easily, independently, and safely. Ramps, stairs, platforms, and slopes of varying heights can provide easy accessibility for all children.

The outdoor environment should have a variety of surface features and equipment to maximize opportunities for development and enjoyment. Multidimensional levels, inclines, partially enclosed spaces, complex space, interconnected play areas, and natural features should all be available.

Children enjoy climbing and playing on varying levels. Equipment and space of varying heights should be provided, but should also be safe, so that if a child falls from one level to the next she cannot hurt herself. Usually a distance of 18 to 24 inches between levels will prevent injuries from occurring. In addition, provision of soft landing surfaces can reduce possible injuries.

Children also enjoy playing on inclines that encourage them to run, climb, crawl, and slide. A variety of inclines should be available to provide increasing complexity for older and more advanced children. These inclines should be designed to accommodate more than one child at a time. Safety features, such as tube slides, can allow children of varying abilities to enjoy the experience of playing on inclines such as slides.

Partially enclosed spaces that are easy and safe to get out of can provide children with enjoyment, escape, and opportunities to be creative and imaginative. They encourage activities involving crawling and moving through space but are also ideal for solitary play. Moreover, enclosed spaces should be abstract in design, so that children can be free to role play and use their imagination.

Playground space and equipment should be complex and challenging enough to continue to stimulate the child's interest in the learning environment. A play environment with a high degree of complexity is more likely to increase the amount and quality of continued play than one that is simple in nature. An outdoor design that is challenging to the child provides variation in size and shape of the physical structure, as well as variation in color, texture, and type of materials (Creaser, 1985). Modular play equipment is particularly useful because it can easily be rearranged to provide variety. In addition, a number of children can utilize the same equipment at the same time. Modular equipment is also more conducive to the stimulation of creative, imaginative play. If space is limited, modular play equipment is especially preferred, since it is generally designed to occupy a limited amount of space.

Equipment with movable parts also adds complexity to children's play. Objects of different shapes and texture and sand and water for pouring and shaping provide experiences that are important to the child's overall development. They also provide variety and something for children to act on rather than be acted upon.

Play areas should be interconnected so that children have easy access to all play spaces and equipment. Interconnecting play areas with pathways, inclines, and ramps in safe places also increases the complex nature of the playground.

A well-designed outdoor environment utilizes the natural environment. Small natural inclines, tire swings hung from trees, materials that blend into the environment, and small, low tree houses can be part of the the natural environment playscape. According to an Australian model, playgrounds can become landscapes with sanded areas, rises and gullies, water courses (created with a hose and child-made trenches, for example), jungle area, domestic/cubby area, climbing area, animal runs, amphitheater, shed, and paths (Creaser, 1985).

A sound outdoor learning environment will, of course, include strong, durable equipment that can withstand heavy use and movement by children. It should also feature well-defined boundaries, such as a fence, or natural boundary lines formed by a row of trees. In addition, play equipment should be strategically located so that one set of equipment does not interfere with the safety area of another. However, a safe area need not be a sterile one. Play environments can be exciting yet safe, encouraging adventure and development. Boring playgrounds are probably more likely to cause accidents than interesting ones (Frost, 1985).

Whatever the particular nature or design of the outdoor learning environment, the primary consideration is the degree to which it allows children to move freely, the variety of experiences it offers, the complexity of its arrangement, and the safety it provides. The outdoor learning environment can be as stimulating as the indoor learning environment when children's special needs are considered, and when the importance of developmental play is understood.

Integrating Indoor and Outdoor Environments

The indoor and outdoor environments should be interrelated to form extensions of each other as much as possible (Frost & Henniger, 1979). Outdoor areas can be thought of in terms of classrooms (Creaser, 1985). To facilitate this integration, we can experiment by doing some traditionally indoor activities in the outdoor environment. For example, it is interesting to discover how children will respond to painting under the carport, under the trees, or in the outdoor play area. The variety of activities is endless. Children can do foot painting in swimsuits and then hop into a pool to clean up. With buckets of water and three- or four-inch paintbrushes, children can paint the outside walls. Textures found on outdoor objects can be used to make rubbings.

Leaves, seeds, flowers, and other treasures from nature can be collected, and nature collages can be made on the spot. Children can garden. Dress-up clothes and prop boxes can be taken outside so that children can engage in different kinds of imaginary play—the outdoors can be an excellent theater (Diana, 1985). Children can also experiment with making pottery outside.

Provided that the weather is favorable, children should have equal access to both indoor and outdoor play areas. Sometimes this type of arrangement is not possible because of natural limitations, but whenever it is possible deliberate consideration should be given to easy transitions between the indoor and outdoor play environments.

Learning Activity: Divide participants into two groups. Ask one group to design an ideal indoor learning environment, and the other group to design an ideal outdoor learning environment. Ask each group to use the Child Care Learning Environment Checklist (fig. 6) as a guide when checking their design. Have each group share their product when finished.

Child Care Learning Environment Checklist

Indoor

		Yes	No
1.	Equipment is available for the development of gross motor skills.	___	___
2.	Equipment is available for the development of fine motor skills.	___	___
3.	There is a rich variety of toys and equipment.	___	___
4.	Complex toys and equipment are available.	___	___
5.	Displays are at eye level of children.	___	___
6.	Quiet areas are separate from active areas.	___	___
7.	Space is provided for low-mobility activities.	___	___
8.	Space is provided for high-mobility activities.	___	___
9.	Pathways do not interfere with activity areas.	___	___
10.	Soft areas are balanced with hard areas.	___	___
11.	Open areas are balanced with closed areas.	___	___
12.	Children can move freely through the environment.	___	___
13.	Materials and equipment are well organized.	___	___
14.	Activity areas reflect the needs of children.	___	___
15.	Boundaries are well defined.	___	___
16.	Exposed areas and protected areas are separated.	___	___
17.	Messy areas and neat areas are separated.	___	___
18.	Areas are organized to take advantage of natural light, water, etc.	___	___
19.	Furnishings are suited to the size and developmental stages of children.	___	___
20.	Storage and display areas are easily accessible to children and adults.	___	___
21.	Storage and display areas are compatible with activity areas.	___	___
22.	Shelves are at children's level and are well organized.	___	___
23.	Storage for play items on shelves is easily identifiable to children.	___	___
24.	Each activity area has a distinct mood.	___	___
25.	Electrical outlets and cords are protected.	___	___
26.	Poisonous, harmful substances are out of reach of children.	___	___
27.	Path areas are planned to minimize running.	___	___

Figure 6. *(continued)*

	Outdoor	Yes	No
28.	Equipment is accessible to all children.	___	___
29.	Play area features varying levels of equipment and space.	___	___
30.	Play area includes inclines of varying heights and degrees of complexity.	___	___
31.	Equipment varies in size, shape, color, and texture.	___	___
32.	Some equipment is modular.	___	___
33.	Some equipment has movable parts.	___	___
34.	Sand and water are available for play activities.	___	___
35.	Several children can play on the same equipment at the same time.	___	___
36.	Partially enclosed play spaces are available.	___	___
37.	Play areas are interconnected.	___	___
38.	Natural environmental features are incorporated in the learning environment.	___	___
39.	Play equipment is heavy and durable.	___	___
40.	Boundaries are well defined.	___	___
41.	One set of equipment does not interfere with the safety of another.	___	___
42.	Equipment and space reflect developmental and special needs of children.	___	___

Figure 6. *Checklist for evaluating child care learning environment designs*

Summary

Quality child care facilities are those in which children constantly interact with their environment and learn from it. As careproviders, we are therefore responsible for creating environments that are developmentally appropriate, stimulating, and satisfying. Ideally, we should attempt to integrate the outdoor and indoor environments so that outdoor and indoor learning activities complement each other. The learning environments should be designed to maximize children's sharing, involvement, engagement in various activities, and safety. Environments should also be designed to satisfy children's need for privacy, variety and complexity in materials and equipment, high and low mobility, and organization.

Enrichment Activities

1. Using the Child Care Learning Environment Checklist, analyze the indoor and outdoor environments in your child care facility. Identify specific areas for improvement and specific measures you can take to improve the environment.
2. Keep a running record for a day or two of all unnecessary disturbances by children. Note where and when each occurrence took place and determine whether redesigning the space would reduce or eliminate the problems.
3. Make a scale drawing or a map of your

indoor and outdoor environments. Place cutouts of all equipment and furnishings on the map. Move them around until you are satisfied with the result.
4. Visit other child care facilities and make notations of environmental arrangements that would be useful in your facility. Try as many options as are possible in your facility.
5. Identify the goals and objectives of your child care facility. Analyze to what extent the physical environments encourage or hinder the attainment of each goal and objective. Specify measures you can take to correct a problem area.

Bibliography

Baird, J. C., & Lutkus, A. D. (Eds). (1982). *Mind child architecture.* Hanover, NH: University Press of New England.

This collection of research and thought-provoking articles underlines the importance of building child care environments that are conducive to both care and learning. Child-oriented architecture keeps in mind children's perceptions, recall, spatial understanding, and preferences and thus aids children (and adults) in interacting and operating in special and better ways.

Bender, J. (1978). Large hollow blocks: Relationship of quantity to block building behaviors. *Young Children, 33* (6), 17–23.

An article that should be read by all adults concerned with quality child care. The author states that the development and learning of young children are enhanced by providing an adequate quantity of challenging materials such as large hollow blocks, building blocks, and so on. Large block play affects problem-solving behavior, stimulates imaginative play, and helps develop concepts and structural operations. In the long run, such materials are also economical and can serve a variety of purposes.

Brand, M., & Fernie, D. E. (1983). Music in the early childhood curriculum. *Childhood Education, 59,* 321–26.

An insightful examination of the importance of music in the environment and curriculum of early childhood programs.

Cataldo, C. (1978). Activity organization to enrich infant-toddler programs. *Day Care and Early Education, 5* (4), 29–32.

The author suggests that space in day care centers be utilized effectively by arranging a large number of activity areas. Such an arrangement can stimulate infant interest and enhance infant learning.

Creaser, B. H. (1985, Summer). The outdoors as a learning area: Experiences of Australian teachers. *Beginnings,* pp. 3–6.

The author advocates the integration of outdoor and indoor learning environments, because children learn wherever they are. An interesting playground is a safer playground. Long-term planning must accompany the construction of a good outdoor environment. Considerations include access, buildings, land, shelter from certain types of weather and seasons, planting, drainage and soil type, security, and storage. The author further suggests a variety of ways in which a playground can be transformed into a landscape to provide maximum benefit for children.

Diana, M. S. (1985, Summer). Why teach it outdoors? *Beginnings,* pp. 27–29.

Play and work outdoors can be very satisfying and stimulating. Children experience a sense of space, can analyze and observe a wide variety of objects, and can do an infinite number of unusual art projects that extend their understanding of the natural environment.

Frost, J. L. (1985, Summer). Safety and playability in play environments. *Beginnings,* pp. 11–14.

Designing playgrounds that are both safe and exciting is a challenge involving site selection and preparation, equipment design, selection and installation, and playground maintenance. Both physical and human resources must be taken into account. Good playgrounds provide many play options. They provide stimulating and safe play when adults discuss appropriate play behavior and potential hazards with children. A useful checklist is included to help teachers in routine monthly checks of the playground.

Frost, J. L., & Henniger, M. L. (1979). Making playgrounds safe for children and children safe for playgrounds. *Young Children, 34* (5), 23–30.

The authors provide a thoughtful look at creative and adventurous playgrounds designed to challenge and stimulate children at play. They warn against hazards that cause injuries and cite standards for safety. They also recommend teaching these standards to children, striving for active adult-child interactions, helping children realize their own limitations, mixing various types of materials and equipment, keeping different developmental needs and levels in mind, and providing enough time for play.

Frost, J. L., & Klein, B. L. (1983). *Children's play and playgrounds.* Austin, TX: Playgrounds International.

Play is developmental, and it is therefore important to design outdoor playscapes that can optimize development through play. The authors discuss adventure playgrounds, playgrounds for children with special needs, and provide a rating scale for programs.

Gandini, L. (1984, Summer). Not just anywhere: Making child care centers into "particular" places. *Beginnings,* pp. 17–20.

Environments that have personality are stimulating and encourage individuality. The author describes an Italian program that uses space to enrich the personal and cultural histories of children and teachers. The program takes into account a sense of personal space, community life, the school's history, and surrounding space. Teachers, parents, and children work together to build a joyous and rich environment.

Greenman, J. (1985, Summer). Babies get out: Outdoor settings for infant toddler play. *Beginnings,* pp. 7–10.

Being outdoors is an enriching and valuable experience for very young children. However, playgrounds for babies need to be different from those for older children. Various considerations should be kept in mind, such as the nature of infants and toddlers, the nature of caregivers, and specially designed landscapes that fulfill the requirements of safety and nurturance. Finally, adults in the environment are key figures in making outdoor time meaningful and successful.

Infant-toddler growth and development. (n.d.) St. Paul, MN: Toys 'n Things Press.

Parents and teachers will find this a helpful guide to normal child development. Information is also provided about appropriate activities, toys and equipment, and safe and satisfying environments.

Kinsman, C. A., & Berk, L. E. (1979). Joining the block and housekeeping areas: Changes in play and social behavior. *Young Children, 35* (1), 66–75.

The article deals with two early childhood program environments that can influence the play and social behavior of young children. These are the block and housekeeping centers. The researchers examine changes in play patterns and behavior in relation to the arrangement and rearrangement of such areas.

Kritcheusky, S., Prescott, E., & Walling, L. (1977). *Planning environments for young children: Physical space.* Washington, DC: National Association for the Education of Young Children.

This useful, concise book guides teachers in planning indoor and outdoor space for children. It suggests ways to decrease traffic jams, keep children occupied while playing, and organize space so as to make a difference.

Langstaff, N., & Sproul, A. (1979). *Exploring with clay.* Washington, DC: Association for Childhood Education International.

A fascinating book. The authors feel that in an environment that encourages art and the manipulation of such materials as clay, the child experiences integrated and enjoyable learning in such areas as the language arts, math, movement, music, science, and social studies. A classroom where such learning took place is described in detail. This was a classroom in which the environment was enriched by a generous supply of clay. A guide to supplies and equipment and an annotated bibliography are provided for further reference.

Loughlin, C. E., & Suina, J. H. (1983). Reflecting the child's community in the classroom environment. *Childhood Education, 60,* 18–21.

The authors argue convincingly that the physical environment of classrooms should reflect the environment, communities, and cultures of the children in it. The way certain communities use space, materials, and equipment can influence the child's attitude about these and affect learning and development associated with them. Schools and teachers who keep these factors in mind will help minimize the discomfort, even shock, of daily transitions from home to school and encourage learning, including the learning of multicultural values.

Lovell, P., & Harms, T. (1985). How can playgrounds be improved? A rating scale. *Young Children, 40* (3), 3–5.

Outdoor play is essential for the development of children's motor skills, but it also influences the growth of social and communication skills and has been found to foster independence and self-esteem. Carefully planned and well-equipped playgrounds are therefore important in a good child care program. The writers point out that playgrounds meeting developmental goals are more valuable than those that are merely attractive and eye-catching.

Ostroff, E., & McGuiness, K. (1984, Summer). Adaptive environments: Classrooms for all kinds of children. *Beginnings,* pp. 26–28.

Teachers who work with a wide range of children frequently need to adapt the learning environment of their centers to different children's requirements. The authors discuss ways of responding to everyone's learning by adapting material organization, equipment, and what is taught. Adapting to how children think is also essential. Adaptation encourages a variety of ideas and resources, a clear set of goals, and a stake in program outcomes.

Pangrazi, R. P., & Dauer, V. P. (1981). *Movement in early childhood and primary education.* Minneapolis: Burgess.

The importance of movement education and physical activity in children's development is stressed. Helpful suggestions are also offered on equipment and materials.

Prescott, E. (1984, Summer). When you think about spaces. *Beginnings,* pp. 3–5.

Dimensions of the learning environment are discussed, and ways to deal with problems environmentally are suggested.

Saunders, R., & Bingham-Newman, A. M. (1984). *Piagetian perspective for preschools: A thinking book for teachers.* Englewood Cliffs, NJ: Prentice-Hall.

A thoughtful and comprehensive book that should be read by all teachers of young children. The learning environment, choice of materials, equipment, and interaction in a Piagetian classroom are extremely important. Such classrooms incorporate activity and variety accompanied by intellectual realism and honesty into the entire learning and developmental system. Charts are also provided to clarify and illustrate these ideas.

Stewart, I. S. (1982). The real world of teaching two-year-old children. *Young Children, 37* (5), 3–13.

Two-year-olds are busy people, and the author of this article explains how their active seeking for experience can be used to promote learning and development. To accomplish maximum learning, the physical environment must be carefully planned and prepared, materials must be well organized and arranged to allow activity and skill extension, and the school day itself must provide a framework suitable for development. Appropriate developmental, cognitive, and social activities can flourish in such favorable environments.

Stiles, D. (1977). *Huts and hideaways.* Chicago: Henry Regnery Company.

A good resource book that offers detailed instructions and diagrams for building outdoor structures of all varieties—rafts, huts, lean-tos and so on—for children.

9

Play for Children

GIVEN the amount and scope of theory and research on play, few early childhood programs, child care settings, or teachers can underestimate the importance of play in the child's physical, cognitive, emotional, and social development. Through play, children learn to come to terms with their environment. Through a variety of play experiences they learn more about the world and how to operate in it.

Children's play reveals their developmental levels and inner lives to their teachers and other adults. Play has, in fact, been called "the window into a child's life" (Cliatt, 1980) and can thus serve as a valuable vehicle for observation and assessment.

In the child care setting, play should be an integral part of the program. Each play interaction and situation can serve as a learning experience, and well-designed programs utilize and organize play to accomplish this goal. The teacher who observes children and participates in appropriate play with them is performing an important role in the development of children in her care.

Objectives

The overall purpose of this chapter is to emphasize and analyze the importance of play in the lives and development of children. We will attempt to define the functions of play, identify types of play, and stress its significance for all aspects of development. We will examine the nature of appropriate play, review guidelines governing the selection of good toys and activities, and discuss the role of adults in the play situation. Finally, on the practical side, we will specify various ways to obtain materials and resources.

Key Ideas

It is difficult to define play precisely, but by understanding what it does and does not do we can utilize play wisely for the development of the children for whom we care. Play teaches children about the world, about people, and about acceptable behavior. There are various types of play—physical, manipulative, imaginative, and rule conforming. There are also several ways in which children play—that is, they engage in solitary, parallel, or cooperative play. To a large extent, the way children play, and the types of play they indulge in, are determined by their ages and stages.

Play influences the physical, cognitive, linguistic, emotional, and social development of children. It affects their activity and ability to distinguish reality from fantasy. Therefore, programs that will optimize all aspects of children's development through play are needed. Appropriate play helps children develop significantly. It involves guidance, participation, but very little interference on the part of adults. Appropriate play activities can be either adult-selected or child-selected.

Toys add to the richness of play. Good toys have special characteristics that we should keep in mind when selecting and obtaining them. We can obtain good toys, materials, and resources for our child care programs from a variety of sources.

What Is Play?

Play is not at all easy to describe. Play means different things to different people, and while some believe it is essential to human growth and development, others firmly believe it is superfluous and irrelevant to the serious side of life.

One way to approach the definition of play is to determine what it is not (Chance, 1979). Play is not something frivolous or silly that children do after more important tasks are completed. Play is not something children indulge in while still too young to work. Finally, play is not something adults do only when other demands have been met.

Learning Activity: Divide participants into small groups and ask them to describe what play is. Reconvene and discuss responses.

In essence, play is the means by which children learn about the world (Eheart & Leavitt, 1985; Piaget, 1952, 1962; Piers & Landau, 1980) and come to terms with their own personal experiences (Almy, 1984). Furthermore, it is through play that children learn acceptable behaviors and ways to interact in their environment.

Through play the child gains an understanding of how the world operates, how people respond to various actions, and how to get desired results from specific actions (Piaget, 1952). For example, the 6-month-old baby learns several things by dropping a spoon from a high chair over and over again. He learns how to use his hands in a particular way, how to manipulate an object in a particular way, what sound follows, and how others react and respond. Once he has learned enough from this activity, he will stop doing it. In other words, the child explores his environment, gets feedback from the environment and reactions of others when he performs certain actions, and, depending on his stage of development, learns various things from the feedback (Caruso, 1984).

As babies become young children, play greatly facilitates the learning of self-help and social skills. The child care environment can be a perfect place for a child to learn such skills. Taking turns, helping with chores, and learning self-care routines are all behaviors that can be taught through play and are easily incorporated into the daily routines of child care programs.

Another way to define play is to identify various types. Play can be physical, manipulative, symbolic, or governed by rules, as in the case of games.

Physical play is the most obvious type of play, generally recognized by evident activity such as running, hopping, sliding, or riding a tricycle. This kind of play is very satisfying to children, and children of all ages engage in it. It is especially useful for gross motor development and control over one's physical movements.

Play can also be manipulative, allowing children to gain control over the environment. Puzzles, books, and toys can be taken apart and put together to provide endless hours of play in which children can figure out how things work (Piaget, 1952, 1962). Children of all ages engage in manipulative play.

Play can also be imaginative in nature. This kind of play is a natural part of children's growth and development (Fein, 1979; Garvey, 1977; Pulaski, 1981; Segal & Adcock, 1981; Yawkey & Trostle, 1982). When children engage in symbolic or pretend play, they are able to fantasize and manipulate the world in their minds (Vygotsky, 1967). Symbolic play allows children to attain complete control over their world. Children as young as 2 years of age engage in symbolic play.

Games and game activities are important factors in social interaction (Bogdanoff & Colch, 1979), a skill of life all children need to acquire. Game playing includes rules and teaches children that their world has certain limitations and restrictions. Games also teach the relationship between cooperation and competition, which is a necessary skill for functioning effectively in the world (Piaget, 1962). Even babies and toddlers experience the rudiments of games through imitative play with their parents. As children get older, games naturally become more sophisticated and complicated.

Yet another way to define play is to describe its outstanding characteristics. Play is enjoyable and provides endless hours of fun and delight for children. It is relaxing and can bring relief from stressful situations. It is also challenging and is best when it matches the developing skills of the child.

Another definition of play takes into account the way children play together. The developmental level of children determines, to some extent, the way in which they play with others. Children generally engage in solitary, parallel, and cooperative play.

When children play alone, they indulge in solitary play. Although this type of play can occur at any stage of development, it is especially prevalent during infancy and childhood. During this stage, children seem to prefer their own activities and toys to socialization, especially with other children.

Question Starter: Can you provide some examples of how children engage in solitary play? (Responses may include: sandbox play; reading a book; playing with dolls or puzzles.)

At times a child plays alongside another child or adult, with little or no interaction. Two children may play side by side in a sandbox, sometimes involved in separate activities, sometimes doing the same thing, sometimes watching each other. When children are playing alongside each other, but not with each other, they are involved in parallel play. Some examples of parallel play are stringing beads and riding tricycles.

As children grow older, they learn to cooperate and interact with each other in a play situation. This is called cooperative or associative play. Such play involves observing general guidelines, such as acting within certain roles while playing house or following specific rules as in games that require taking turns. In both cases, there is some agreement before play begins as to what the guidelines or rules will be.

Children's ages and stages of development determine, to a large extent, the type of play and games in which they are most likely to engage (Piaget, 1962; Bogdanoff & Dolch, 1979). Toddlers are not yet capable of cooperative play but frequently engage in parallel play. Kindergarten children can easily participate in many types of cooperative play but sometimes choose solitary play. Children of all ages need opportunities to participate in various types of play for which they possess capabilities. They should not, however, be pushed into activities for which they are not ready. A well-planned program will include a wide variety of play experiences for each child and will take into account each child's age, interests, and stage of development.

By understanding types of play and the ways in which children play, we are better able to plan appropriate play environments. This understanding also provides us with a basis for selecting and planning activities.

Importance of Play

Play contributes to the overall growth and development of the child in a very meaningful way. Conversely, it is a natural outcome of the process of an individual's cognitive and physical growth (Garvey, 1977). Because of the wide-ranging implications play has for the child's physical, cognitive, linguistic, emotional, and social development, parents, teachers, and educators need to pay serious attention to it.

Play contributes to the physical development of children by giving them the opportunity to develop large and small muscles that are necessary for the healthy growth of the body. Play also helps children develop perceptual skills. Through play children learn to judge distance, achieve balance and coordination, discover what works and what does not work, and begin to interpret language related to physical movement.

Through play children develop their cognitive skills. They learn to make sense out of the world. By interacting with objects and people in the environment, children gain knowledge, discover cause-and-effect relationships, experience success and failure, and learn that objects have meaning. Play, precisely because it is fun for the child, helps solidify learning. It provides the foundation for future development through endless repetition of activities that leads to mastery of skills necessary for succeeding stages of growth. Play is, moreover, a significant means of attaining problem-solving abilities that are vital for intellectual development (Almy, 1984; Bruner, 1983; Gotz, 1977).

Children's language development can also be enhanced through play. From a very early age children babble, experiment, and play around with sounds, syllable shapes, intonation, and stress patterns (Garvey, 1977; Weir, 1962), eventually accomplishing adequate verbal fluency and the ability to deal with situations calling for self-expression and creativity. Language play gives pleasure, provides practice, and lets the child control and manipulate experience (Schwartz, 1981). As children grow older, meaning and verbal games are a vital part of their cognitive and linguistic development.

Play also contributes to the emotional development of children. It allows them to experience many aspects of life in a nonthreatening way, helps them cope with emotional conflicts, and offers escape from unpleasant life situations. Play allows children to express themselves (Almy, 1984; Cliatt, 1980). Therefore, it has a valuable therapeutic function (Bruner, 1983; Butler, Gotts, & Quisenberry, 1978; Erikson, 1950, 1972). In pretend play, children gain a clearer idea of what is real and what is not. They also learn about themselves, their strengths and their limitations.

Through play children learn important social skills, such as sensitivity to others, how it feels to be in someone else's place, the rules that govern interactions, and cooperation (Griffing, 1983). They also learn about power, hierarchies, competition, and leadership and following skills.

Through play the roots of creativity are nurtured. Play itself is an expressive activity in which children have many opportunities to try out new ideas in a nonthreatening manner. Children feel free to imagine and pretend, are encouraged to choose what they will create and/or act out, and decide how they should respond to certain situations.

Appropriate Play

Although all play experiences can contribute to the developmental growth of children, in the child care setting appropriate play is play that is purposeful. Therefore, activities should be designed to enhance the developmental growth of each individual child. Since all children's play needs are based on their developmental levels, activities should be planned to meet those needs. Purposeful play can be either adult-selected or child-selected. It can also be free but occurring in an environment rich in opportunities for learning, creativity, and development.

Play, we have seen, should be individually oriented to meet the developmental needs of each child. We can obtain information about these needs by maintaining an ongoing assessment of the child's developmental growth through attentive observation (Cliatt, 1980). For example, if we observe that Mary has trouble stacking blocks, we can plan experiences that will give her practice in performing this activity.

The best way to ensure that purposeful play occurs is to keep careful records of children's accomplishments in relation to the kinds of activities they should be able to accomplish at any given age. Numerous developmental checklists are available, but we can develop one especially suitable for the children in our care. The checklists can be as lengthy as necessary for individual purposes.

Another way to promote purposeful play in a child care facility is to develop daily lesson plans that are rather specific. The daily lesson plan should include objective(s), activities to accomplish the objective(s), relevant skills and concepts, procedures for accomplishing the objective(s), and needed materials and equipment. The value of lesson plans is that they provide ways of organizing for purposeful play.

Appropriate play naturally includes a rich variety of activities designed for a specific child or group of children. These activities can be selected by either the child or the adult, but the adult is instrumental in the planning and setting up of materials, environment, and events. As we have seen, we should select activities that reflect the developmental needs of children and have a clear purpose in mind (Butler, Gotts, & Quisenberry, 1978). These activities should be rich in variety and challenging enough to sustain the child's interest. Quiet activities should be balanced with more active ones—for example, activities such as reading should be interspersed with activities that require considerable movement.

Child-selected activities are equally important in children's growth, learning, and maturation (Eheart & Leavitt, 1975). Because we are concerned about children's development and learning, we often fall into the trap of placing a strong emphasis on teacher initiated activities. However, a well-planned child care program should reflect a balance of self-selected activities and more structured adult-selected activities.

Since one aspect of play is the spontaneity and pleasure of the activity, it is extremely important that children of all ages have the opportunity to select some of their own play situations. Indeed, some people believe that play is truly play only when the activity is self-selected. However, in addition to the sheer enjoyment of experiencing what they want and choose to do, children learn a lot from the process involved in choosing among free-choice activities. By selecting some of their own play experiences, children learn to make decisions at a young age. At first, children choose activities and objects because they want bright colors, interesting shapes, something new and different, or because someone else has something similar. Later, as they become more discriminating, children choose activities because they are interesting, stimulating, and challenging. In general, children select activities from which they can learn.

When given the chance to choose their own activities, children have the opportunity to build self-motivation, an important adult characteristic. Making decisions reinforces children's feeling of worth as individuals. Following through with these decisions increases their responsibility and motivates completion of the task.

Much learning can take place in unstructured, child-initiated activities. In such play, the teacher does not specifically plan a lesson but plans options for activities that contribute to the child's growth and development. The adult is, of course, always available to stimulate and to challenge. Consequently, child-selected activities, or free play, can be quite goal-directed, and tactful adult intervention can be extremely stimulating to the child's development. Teachers who do not recognize free-play situations as opportunities to encourage learning may be missing valuable opportunities.

Whether play is child-selected or adult-selected, there should be a balance of activities. A varied program should include a balance of games, meaningful sensory and language experiences, challenging task-oriented activities, and some activities that are repetitious. Children enjoy and learn from a variety of situations.

The classroom and play environment can have a direct influence on the quality of children's activities and play (Kinsman & Berk, 1979). In addition to a variety of activities from which to choose, children need freedom to move through the environment to select materials and activities of interest to them. The roots of curiosity are nurtured by the ability to move freely indoors and outdoors, and the individual growth of the child is promoted. Restricted environmental boundaries inhibit growth; freer environments encourage movement and development.

Adult Role in Play

Question Starter: What role do adults play in enhancing children's play? (Responses may include: supporting; facilitating; planning; participating; responding; and role modeling.)

Adults have an important role in enhancing children's play (Bruner, 1983). We do not simply provide toys and set up the play environment. We are an integral part of the play situation—supporting, facilitating, observing, and planning as well as modeling play behavior (Segal & Adcock, 1981). In some countries teachers are thought of as "playleaders" who observe, participate nonobtrusively, prompt —but only if the need arises—design, and provide creative and appropriate materials (Blalock & Hrncir, 1980).

The adult role consequently involves not merely offering instruction but playing with children. An adult influences the quality of a child's play by being a good play model. A child learns a great deal by observing an adult's play behavior. Since children tend to imitate adults, the more elaborate the adult is, the more the child will expand on what the adult does. For example, the teacher can bring two or three different toys together and create a complex learning situation. The child will often repeat the same thing.

Adults also influence children's behavior when they are responsive in the play situation. That is, when we respond to a child's actions, the child realizes that her behavior, even in play, is meaningful and has consequences (Chance, 1979). In this respect, the more we play with the child, the better.

Adult intervention and participation should not, however, be too obtrusive. While playing with children is important, we should also allow them freedom to play alone or with other children, although we should be present in a supervisory capacity. Whether we actively engage in play with children or guide them in a subtle manner, we should do our best to encourage and enrich the quality of their play experiences (Bruner, 1983; Singer & Singer, 1977).

Adults should plan play with the individual child in mind (Gordon, Guinagh, & Jester, 1972). Since children are different, they have different play needs that we should observe and respect. Play should be a challenge, but never an impossible challenge that frustrates the child and damages his self-esteem. Physical maturation influences the extent of the challenge to some degree, but individual children are also challenged by different things. Thus, a well-planned program of play addresses the needs of individual children.

Selecting Toys

Children are curious and inventive by nature. They play with all kinds of objects and learn a great deal from them. Every object a child plays with need not be a toy specifically designed for certain types of play. However, a well-designed program of play usually includes a rich selection of good toys. Good toys have a variety of characteristics that make them valuable. A good toy should accomplish several of the following objectives: encourage involvement; foster creativity; provide information; encourage problem solving; help children develop motor skills; help children develop social skills; provide experiences of frustration, patience, and success; teach paying attention to a task and completing it; encourage exploration, discovery of what goes together, and creation of order; allow children to practice and improve skills; provide opportunities to hear and use language; help children learn about feelings; provide enjoyment.

Learning Activity: Divide participants into small groups. Ask them to list several typical toys and specify their potential value to a child. Have them evaluate the toys in relation to the criteria listed above. Reconvene to discuss participant input.

The manner in which children view certain toys makes a difference in how much they learn from them. New toys should be introduced in a positive way. They should, initially, arouse the child's interest and continue to challenge him in some way. The child should also want to play with a toy at a particular time. For example, if we insist that Gino play with a ball today because he played so well with it yesterday, we not only may be creating a discipline problem but may be giving the child negative feelings toward a certain toy.

We should also keep in mind that while good toys promote learning, they should also provide fun and satisfaction. If they do not, children will not play with them. Indeed, materials that are fun will satisfy the child's urge to explore, manipulate, experiment, discover, and create.

There are a number of ways in which we can help children get maximum benefit from playing with toys. We can arrange toys so that selection is facilitated. We should, of course, match the toy with the child's developmental level. Through toys we can help children learn about other children and cultures. We can rotate toys so that they are manageable and continue to stimulate interest. We can involve children in the cleaning-up process as a part of play. For this purpose we should provide containers which children can use to store toy pieces, and which they can conveniently carry and put away. We should have a suitable place for every toy on shelves that are low, open, and easily accessible to small hands. We can, moreover, attempt to provide a rich variety of toys and make them available to both boys and girls. With the help of toys we can teach children about competition and cooperation. Finally, we can increase the complexity of toys by combining them or using them in novel ways to stimulate and challenge (Chance, 1979).

Careful thought should be given to the selection of toys, since there are many from which to choose, and some are rather expensive. Safety considerations, care for the toy, and where and how it can be used should be kept in mind. The Toy Selection Checklist (fig. 7) can be used to evaluate toys in any child care facility. The checklist can also be useful in selecting toys that will provide appropriate experiences for children.

Toy Selection Checklist

Directions: Evaluate toys according to these criteria.

Does the toy

		Yes	No
1.	encourage adult-child interaction?	____	____
2.	encourage child-child interaction?	____	____
3.	meet safety standards?	____	____
4.	make the child feel good about self?	____	____
5.	work well?	____	____
6.	fit into available space?	____	____
7.	add another dimension to existing toys?	____	____
8.	help child learn and grow in a variety of ways?	____	____
9.	appeal to children of different ages?	____	____
10.	meet the developmental needs of the child?	____	____
11.	encourage problem solving?	____	____
12.	help build social skills?	____	____
13.	cost too much?	____	____
14.	clean up and repair easily?	____	____
15.	appear to be made of suitable, sturdy material?	____	____
16.	provide more than one type of learning experience?	____	____
17.	stimulate curiosity, imagination, creativity?	____	____
18.	develop muscular coordination, freedom of movement, manual skills?	____	____
19.	promote growth toward independence, exploration, group activity?	____	____

***Figure** 7. Criteria checklist for evaluating toys*

Resources and Materials

Play items can be either purchased new or obtained in other ways. Since toys and supplies are rather expensive, it is wise to consider alternative ways of obtaining play items and of providing experiences for children. Before selecting and purchasing or obtaining toys or supplies, several guidelines can be applied. We should, for example, carefully consider what toys are really needed before adding to the current supply. It is also a wise policy to be aware of what is available in the community. Moreover, we should know the needs of everyone involved in the situation: the children, other staff persons, and our own.

Toys and supplies can, in fact, be obtained in several ways. We can, first of all, use local libraries, which are excellent resources for child care facilities. Not only do they contain books for children, but many now have toy-lending facilities, the use of which can serve as a good way to rotate toys on a weekly or biweekly basis.

Another means of obtaining toys is by purchasing them inexpensively at rummage sales, moving sales, and thrift shops. Broken parts of toys or missing pieces of equipment can sometimes be replaced when found at sales.

Child care facilities in many communities utilize a toy-sharing system. That is, toys are shared on a rotating basis by several child care operations. This type of system offers an excellent opportunity to increase the numbers and variety of toys with which children can play.

For teachers who have the time and enjoy doing it, making toys is another good option. Some parents also enjoy this type of activity. Even children can help make simple toys. Free and inexpensive materials for making toys can be obtained in a variety of ways. Only our creativity limits the way we utilize available materials. Boxes, crates, and cartons are available from all kinds of retail outlets and can be used to make bookcases, toy storage, and play items such as stores or doll corner furniture. Adding castors to a box can make it into a wagon or pull-and-push toy. Rubber tires and inflated innertubes can be made into swings or stepping-stones. They can also serve as a sand enclosure. Milk cartons can be used to make bird nests, planters for seeds or small plants, storage bins for marbles, spools or other small items, or for housekeeping and store play. Spools can be used for stringing items such as wheels for pull toys, or they can be combined with small sticks or pipe cleaners for construction activities. The tops from plastic milk jugs can become play money or objects for counting games. Old locks, keys, fasteners, switches, chains, and doorknobs can be used to create a gadget board. Egg cartons could be used for storage of small items or cut apart for various art projects. The cardboard from new shirts can be used to make backings for pasting projects or for drying clay work. Corks can be used for block printing, and old sponges for painting or water play. We can insert pebbles into paper plates stapled together to make a shaker or a tambourine. Any kind of stick can become a rhythm stick. Juice or coffee cans can be turned into drums. All we need to do is look around and think creatively about how surplus items can be used. We can obtain additional craft and usage ideas from magazines and newspapers.

The community itself is often a good resource from which to obtain play items. Businesses within the community may be willing to provide free materials. For instance, many materials for art projects can be obtained from grocery stores, fabric shops, or carpet shops. Play items can sometimes also be obtained from parents and friends. Requests for toys and supplies can be made through newsletters or special announcement sheets posted on the bulletin board, or even by word of mouth.

Household objects can provide excellent fun and good learning experiences for children. For example, children enjoy playing with discarded purses, shoes, clothes, belts, measuring cups, cartons, and old typewriters. These, too, may be collected from local businesses, friends, and parents.

Summary

Play is children's work. Children learn to make sense of their world and function as human beings through a wide variety of play experiences. Enjoyable play situations are conducive to learning, while quality of the environment and the materials available affect the play and learning experiences of young children. As teachers, we have a major responsibility to provide the best play environment possible with a rich variety of materials and activities that are appropriate to children's ages and stages of development.

Enrichment Activities

1. Select one child for whom you will develop a set of developmental activities. Identify the age and the developmental level of the child in each of the following areas: physical/motor (gross, fine); cognitive (concept, including size, number, color, generalization, classification, sequencing, and memory); language (listening, verbal, sociodramatic play, letter/sound recognition); and social/emotional (empathy, imagination, and group dynamics). Specify activities that you would plan to enhance this child's emerging development in each of the areas.
2. Devise a recordkeeping system for keeping track of the activities in which each child engages. Use the system to modify activity choices that you plan for children.
3. Make a five-day plan that includes all the components of a good lesson plan: objectives, activities, skills and concepts, procedures, and materials and equipment.
4. Keep an ongoing list of materials and equipment that you can collect from community resources, parents, and others. At the end of each year, figure out how much you save by taking advantage of these resources.
5. Use the Toy Selection Checklist to evaluate some of the toys in your child care facility. Use the checklist to assist in selecting new toys for purchase.
6. Identify toys that are appropriate for the ages of children with whom you work. Analyze the value of each toy by determining what the child experiences while playing with it.
7. Become aware of the functions of play items in your child care facility by listing the items that respond to each of the following developmental needs: promote large and fine motor activities; stimulate other activities; promote language growth; provide meaningful sensory experiences; promote social skills; encourage exploration, discovery, and problem solving. Is there a balance of different kinds of play items, so that children are encouraged in all areas of growth?
8. Assess the nature of play in your child care facility by responding to the following: *(a)* list and describe activities that adults direct with children; *(b)* list and describe activities that children engage in during free-choice play; *(c)* specify provisions for safety; and *(d)* list ways in which play can be improved in your child care facility.

Bibliography

Baker, K. R. (1966). *Let's play outdoors.* Washington, DC: National Association for the Education of Young Children.

This concise book describes the components of a good play area. It details the types of equipment and experiences that make outdoor play valuable.

Barber, L. W., Strother, D. B., & Duckett, W. (1982). The importance of play. *Practical Applications of Research Newsletter.* Bloomington, IN: Phi Delta Kappa's Center of Evaluation, Development and Research.

Stressing the importance of play in child development, the authors state that not enough scope or significance is given to it in today's preschools, kindergartens, and schools. Definitions and theories of Montessori, Freud, and Piaget are given. Research is cited on play and cognitive development; play, reconstruction, and comprehension; play, language acquisition, and expansion; symbolic play, empathy, and abstract thought; and play and socialization. Practical applications of these theories by parents and teachers are recommended. The importance of choosing toys and environments conducive to creativity is stressed. The therapeutic value of play is noted.

Blalock, J. B., & Hrncir, E. J. (1980). Using playleader power. *Childhood Education, 57,* 90–93.

Emphasizing the value of play, Blalock and Hrncir give examples of successful "playscapes" in Denmark and other European countries. The authors describe the role of the teacher as playleader. The teacher is an observer, a participator (although not obtrusively), a prompter (but only when needed), and a provider of appropriate and creative materials.

Brown, J. F. (1982). *Curriculum planning for young children.* Washington, DC: National Association for the Education of Young Children.

Taken from the best of *Young Children,* this book provides a composite of useful ideas for curriculum planning for young children. It emphasizes the importance of play to children's learning and the need to intentionally emphasize play in the curriculum.

Bruner, J. S. (1983). Play, thought, and language. *Peabody Journal of Research, 60* (3), 60–69.

Bruner discusses the organization of play activity into playgrounds to help children "realize their potential and live more richly." Distinguishing between play and learning, he states that play projects the inner life onto the outer world. Learning, on the other hand, is an interiorizing of the external world to make it part of oneself. Adults often subtly structure play to teach children cultural values. Play is also therapeutic and helps improve the intellect. And play encourages mastery over language. Rich and extended experiences stem from play with constructive materials without adult direction. However, adult presence in the environment reassures children. Children do not play best when alone, although they need solitude sometimes. When alone they cannot combine ideas, and for Bruner the combinatorial aspect of play is essential. Two children play better than one or three, but certain periods of the day should include group activity of high intellectual quality.

Butler, A. L., Gotts, E. E., & Quisenberry, N. L. (1978). *Play as development.* Columbus: Charles E. Merrill.

This comprehensive and useful book stresses the value and significance of play in the child's life, development, and education. Part 1 deals with theories of play and attitudes—both historical and current—toward its utilization. Part 2 details practical applications of play to encourage development and support adaptation to the physical and social environment. Special and therapeutic applications of play are also examined and explained. Supplementary material on field trips, excursions, and equipment provide guidance for teachers and centers.

Chance, P. (1979). *Learning through play.* New York: Johnson & Johnson.

The book summarizes a pediatric round table conference in which the value of play in a child's life is discussed. Good play is defined, and ways to improve it are suggested. A readable and informative book.

Cliatt, M. J. (1980). Play: The window into a child's life. A checklist for observing children's play. *Childhood Education, 56,* 218–20.

A valuable article for those who observe children's activities to learn and understand more about children and their needs. Play frees children to express themselves: it therefore provides a natural means for teachers to listen, observe, and evaluate language skills, social behaviors, and emotional development. A useful checklist is provided to assist observation. The checklist is comprised of searching questions, which are themselves based on sound developmental ideas.

Cowe, E. G. (1982). *Free play: Organization and management in the pre-school and kindergarten.* Springfield, IL: Charles C. Thomas.

Another practical book on activities for both outdoor and indoor free play. Although organizing and managing are terms that indicate the limiting of free play, the learning outcomes and techniques for improving the quality of play that are described will provide helpful information for teachers.

Eheart, B. K., & Leavitt, R. L. (1985). Supporting toddler play. *Young Children, 40* (3), 18–22.

The writers assert that child-directed play is essential to a dynamic curriculum. Toddlers learn by participating and experiencing freely in their environment. While allowing children to take the lead, adults need to support and expand the scope of children's play. This can be done by observing children's play; taking advantage of opportunities for expanding play; encouraging children to explore materials with the least amount of directions; allowing independence; avoiding interrupting play unless absolutely necessary; showing interest in what children want to tell about their play; being available when assistance is needed; and avoiding needless conversation with other adults. The environment should be designed to provide appropriate experiences, and activities should promote development.

Engstrom, G. (Ed.). (1971a). *Play: The child strives toward self-realization.* Washington, DC: National Association for the Education of Young Children.

Pioneers in the field, such as Sutton-Smith, Curry, and Smilansky, discuss the values of play for young children. The writers stress that children grow and learn through play.

Engstrom, G. (Ed.). (1971b). *The significance of the young child's motor development.* Washington, DC: National Association for the Education of Young Children.

This concise book describes the importance of physical activity in early childhood. It examines research regarding motor development and explores the relationship between motor development and emotional, social, and intellectual growth. It presents ideas for an appropriate environment to facilitate the motor development of young children.

Fein, G. G. (1979). Pretend play: New perspectives. *Young Children, 34* (5), 61–66.

A useful resource that provides a comprehensive review of research in the field. Imaginative play, symbolic play, and sociodramatic play are defined. Major research is cited and discussed, including that of Piaget, Vygotsky, and a host of others.

Forman, G. E., & Hill, F. (1980). *Constructive play: Applying Piaget in the preschool.* Monterey, CA: Brooks/Cole.

An unusual, fascinating, and practical book that seeks to apply Piagetian principles to preschool play. The authors recommend a wide variety of activities to help children construct knowledge about their world. Play materials (of a rather uncommon nature) are described. Activities are discussed according to their content, the progress they should encourage, and the process children go through while playing. Photographs, diagrams, records, and behavioral observations highlight the book.

Forman, G. E., and Kuschner, D. S. (1983). *The child's construction of knowledge: Piaget for teaching children.* Washington, DC: National Association for the Education of Young Children.

The authors explain how to apply Piaget in settings with young children. They introduce a number of learning situations to intrigue children from 2 through 5, linking theory and practice.

Garvey, C. (1977). *Play.* Cambridge: Harvard University Press.

"Play," believes Garvey, "is a natural product of the processes of physical and cognitive growth" (p. 123). For those interested in child development, the study of children's play provides valuable information about their newly acquired abilities and competencies. Garvey identifies three types of social play: spontaneous, which is most often characterized by rhyme and wordplay; fantasy and nonsense; and play with conversation. Make-believe and the effects of "tutoring in imaginative play" are also discussed.

Greenlaw, J. M. (1984). Facilitating play behavior with children's literature. *Childhood Education, 60,* 339–44.

This article should be especially useful in reminding parents and teachers of the kinds of books that can be combined with imaginative play to help children of different ages explore feelings and adapt themselves to their environment. Rhymes, for example, can be acted out by toddlers, while preschoolers and older children can use nonsense rhymes and stories to canalize aggression. As children grow older, fairy tales and stories with monsters and other horrors serve as an outlet for aggressive feelings. Greenlaw also cites many books that will be useful in children's imaginative play.

Gordon, I. J., Guinagh, G., & Jester, R. (1972). *Child learning through child play.* New York: St. Martin's Press.

An offering of games and activities to help very young children develop physically and intellectually. Useful for both parents and teachers.

Gotz, I. (1977). Play in the classroom: Blessing or curse? *The Educational Forum, 41,* 329–34.

Observing that parents often question the educational merit of games and play, Gotz points to several important functions of play: it aids problem solving; it encourages self-assertion; it permits the expression of taboo subjects and impulses; it allows children to experience a wide range of activities and roles; it releases tension; and it allows creativity.

However, Gotz criticizes the uses made of play in the classroom, where play is often turned into work and directed towards an end. Thus spontaneity is lost. Play should be its own end: "non-serious, self-contained, worthwhile in itself." Gotz feels strongly that play should not be destroyed in the name of learning. However, attitudes of play can be applied to learning activities that make them more enjoyable to children.

Griffing, P. (1983). Encouraging dramatic play in early childhood. *Young Children, 38* (2), 13–22.

The article underlines the importance of dramatic and sociodramatic play and gives teachers many practical suggestions on how to facilitate such play in the classroom. Some benefits of dramatic play are: it is rich in symbolic activity; it is cognitively complex; it involves extensive social interaction and verbal communication; and it develops flexibility regarding views of others. Teachers can observe children's play to see where they are developmentally and to guide and enhance play experiences. Ideas on creating good physical settings are offered, as are practical suggestions on how to enrich and enhance play. The teacher is seen chiefly as a resource person rather than an actual participant in this type of play. The teacher should respect individual styles in play, as in other learning situations.

Hill, D. M. (1977). *Mud, sand, and water.* Washington, DC: National Association for the Education of Young Children.

This short book explores ways in which the teacher can incorporate the use of mud, sand, and water in the curriculum. It explains the importance of using natural materials for learning.

Hirsch, E. S. (1985). *The block book.* Washington, DC: National Association for the Education of Young Children.

This book addresses the importance of blocks in young children's development. It explains why blocks are an integral part of children's learning through play.

Holt, G. G. (1977). *Science with young children.* Washington, DC: National Association for the Education of Young Children.

This practical guide offers a wealth of suggestions for implementing science activities with children. Everyday items can be used to teach science concepts.

Isenberg, J. P., & Jacobs, J. E. (1982). *Playthings as learning tools.* New York: Wiley.

A practical guide for parents (and teachers) of preschool and middle years children. Play materials and play activities that encourage learning are described, and learning outcomes are detailed. Adult-child interaction is stressed. Major theories and research are provided in a readable way. A glossary and resource guide provide useful information.

Kamii, C. (1982). *Number in preschool and kindergarten: Educational implications of Piaget's theory.* Washington, DC: National Association for the Education of Young Children.

This book provides hundreds of activities that are better than counting by rote and filling in work sheets. It shows how children can learn about numbers by voting, dividing snacks, playing games, and even cleanup.

Kamii, C. (1984). *Young children reinvent arithmetic: Implications of Piaget's theory.* Hagerstown, MD: Teachers College Press.

Translating Piagetian theory of logico-mathematical knowledge into a concrete program, the author discusses how to make games and activities, how to use them, and their rationale and objectives. The focus of attention is on Piaget's theory of number as it relates to how children reinvent it.

Kamii, C., & DeVries, R. (1980). *Group games in early education: Implications of Piaget's theory.* Washington, DC: National Association for the Education of Young Children.

The authors explore the place of group games in early childhood, linking Piagetian theory with practice. They identify good group games, examine the rationale for using group games, explain how competitive games contribute to children's development, and provide ready-to-play directions for many new and favorite games.

Lasky, L., & Murkerji, R. (1980). *Art: Basic for young children.* Washington, DC: National Association for the Education of Young Children.

The authors provide a rationale for understanding why coloring workshops, cutting out patterns, and similar teacher-directed activities are not art. They provide many ideas for teachers to try to get children involved in the art process.

Marzolla, J., & Lloyd, J. (1972). *Learning through play.* New York: Harper and Row.

This book was written for parents of very young children but should be extremely useful for teachers as well. The activities presented are based on sound educational principles and include most areas that can be developed through the medium of play—language, the senses, early literacy, problem-solving, creativity, and so on. The writers emphasize a point parents and teachers should always keep in mind: children learn at their own pace and should not be pushed. If a child cannot or will not participate in an activity, let it be—try another.

McDonald, D. F. (1979). *Music in our lives: The early years.* Washington, DC: National Association for the Education of Young Children.

The author presents ways in which the teacher can incorporate music in the early education program even when skills are limited. The book demonstrates how to teach children to sing, listen to good music, and play instruments.

Piaget, J. (1962). *Play, dreams and imitation in childhood.* New York: Norton.

A detailed, systematic, and influential study of child development in terms of imitation, which is related to accommodation, and play, which is related to assimilation. The evolution of play, according to Piaget, parallels the cognitive development of children. Three important stages are practice play, symbolic play, and play with games and rules. Through these succeeding stages, children come to terms with their world. An interesting feature of the book is Piaget's account of the behavior of his own children. His observations were made on a day-to-day basis and give this otherwise somewhat difficult-to-read book a personal touch.

Piers, M. W., & Landau, G. M. (1980). *The gift of play: And why young children cannot thrive without it.* New York: Walker.

Play "is the only good and lasting way of learning for the young child." The authors attempt to substantiate this claim by presenting significant research findings and data on children's play. Included are discussions on aggression, violence, and sex play. These factors are part of children's development, and parents and teachers should not be alarmed when such behaviors occur. Proper handling of situations involving aggressive behavior should alleviate problems. Play is also instrumental in encouraging problem solving and is often therapeutic in nature. The authors feel somewhat strongly about television. Too much television can be harmful and inhibiting: children would be much better off playing. Finally, the authors make useful suggestions on how to choose good nursery schools for children.

Pulaski, M. A. S. (1981). *The rich rewards of make-believe.* In R. D. Strom (Ed.), *Growing through play* (pp. 8–18). Monterey, CA: Brooks/Cole.

Make-believe plays "an intrinsic part" in normal growth. It affects language fluency, waiting ability, concentration, positive attitudes in originality, creativity, and flexibility. The writer describes an experiment involving the use of simple, unstructured materials like clay, paints, and old clothes, and highly structured materials such as sophisticated dolls (Barbie, GI Joe). Results revealed that children who were high fantasizers played imaginatively with all materials, while those who were low fantasizers generally "fooled around." High fantasizers were more able to switch from activity to activity. Teachers might be interested in observing children to see if these findings are borne out. Moreover, they may wish to go further and see why some children are low fantasizers. They may also wish to attempt to raise the level of fantasy play of young children.

Rowen, B. (1982). *Learning through movement: Activities for the preschool and elementary grades* (2nd ed.). Hagerstown, MD: Teachers College Press.

The author explores the role of movement in the teaching of science, number concepts, language, history, and geography. Practical suggestions for ways to make constructive use of children's natural desire and need for movement are offered.

Schickedanz, J. (1985). *More than the ABCs: The early stages of reading and writing.* Washington, DC: National Association for the Education of Young Children.

This book demonstrates how to plan for literacy learning and how to give it a prominent place in children's lives. It utilizes a child development approach that dispels common myths about learning to read and provides information about introducing children to print.

Schwartz, J. I. (1981). Children's experiments with language. *Young Children, 36* (5), 16–26.

The article deals with the importance of language play to children's cognitive and emotional development. Language play gives pleasure, provides practice, and allows the child to control experience. By experimenting with and exploring the rules and patterns of their language children gain mastery over it and learn to manipulate it as a social tool. Some aspects of language play discussed are sound play, pattern play, grammatical or structured play, and meaning play and verbal games. Schwartz suggests that teachers support and enhance language play but not deliberately teach it, as that would detract from its spontaneity.

Segal, M., & Adcock, D. (1981). *Just pretending—ways to help children grow through imaginative play.* Englewood Cliffs, NJ: Prentice Hall.

A book for parents and teachers to enjoy and learn from. The authors emphasize the role of play, especially pretend play, in social development and in children's growing ability to manipulate objects symbolically. The adult role in children's pretend play is stressed. Adults can support and facilitate play. They can serve as observers, planners, and models. Techniques to help them in these roles are suggested.

Singer, D. G., & Singer, J. L. (1977). *Partners in play: A step-by-step guide to imaginative play in children.* New York: Harper and Row.

The authors examine games, activities, and exercises that expand the imagination of preschoolers and help them enjoy play more. The book is designed to help parents and teachers encourage and enrich play, but it is also meant to develop children's own imaginative resources (again, with some adult help). Along with the wide variety of activities and games, the Singers suggest ways to use television effectively and recommend various useful and creative materials for children between the ages of 2 and 5.

Singer, J. L., & Singer, D. G. (1984). *Make believe: Games and activities to foster imaginative play in young children.* Glenview, IL: Scott, Foresman.

An extensive offering of interesting games and activities to enrich the quality of children's play.

Skeen, P., Gauner, A. P., & Cartwright, S. (1984). *Woodworking for young children.* Washington, DC: National Association for the Education of Young Children.

The authors explore the use of woodworking in programs for young children. They describe what woods are easiest to use, what kinds of hammers and nails are best, and how to teach children woodworking.

Sobel, J. (1982). *Everybody wins: 393 non-competitive games for young children.* New York: Walker.

A wise, refreshing, and radical educational approach is brought to the playing of games through what the author calls cooperative play. Play should be for fun, not for competition. Children should not be made anxious about winning or losing. They should learn to get along together through play activities. In providing the reader with a wide range of activities, Sobel modifies the structure and rules of many old games, and creates some new ones to fit his system. He suggests that children themselves be allowed to modify rules as they go along—this leads to creativity and thought on their part. He feels that freedom to move and to innovate is essential for children's development and should be the only prerequisite for children's games.

Sullivan, M. (1982). *Feeling strong, feeling free: Movement exploration for young children.* Washington, DC: National Association for the Education of Young Children.

This book provides a step-by-step approach for working with children from 3 to 8. It demonstrates how teachers can bring children together, warm up, and begin movement sessions.

Yawkey, T. D., & Trostle, S. L. (1982). *Learning is child's play.* Provo, UT: Brigham Young University Press.

Imaginative play is an important element of children's physical, cognitive, and social development. Parents and teachers will find relevant and helpful information on play material that can be made and used at home or at school, on techniques for guiding play, and on using imaginative play to enhance language learning and communication skills.

Vygotsky, L. S. (1967). Play and its role in the mental development of the child. *Soviet Psychology, 5* (3), 6–18.

Vygotsky believes in developing symbolic play and freeing individual meaning and thought from concrete objects. When children act by responding to ideas rather than to objects, they have developed the ability to symbolize. In pretend play children at first need an actual object that they substitute for reality, but later on the necessity for a signifier or substitute disappears. The child practices substitution until true symbolism appears and meaning is free of matter.

10

Nutrition for Children

RESEARCH shows that good nutrition is essential for physical, mental, and behavior development (Stevens & Baxter, 1981), and planning for and providing proper nutrition is one of the signs of a quality child care program. As the demand for and use of child care facilities increases, we need to become familiar with, and proficient in, the basic concepts of nutrition for children. As teachers of young children, we need to know what the components of a good diet are, what foods provide required nutrition, and what amounts of food children of different ages need. Moreover, we should be aware of, and know how to deal with, the individual and special needs of certain children. Finally, we should strive to provide children with a sound nutrition education, so that good habits are established early in life.

Objectives

In this chapter we will survey the components of a nutritious diet and review certain myths associated with children and food. We will examine the factors that influence people's eating habits and see how good habits can be instilled. We will study the goals, concepts, and methods of nutrition education and examine the teacher's role in the nutrition process. Finally, we will discuss ways in which parents can be involved in a successful food program.

Key Ideas

Proper nutrition is essential to the growth and development of young children. Four basic food groups serve as sources of nutrients, and a knowledge of these groups helps us plan, prepare, and provide nutritious food for children.

Eating habits are established early in life and have long-lasting effects. Social, religious, ethnic, cultural, and economic factors influence the eating behaviors of people. However, education can alter food habits. Adult and parental influences also shape the eating habits of children.

Our work with young children includes the important role we play in organizing successful food programs, planning menus, buying food, managing budgets, and involving parents in the project. By setting good examples, by allowing children to help in food preparation, and by making mealtimes pleasant, we can teach children to enjoy eating while learning to appreciate nutritious foods. We can help children acquire sound nutritional practices by using a variety of approaches and incorporating nutrition into all aspects of the curriculum.

Four Basic Food Groups

As teachers of young children, we need to be aware of the principles of good nutrition, not only because we have to feed the children in our care, but because we want optimal physical and mental development for them, and because we want them to learn to make the right choices regarding food. Thus, we should understand several basic facts about nutrition. We should know, for example, that all people need the same nutrients throughout life, but that the amounts needed by adults and children are different. The nutrients we all need are starches or carbohydrates, proteins, fats, vitamins, minerals, and water. We could not live or maintain our bodies if our regular diets were lacking in even one nutrient. Therefore, we must select our diets carefully.

Each individual needs nutrients contained in the four basic food groups, although the amount needed will vary depending on age and other factors. The Basic 4 is a tool developed to help make the selection of a balanced diet easier. The four food groups in the Basic 4 are milk and dairy products such as cheese, cottage cheese, yogurt, and fluid and instant milk; meat and protein foods consisting of meat, fish, poultry, eggs, nuts, peanut butter, dried beans, peas, and lentils; bread and cereal products, comprising all types of whole-grain or enriched breads, cereals, crackers, and baked goods, as well as pasta such as rice, noodles, spaghetti, and macaroni; and fruits and vegetables, such as citrus fruits, berries, melon, yellow vegetables, and green and leafy vegetables. Some foods, such as jelly, salad dressings, candy, sugar and oils, do not fit into any of these groups. These foods are not basic to our diets, because they provide very little nutrient value.

At first glance, some foods are difficult to classify according to the Basic 4. For example, where does pizza belong? Actually, the ingredients found in pizza come from all of the Basic 4: cheese, from the milk and dairy group; pepperoni, from the meat group; crust, from the bread and cereal group; and mushrooms, green peppers, tomato sauce, all from the fruit and vegetable group.

While thinking of food, we should not forget water, which is essential for life. Infants and children require more water than adults, because a child's body surface area is proportionately larger, and more water is lost through evaporation (Endres & Rockwell, 1980). We should offer plenty of water and other liquids to young children.

Myths about Food Habits

Recent research on food habits has revealed some interesting insights into commonly held ideas concerning children and food (O'Brien, 1978). These studies have demonstrated that children do not necessarily get the nutrients they need in the ways in which we might think.

First, we may think that serving well-balanced meals will guarantee that children's nutrient needs will be met. This is true only if children eat the food, not if it is left on the plate—as it often is. However, certain foods children generally like and usually eat, such as fruits, cheese, cereals, meat loaf, and raw vegetables, do provide essential nutrients and should thus be served frequently.

Second, we may believe that insisting that children clean their plates results in their learning to like a lot of different foods. There are, however, usually no long-lasting effects when children are forced to eat everything on their plates. It is best to ask children to taste certain foods, rather than insist that they finish everything.

Third, we may think that children need

a hot lunch. Actually, children can obtain the same nutrients from cold food or food served at room temperature as they can from hot food. Children also enjoy salad bars from which they can select their own vegetables. Salad not eaten can be refrigerated and eaten the following day.

Fourth, we may feel that children will eat more if we give them small portions. Although small portions reduce waste, children eat about the same amounts of food, whether it is served in large or small portions.

Finally, we may believe that children are bound to eat certain types of food if we serve them over and over again. Rather than repeatedly serving food that children noticeably dislike, it is best to introduce an unusual or unpopular food only occasionally, since children are not likely to undergo drastic changes of taste. It is best to serve nutritious food that children will eat.

Influences on Eating Habits

Our eating habits are influenced by many factors. We are not born liking certain foods and disliking others. We are, instead, influenced by other concerns. It is important that we know and understand the factors that influence our own and children's eating behaviors.

Why do we eat what we do? First, we eat for social reasons. For example, we eat what others eat when we are their guests. We taste different foods because someone recommended them. The social setting thus strongly influences what we eat.

We eat certain foods because of our religious beliefs and practices. Some religions forbid the eating of certain kinds of foods. We may also be influenced by religious and nonreligious convictions, such as those that lead some people to become vegetarians.

Ethnic and cultural customs and traditions influence our eating habits also and determine whether we eat a particular food and in what form.

Economic considerations influence the kinds of foods we eat. For example, we may buy what is on sale at the store to save money. We may not buy prepared food because it is too expensive. In fact, research shows that income has a direct influence on nutrition and thence on growth and development (Stevens & Baxter, 1981).

Education influences our eating habits. Food habits are, to a great extent, learned. We are not born liking or disliking liver or spinach. We learn to enjoy or avoid certain foods from those around us.

Finally, some children's eating habits are shaped by specific dietary and health considerations, such as lactose or milk intolerance or a disease such as diabetes. In such cases, special diets are required, and we should cooperate with parents and professionals to provide appropriate food for the affected child.

Adult influence on children's behavior and attitudes is naturally very strong. Thus, parents and other adults help shape the eating habits of children, who are influenced by eating with adults and listening to what they say about the foods they choose to eat or not eat. Children also learn that they can manipulate adults by eating or refusing to eat certain foods.

It is important for us to set a good example for children. We can model positive eating habits by being willing to try new foods, by eating a variety of foods, and by pointing out the enjoyable aspects of different foods—for example their color, texture, taste, aroma, nutritional value, and variety. It is also important for us not to do things that teach children to manipulate or fear mealtime situations. For example, when bribery is used, it teaches children to hold out for something better and to use food as a means of getting something they want. Scare tactics and punishment, when used, can make eating a negative experience and teach children to dread mealtimes.

Promoting Positive Eating Habits

A variety of strategies for serving food to young children can make mealtimes pleasant experiences for both children and adults. These strategies can help form good eating habits and provide learning experiences as well.

Children's appetites, like our own, vary from meal to meal. Thus, we should not expect children to eat every meal with the same enthusiasm. In addition, small children may go through periods of wanting to eat the same food over and over, then quite suddenly stop eating that food. These trends are usually temporary if adults do not overemphasize them, and they will generally run their course.

It is a mistake to insist that children eat everything on their plates, or that they try a new food. Children need encouragement and a good example to follow, but coercion usually backfires. Desserts or other foods should not be withheld as punishment or always saved to be eaten last. If the dessert contributes to nutrition, as it should, it may be eaten anytime, even first. When sweets are used as rewards, children learn to value them more than other foods. This is not the nutrition lesson we want to teach.

Eating should be as easy as possible. Food should be served in a form that is easy for young children to manage. Bite-sized pieces and finger foods are liked by children, and suitable for small hands. Meat, vegetables, fruit, and bread can be cut into bite-sized chunks, strips, sections, or pieces that are easy to handle. Since young children will use their hands for much of their meal, hands should be carefully washed before children come to the table.

Dishes and eating utensils for children should be attractive, durable, and suited to small hands. Milk and other beverages should be served in small glasses or cups with handles. Since children are not as skillful as adults in their eating, spills are likely. We should be prepared by using washable table tops and chairs, and having sponges and towels handy. Children need to be allowed to explore food and learn to enjoy eating. Neatness will come later.

The dining area should be comfortable and equipped with suitable child-sized tables and chairs. Seating children in groups of four to six with an adult helps to make mealtime a social occasion and one that is easily managed.

Children should be served as soon as they are seated at their tables. Waiting results in restless children who are more likely to disrupt the mealtime atmosphere.

Food can be served family style, with adults helping children to serve themselves. First portions should be small to moderate, with the understanding that more is available. An adult who usually eats with children will soon learn to judge appropriate portion sizes for the children at the table.

Children should be introduced to new foods. They need the opportunity to eat a variety of foods. Serving less familiar foods occasionally and encouraging, but not forcing, children to try them helps to build good attitudes and habits. If a new food is introduced in a very small quantity, along with more familiar foods, children are more likely to try the new food. The behavior of the adult in introducing the new food is critical. Food habits are taught, and adult behavior is a powerful influence. We should not be discouraged if children refuse a new food. We can wait a while and try again. A story or other activity can be used to help children accept new foods.

Eating is a social activity as well as a nutritional one (Aronson, 1985). But it should not be overtaxing. Mealtimes need to be relaxed and pleasant. Some children need a quiet time before meals so that they are not too tired or excited when they come to the table. Adults can teach by example that mealtime is a good time for conversation. We should, however, discourage complaints about personal food dislikes and should try to emphasize positive attitudes.

Small children are ready to leave the table as soon as they have finished eating. They may become grumpy and fidgety if required to remain at the table until everyone has finished. A convenient plan should therefore be devised to help children move with ease from mealtime to play.

Children should be encouraged to help with aspects of meal preparation. Helpers can set the table, fill glasses, pass seconds, clear the dishes, and wipe tables. The amount of responsibility will need to be tailored to the child's age and ability.

Sometimes we need to give special attention to eating problems, such as prolonged eating of a very limited variety of food, or overeating. These problems will not run their course if ignored. In such cases, we need to talk with the parents. Perhaps the problem exists at home or is due to some stress in the child's life. If the underlying problem can be addressed, in time the child's eating habits should improve.

It is probably best to discourage children and parents from bringing snacks to the center unless there is enough for all. Even then, extras should contribute to the overall food and nutrition program—that is, they should provide nutritional value and not just calories for energy. Birthdays can be celebrated just as well with candles in a section of watermelon or other fruit as with a very sweet cake.

Nutrition Education

Nutrition education for young children involves much more than serving meals and snacks. The overall goal of nutrition education is to help children become more knowledgeable about new and familiar foods and learn to choose nutritious foods for meals and snacks (Church, 1979). Nutrition education can also stimulate the young child's cognitive development in a variety of ways (Endres & Rockwell, 1980).

In general, nutrition education for young children involves learning about food through sensory experiences. For example, a child who goes to an orchard and picks apples, then prepares and cooks them to make applesauce is learning where food comes from, what it looks like, what the texture is before and after cooking, and what it tastes like.

The teacher's role and overall goal in the nutrition education process is to help children become aware of nutritious foods. This awareness can best be accomplished through many direct food experiences. We can provide opportunities for children to encounter, assimilate, and, finally, integrate information from sensory experiences with food.

We can make learning about food a varied and interesting experience. Young children are, on the whole, fascinated with food and eating, and we can use each area of the curriculum to teach them about nutrition. We can provide learning experiences involving food and food preparation and integrate nutrition concepts into all program activities: fine motor, gross motor, language, science, physical education, social studies, music, art, and mathematics.

Question Starter: What are some activities we can plan to teach nutrition education in the child care setting? (Responses may include: field trips; gardening; cooking; planning menus; incorporating multicultural foods in meals.)

We can take children on field trips that help them become aware of the food and nutrition activities going on around them. Trips to gardens, farms, orchards, markets, grocery stores, packaging plants, and bakeries help make children aware of many different aspects of food and food preparation.

Children also learn by planting and preparing food. They learn about fruits and vegetables by seeing the plants as they grow, and later, as they are cut, peeled, or sliced in preparation for serving. Children especially enjoy planting seeds, watching them grow, harvesting their own plants, and preparing food they have grown. Planting gardens in the summer is an excellent way for children to learn about food and food processes. They are also more likely to eat foods that they have planted and prepared.

Even when they have not planted the food, children learn about it when they assist in meal or snack preparation. Children particularly enjoy making peanut butter, applesauce, and other simple foods. They also learn to cooperate and follow instructions and discover what works and what does not when they are given the chance to help prepare the food they eat.

Food experiences can involve a wonderful variety of activities with even a single food. For example, oranges can be peeled and sectioned, cut in half and eaten with a spoon, or squeezed for juice. Children can visit stores to buy oranges, look at pictures of orange trees, examine the seeds, and talk about growing oranges and varieties of oranges.

Children can also expand their language concepts by engaging in food activities. They learn new words, colors, shapes, terms, and numbers. For example, after a trip to the grocery store, children can dictate their experiences to an adult who writes down their story. We can help children enlarge their vocabularies by introducing new words, such as "stem," "seeds," "peelings," and so on.

Math concepts can be introduced through food experiences. As children prepare food, they learn about adding ingredients and using measurements. For example, children can learn the concept of division when the food they have prepared is divided. Through food experiences, we can introduce metric as well as conventional terms.

Children can get multicultural and cross-cultural education through food experiences (Munsch, 1983). They can learn about food customs and about types of foods eaten by different people and by different children in their group. Cooking can, in fact, become an exciting and effective learning tool. As Kositsky (1977) points out, it can be a satisfactory means of getting even young children to appreciate different eating practices in America and elsewhere. Parent involvement can be a great help and resource in this endeavor.

Other examples of nutrition education activities include: exploring where foods come from; guessing games (What is the food? Where does it come from? What do we get from trees or cows?); matching games (colors with food, animals with food, names with pictures of food); word games (describing names, colors, feel, smell, shape, taste, how food grows, positive food experiences); and flower pot gardens.

Learning Activity: Divide participants into small groups, and ask them to select a food or foods and describe how the food(s) can be incorporated into all areas of the curriculum as a learning experience: science; art; music; social studies; language; math; sensory motor development; consumer education; and personal social skills. Ask the groups to share their experiences when finished.

Successful Food Programs

Successful nutrition programs in child care facilities rely heavily on active and informed adult involvement, on practical and sound menu planning, and on effective financial management.

Basically, as careproviders we play an active and supportive role where nutrition is concerned (Endres & Rockwell, 1980). An essential part of child care programs is the feeding of children. However, our responsibility is much more than just having something for children to eat. Our job is to select food that will meet children's nutritional needs, to prepare it so that its value and flavor are retained, to serve it attractively, to encourage children to eat by our words and actions, and to make mealtime a pleasant social occasion. We need to remember that food habits stay with children throughout life.

We can help children to develop healthy bodies by designing a food program that will benefit them. We can help by being alert for signs of good or poor nutrition; by providing foods children require to meet their nutritional needs; by fostering good eating habits as we set positive examples; by planning projects, activities, and experiences that help children learn about food and how to appreciate what it does; and, finally, by providing nutritious, appealing meals and snacks within the constraints of budget, resources, and regulations of licensing or government reimbursement programs.

Meals and snacks served as part of child care programs should be planned with the total daily needs of children in mind. The number and kinds of meals and snacks served at the center will depend on the length of time children are away from home, and what and when they ate before arriving. If possible, meals eaten at home and away from home should complement each other. As a guide, children in group care from five to seven hours should receive meals and snacks that provide one-third to one-half of their nutritional needs. Children spending eight to nine hours at the facility should receive at least two-thirds of their daily nutritional requirement. Parent conferences and posted menus, which take into account both meal and snack times, inform everyone about what children are eating.

Like regular meals, snacks should be a planned part of the day, and should help meet the child's nutritional needs. Snacks can be simple and nourishing: for example, apple slices, plain crackers, and juice, or vegetable strips and milk. If served at least one and one-half hours before meals, snacks should not diminish appetites.

Question Starter: What kinds of nutritious snacks have you prepared that children really like? (A wide range of responses are possible.)

Menu Planning

Menus and snacks should be planned with several considerations in mind. Menus should, first of all, be planned to meet children's nutritional needs while remaining within the limitations of budget, staff, time, and equipment. As food prices continue to rise, planning becomes critical. Factors such as shopping for food, storing it, and preparing it properly can all contribute to staying within the budget.

We should also plan for variety. That is, we should review the menu for color contrasts and eye appeal, size-and-shape contrasts, flavor combinations, and textures that appeal to children, such as crisp, soft, and chewy. Lumpy, gummy foods and stringy items should be avoided. Combinations of foods should be varied so that children can learn to appreciate pork and dressing as well as turkey and dressing. Methods of preparation should also vary: potatoes can be baked, broiled, mashed, hashed, creamed, and so on. New foods should be included occasionally.

The same menus should serve children and staff. Children learn a great deal from the examples set by adults, thus it is very important that they see adults eating the same foods as themselves.

Planning ahead saves time and money. One system of planning is called cycle menu planning. Cycle menus are a set of menus that can be repeated every few weeks. Cycle menus can be developed for each season to add variety and to take advantage of seasonal bargains.

Several steps are involved in planning cycle menus. The first step is to select the length of time and season the cycle will cover. Four weeks is a typical time period.

The next few steps involve choosing foods that satisfy daily nutritional requirements. A protein-rich dish should be planned for each and every day of the cycle. These dishes are selected from the dairy and/or meat group—for example, macaroni and cheese, peanut butter sandwiches, barbeque pork cubes. This selection is in addition to milk for drinking. Different methods of preparation can be used. Using recipes ensures the same quality each time.

Vegetables and salads should also be selected for each and every day. A source of vitamin C needs to be included daily, and a source of vitamin A every other day. Seasonal favorites and specials can be taken into consideration. A finishing touch, such as a fruit or pudding, can be chosen to round out the meal. Again, we can take advantage of opportunities to add variety of taste, texture, and color to balance the nutritional value and attractiveness of the meal.

Bread, butter, and beverages are other considerations. We should use whole-grain or enriched breads, crackers, and rolls. New items such as rye bread, different kinds of cheeses and crackers, or whole wheat or bran muffins can be tried occasionally.

Snacks should also be planned. Interest and variety should be kept in mind. Snacks may be planned around other child care activities such as stories or field trips. Snack time can be a good time to introduce new sensory experiences with foods such as green peppers or less familiar types of fruits and melons.

Menus should be reviewed carefully and checked for nutritional adequacy, variety of color, taste, texture, and ease of preparation. It is a good idea to plan a few emergency menus. One never knows when the cook will be ill, or the power will go off.

Finally, market orders should correspond to the menus and the frequency of shopping trips. Shopping trips should be planned on a regular basis, depending on food storage facilities. As the menus are used, any changes made or problems encountered should be recorded. This information will help update the menus before the cycle begins again. An example of a three-week cycle menu is shown in figure 8.

It is essential that we handle all aspects of meal and snack time with an eye toward safety and cleanliness. Food must not be allowed to spoil or become contaminated. Equipment, dishes, utensils, floor, and walls need to be kept clean and in good repair. Everyone who handles food should take health and safety precautions. Washing hands, including those of children, and protecting food from smoke,

Three-Week Cycle Menu

Week 1

Breakfast	*Lunch*	*Snack*
Monday		
Hot oatmeal with raisins, 1/2 cup Milk, 1/2 cup Juice, 1/3–1/2 cup Whole wheat toast, 1/2 slice Margarine, 1/2 tsp.	Tuna rice casserole 1-1/2 oz. tuna 1/4 cup rice Cream of mushroom soup Broccoli, 1/2 cup Beets, 1/4 cup Whole wheat bread, 1/2 slice Milk, 1/2 cup	Deviled eggs, 1/2 Whole wheat crackers (3) or popcorn Milk, 1/2 cup
Tuesday		
Cold cereal, 1/2 cup Milk, 1/2 cup Whole wheat toast, 1/2 slice Peanut butter, 1 tsp. Fresh fruit (variety), 1/4 cup	Beef stroganoff over noodles 1-1/2 oz. beef 1/2 cup gravy 1/4 cup egg noodles 1/4 cup baby lima beans Orange raisin salad 1/4 cup fresh orange 1 tbs. raisins Whole wheat bread w/marg. Milk, 1/2 cup	Cottage cheese, 1/4 cup Pineapple chunks, 1/4 cup Milk, 1/2 cup
Wednesday		
Whole wheat pancakes Yogurt, 1/4 cup Fruit (strawberries, blueberries, etc.), 1/4 cup Juice, 1/3 cup Milk, 1/2 cup	Baked turkey, 1-1/2 oz. Stuffing, 1/4 cup Sweet potatoes, 1/4 cup Peas, 1/4 cup Biscuit Milk, 1/2 cup	Orange slices, 1/4 cup Cheese crackers (4) Milk, 1/2 cup
Thursday		
Cold cereal, 1/2 cup Milk, 1/2 cup Whole wheat toast, 1/2 slice; w/marg., 1/2 tsp. Fresh fruit (variety), 1/4 cup	Chili, 1/2 cup 1 oz. ground beef 1/4 cup beans 2 tbs. tomato sauce Carrots and celery sticks Fruit salad, 1/4 cup Whole wheat crackers	Peanut butter balls (2) Banana, 1/2 Milk, 1/2 cup
Friday		
Scrambled eggs, 1/2; w/cheese, 1/2 oz. Whole wheat toast, 1/2 slice; w/marg., 1/2 tsp. Juice, 1/3–1/2 cup Milk, 1/2 cup	Pork patties, 1-1/2 oz.; w/gravy Peas, 1/4 cup Peaches, 1/4 cup Whole wheat bread, 1/2 slice Milk, 1/2 cup	Whole wheat raisin muffins (1), w/marg., 1/2 tsp. Milk, 1/2 cup

***Figure 8.** (continued)*

Week 2

Breakfast	*Lunch*	*Snack*
Monday Cream of wheat w/honey, 1/2 cup Milk, 1/2 cup Whole wheat toast w/marg., 1/2 tsp.	Broiled beef patty, 1-1/2 oz. Creamed corn, 1/4 cup Green beans, 1/4 cup Whole wheat bread w/marg., 1/2 tsp. Milk, 1/2 cup	Apples, 1/4 Peanut butter, 1 tbs. Milk, 1/2 cup
Tuesday Cold cereal, 1/2 cup Milk, 1/2 cup Whole wheat toast, 1/2 slice; w/marg., 1/2 tsp. Fresh fruit (variety), 1/4 cup	Beans & ham 1 oz. ham Beans (variety), 1/2 cup Zucchini salad 1 slice tomato 1 tsp. dressing Cornbread, 2″ slice Milk, 1/2 cup	Tangarines Crackers (2) Milk, 1/2 cup
Wednesday Homemade granola w/fruit and milk Juice, 1/3–1/2 cup Whole wheat toast, 1/2 slice Milk, 1/2 cup	Broccoli-cheese quiche 1/4 cup broccoli 1 oz. cheese 1 egg Crust Tomato slices, 1/2 cup Milk, 1/2 cup	Cornbread w/honey Apple juice, 1/3 cup
Thursday Cold cereal, 1/2 cup Milk, 1/2 cup Whole wheat toast, 1/2 slice w/peanut butter Fresh fruit (variety), 1/4 cup	Chicken livers (fried), 1-1/2 cups Green beans, 1/4 cup Homemade muffin Milk, 1/2 cup	Celery or crackers w/peanut butter or cream cheese, 1 tbs. Milk, 1/2 cup
Friday Eggs in a nest 1 egg in a slice of whole wheat toast Apple crunch Milk, 1/2 cup Juice, 1/3–1/2 cup	Chili mac 1/4 cup macaroni 1/4 cup chili Melon, 1/4 cup Carrot and celery sticks Whole wheat bread w/marg., 1/2 tsp. Milk, 1/2 cup	Whole wheat banana muffins (1) w/marg., 1/4 tsp. Milk, 1/2 cup

Week 3

Breakfast	*Lunch*	*Snack*
Monday		
Malt-O-Meal w/raisins, 1/2 cup Milk, 1/2 cup Whole wheat toast, 1/2 slice Peanut butter, 1/2 tsp. Juice, 1/3–1/2 cup	Cheese toasties 1 oz. cheese 1 whole wheat bread Oven browned potato, 1/4 cup Raw cauliflower and celery, 1/4 cup Milk, 1/2 cup	Mock sour cream dip Sliced celery, cucumber, and carrot sticks Milk, 1/2 cup
Tuesday		
Cold cereal, 1/2 cup Milk, 1/2 cup Whole wheat toast, 1/2 slice; w/marg., 1/2 tsp. Fresh fruit (variety), 1/4 cup	Mad Hatter meatballs Mixed vegetables, 1/4 cup Fruit salad, 1/4 cup Whole wheat bread w/marg. Milk, 1/2 cup	Bread pudding w/raisins Milk, 1/2 cup
Wednesday		
Honey crunch fruit salad Homemade muffin w/marg., 1/2 tsp. Milk, 1/2 cup	Tuna noodle casserole 1 oz. tuna 1/2 oz. cheese (variety) sauce Noodles, 1/4 cup Stir-fried broccoli, 1/4 cup Apple slices, 1/4 cup Milk, 1/2 cup	Wheat crackers w/peanut butter (3) Apple juice, 1/2 cup
Thursday		
Cold cereal, 1/2 cup Milk, 1/2 cup Whole wheat toast, 1/2 slice; w/marg., 1/2 tsp. Fresh fruit (variety), 1/4 cup	Turkey stew 1-1/2 oz. turkey 1/4 cup mixed vegetables Tangarines, 1/4 cup Biscuit w/marg., 1/2 tsp. Milk, 1/2 cup	Fruit salad, 1/4 cup Milk, 1/2 cup
Friday		
Whole wheat pancakes w/fruit syrup Milk, 1/2 cup Juice, 1/3–1/2 cup	Pizza 1 oz. beef 1/2 oz. cheese 1 tsp. green pepper 1 tsp. tomato sauce Whole wheat crust Carrot sticks, 2″–6″ Cucumbers, 2 slices Milk, 1/2 cup	Chex party mix Cereal with milk for infants Fruit juice, 1/3 cup

***Figure** 8. Three-week cycle menu of nutritious and flavorful meals*

hair, and germs can prevent many foodborne diseases and add to meal appeal.

Food Buying and Storage

A successful child care program will include food-buying habits that reflect careful menu planning. Such planning reduces cost and waste and provides a clear-cut basis for setting up shopping lists.

Careful food buying takes into consideration children's likes and dislikes, nutritional needs, budget restrictions, storage space for food, food preparation space and equipment, and licensing or governmental restrictions. For example, although quantity buying can sometimes result in lower prices, it is not appropriate to purchase food if there is no space to store it, or if children do not like it. Foods that children like and eat can result in substantial savings when purchased in season or on special.

Storage of food requires careful planning. Storage areas should, of course, be accessible to preparation areas. Shelf space should accommodate the size of the food items, which should be stored separately from nonfood items. Food storage areas should be dry and relatively cool (60 to 70 degrees Fahrenheit). Commodities should be stored in tightly sealed containers, and perishable food should be stored at 45 degrees or lower.

Parent Participation in Food Programs

A successful food program in a child care facility also includes parents. When parents are well informed about food, food preparation, and the importance of good eating habits, they can help shape the child's food habits and attitudes and reinforce the goals of good nutrition education.

Question Starter: What are some successful ways in which you have involved parents in your food program? What were the results? (Responses may include: parent meetings and conferences; open house; newsletters and bulletin board displays; social gatherings.)

There are a number of ways in which we can involve parents. We can make special efforts to talk to them about the food experiences of their children. Discussions about food can also occur at parent conferences, open houses, and other parent meetings.

Written reports about the child can also be made to parents. These reports should always include some information about foods the child eats. Reports can, moreover, include food activities in which the child has been or could be engaged.

Information about food and nutrition can also be provided through periodic newsletters. Nutritious snacks and recipes children can use may be included in the newsletter or placed on bulletin boards for parents to view.

When parents visit the facility, they can see firsthand what children are learning about nutrition by viewing displayed art work, projects, drawings, and activities about food. And finally, nutritious food that has been planned and prepared by children can be served at social gatherings that parents attend.

Summary

Good nutrition is essential to good health, and teachers are in an excellent position to foster good eating habits in children. Careful attention to nutritional needs of children, menu planning, food buying and storage, and the development of positive attitudes about nutritious foods can contribute to a quality child care food program.

Enrichment Activities

1. Using the steps for planning a cycle menu, devise a four-week cycle menu for your child care facility.
2. Keep a list of all the foods you serve children in your facility for a week. Record the food preferences of children by using the following percentage for each food: 0%–25%; 25%–50%; 50%–75%; 75%–100%. Take into consideration the foods children actually eat and those that are left over. At the end of the week, summarize the results and specify which foods you will consider serving again, and why.
3. Use the questions and rating scale developed by the Food and Nutrition Service of the U.S. Department of Agriculture (fig. 9) to evaluate the menus in your child care facility. Rate your answers: almost always; sometimes; never.
4. Describe at least three ways in which you can improve the food program in your child care facility. Try to implement your recommendations.
5. Introduce a new food to children in your child care facility. Show how the food can be incorporated into all areas of the curriculum.
6. Prepare a list of nutritious recipes that can be distributed to parents in your child care facility.

Menu Rating Scale

1.	Are all components of the meal included?	Almost always	Sometimes	Never
2.	Are serving sizes sufficient to provide young children with the required quantity of meat or an alternate or equivalent? Are two or more vegetables provided?	Almost always	Sometimes	Never
3.	Are serving sizes planned?	Almost always	Sometimes	Never
4.	Are other foods included to meet the nutritional needs of young children and to satisfy appetites?	Almost always	Sometimes	Never
5.	Do meals include a good balance of color, texture, shape, flavor, and temperature?	Almost always	Sometimes	Never
6.	Are most of the foods and food combinations ones children have learned to eat?	Almost always	Sometimes	Never
7.	Are the food combinations pleasing and acceptable to children?	Almost always	Sometimes	Never
8.	Have children's cultural and ethnic food practices been considered?	Almost always	Sometimes	Never
9.	Are food varied from day to day and week to week?	Almost always	Sometimes	Never
10.	Are different forms of food (fresh, dried, canned) included?	Almost always	Sometimes	Never
11.	Are seasonal foods included?	Almost always	Sometimes	Never

Figure 9. *Criteria for evaluating menus in a child care facility*

Bibliography

Aronson, S. S. (1985, March). Infant feeding in child care. *Child Care Information Exchange,* pp. 22–25.

General but important principles about the feeding of infants in child care are discussed. Topics include feeding programs, funding, and nutrition concerns.

Church, M. (1979). Nutrition: A vital part of the curriculum. *Young Children, 35* (1), 61–65.

The author reports on a program aimed at studying and changing the food habits of young children. Through classroom activities and parent education, children's attitudes toward food were influenced. Therefore, Church advocates the implementation of a curriculum that includes teaching children about nutrition and actively involves them in food choices and food preparation.

Croft, K. B. (1971). *The good for me cookbook.* San Francisco: R and E Research Associates.

One of the chief features of this delightful book is that even young children can use the recipes provided to prepare or help in the preparation of healthy and delicious food. The recipes are drawn from a variety of sources and cover all aspects of a nutritious meal.

Endres, J. B., & Rockwell, R. E. (1980). *Food, nutrition, and the young child.* St. Louis: C. V. Mosby.

This informative and comprehensive book deals with the nutritional needs of children from birth to 5 years of age and presents various concepts about food and nutrition, especially as they apply to child care settings. Food and nutrition as a significant part of the curriculum are examined and explained. Nutrition-related problems and controversies are also discussed.

Herr, J., & Morse, W. (1982). Food for thought: Nutrition education for young children. *Young Children, 38* (1), 3–11.

Nutrition education should be an essential part of the early childhood curriculum. The authors list ten basic food and nutrition concepts that can be taught to young children and that can, at the same time, enhance several learning areas such as sensory development, fine and gross motor development, language arts, math, science, dramatic play, art, music, and social studies.

Jacqua, I. C., & McClenahan, P. (1982). *Nutrition for the whole family.* Englewood Cliffs, NJ: Prentice-Hall.

A good resource guide for parents and teachers, this book studies children's eating habits, related health issues, and the parental role in teaching and modeling nutrition attitudes and behavior. Various games, activities, and strategies for teaching children about nutrition are presented.

Kositsky, V. (1977). What in the world is cooking in class today? *Young Children, 33* (1), 23–31.

An enjoyable and enlightening article on how young children can be taught multicultural awareness as well as sound nutrition through the preparation of simple but appetizing and healthy foods in class.

Martin, M. J. (1980). *Role of child nutrition programs in health education.* Paper presented at the American School Health Association Convention, Dallas, TX. (Eric Document Reproduction Service No. ED 195 527)

This document stresses the importance of incorporating nutrition education into school health programs. The necessity for trained health educators and for government concern and funding is also underlined.

McCrea, N. L. (1981). A down-under approach to parent and child food fun. *Childhood Education, 57,* 216–22.

The article gives a detailed description of an Australian workshop series in which children, their parents, and teachers participated, learning about nutrition and health through a variety of fun-filled activities. The activities themselves were drawn from the areas of art, culture, language arts, literature, science, and others. The learning experience was, therefore, integrated and comprehensive and was enjoyed by adults and children alike.

Munsch, A. B. (1983, May/June). What's for lunch? *Child Care Information Exchange,* pp. 36–39.

The article deals with the very real problem in day care centers of matching nutritional needs with children's likes and dislikes and the budget. The writer examines menu planning, standard recipes, cycle menus, and nutritional, educational, operational, and financial concerns. A sample cycle menu is provided.

O'Brien, M. (1978). Facts and fancies about children's foods. *Day Care & Early Education, 5* (4), pp. 10–11.

Many of the ideas adults have about children's nutrition and eating habits are erroneous or mere fancy. The article will make interesting reading for parents and teachers.

Pipes, P. L. (1977). *Nutrition in infancy and childhood.* St. Louis: C. V. Mosby.

This practical book gives useful information about the sources of good nutrition and the development of good food habits in children.

Reinisch, E. H., & Minear, R. E. (1978). *Health of the preschool child.* New York: John Wiley and Sons.

This comprehensive and readable book will be welcomed by administrators, teachers, and parents concerned with the health of young children. It provides information on policies, health programs and assessment, care of sick children, behavioral problems, first aid, and safety. The chapter on nutrition, although brief (pp. 61–76), presents useful information on nutrients and their use, sources of nutrients, food groups, serving nutritious food to children, and the effects of malnutrition.

Stevens, J. H., & Baxter, D. H. (1981). Malnutrition and children's development. *Young Children, 36* (4), 60–71.

A discussion of important research, both in the United States and abroad, on the effects of malnutrition on the development of children. Implications for teachers and society are also considered, and it is stated that programs enabling parents and centers to provide an adequate diet for children should be a priority with policy makers.

Vonde, D. A. S., & Beck, J. (1980). *Food adventures for children.* Redondo Beach, CA: Plycon Press.

This interesting book presents a variety of activities and safety measures that can be taught to young children during the preparation and eating of nutritious food. Food preparation can be a wonderful learning and developmental resource: while they learn about food itself, children also learn about color, texture, smell, size, shape, and weight. Language growth is stimulated, motor skills are reinforced, and social skills are attained.

Wanamaker, N., Hearn, K., & Richarz, S. (1979). *More than graham crackers: Nutrition education and food preparation with young children.* Washington, DC: National Association for the Education of Young Children.

The authors provide ideas on how teachers can help children learn to select, prepare, and enjoy nutritious foods. Recipes, finger plays, and teaching ideas are presented.

11

Health and Safety for Children

AS the need for and use of child care outside the home grows, it is becoming increasingly obvious that adults who work with young children play a significant role in maintaining and managing children's health, safety, and well-being. We find ourselves responsible for providing a safe environment, monitoring and assessing the health of our charges, constantly being prepared to manage emergencies, and serving as part of a larger system or team consisting of health professionals, parents, and teachers. It is, therefore, important to be informed about children's health and safety needs.

Objectives

The overall purpose of this chapter is to explore the measures we should take to protect the health and safety of children. We will review the components of health policies, procedures, and programs that should be developed and made known to all concerned. We will identify the infectious disease process and examine strategies for preventing and managing the spread of disease in child care settings. We will explore ways to make playgrounds and the environment safe for children. Finally, we will discuss preparedness, first aid, and the teaching of safety rules and habits to children.

Key Ideas

There is a great deal that we can do to assure the health and safety of children in our care. We can work with parents and other professionals in the community to foster the well-being of children. Furthermore, if our child care facilities have established sound health policies and procedures, we will be well equipped to deal with all aspects of the management and prevention of disease and accidents.

Young children are susceptible to many types of infectious diseases. Understanding the infection process and controlling and managing the spread of infectious diseases are an important part of the teacher's role. A knowledge of the principles of good sanitation and hygiene and an adherence to sanitary standards and regulations are essential for everyone who works in a child care facility.

We need to be aware of all hazards that pose a potential threat to the safety of children. It is essential to take precautions to prevent accidents and injuries. By being alert, vigilant, and prepared, we can eliminate or reduce many accidents and injuries to children. As teachers, we also need a sound knowledge of the elements of first aid and of taking care of sick children.

Health Programs and Policies

Developing and establishing firm guidelines for a sound health program should be a priority for center administrators and staff. Clearly stated policies and procedures should be in place in child care settings, and it is essential that all staff and parents understand them. The programs, policies, and procedures should be worked out cooperatively, with health care professionals, teachers, and parents playing active roles to ensure that the best interests of all concerned are met. Thus, a jointly developed, ongoing health program can protect the well-being of both adults and children, while clearly specified policies will help everyone know how to manage emergencies and other health and safety related problems.

Question Starter: What types of information should be included in the health care policies of a child care facility? (Responses may include: inclusion and exclusion of sick children; daily health checks; illness and accident management at the facility; medication guidelines; sanitation procedures.)

Aronson (1983) points out that although the policies of each child care program may be developed to suit its specific needs, certain general areas need to be covered in most programs. There should be, for example, policies and guidelines concerning the inclusion or exclusion of children at the time of enrollment owing to health-related factors, since caring for certain groups of children, such as those who are deaf or blind, may be beyond the capacity of the facility. Other guidelines should include: daily health surveillance of children and recognition of illness symptoms; exclusion and/or care of sick children; management of injuries; first aid, and preparedness for emergencies; environmental safety awareness and surveillance; administration of medication; routine health assessments for children; nutrition and feeding; sanitation and cleaning procedures; care and maintenance of equipment; dental hygiene; health education; transportation; and a mechanism for the review of policies and procedures. Teachers, parents, and health professionals should review the statement on health policies as it is developed.

The issue of adult health is of utmost importance in child care programs, and clear policies regarding it should be outlined and explained. Specific job-related factors that influence or are influenced by health exist in many professions, and child care is more vulnerable than most. Thus, health considerations that could affect job performance need to be kept in mind. An adult who is not well cannot function properly and could contribute to risk factors in the facility.

Regular health examinations and appraisals of center staff and personnel should be a requirement, and special attention should be given to those features that are especially relevant to the special nature of child care, such as hearing, vision, and other sensory abilities. While physical and emotional fitness need attention, policies on habits that could be harmful, such as smoking at work, should also be clearly defined.

Finally, the legal implications of failing to comply with laws, regulations, and established standards should be known and understood by all concerned. Noncompliance with specified teacher-child ratio standards, negligence in adequately supervising children, and failure to reduce or remedy hazardous conditions could result in liability suits. We should remember that while having liability insurance is critical for centers, preventing accidents—to the best of our ability—is much more important.

Policies on a comprehensive health and safety program and continuous health supervision of children and adults in the program should, therefore, be devised. Guidelines on how to carry out daily observations and checklists for staff to use should be provided. Managing accidents, sicknesses, and specialized problems should also be covered in the policy, and programs on nutrition, safety, accident prevention, and other elements of health education should be set up.

Infectious Diseases in Child Care

Infectious diseases are a fact of life for most people but especially so for young children who are more susceptible to disease than adults. Child care centers are especially at high risk so far as infectious diseases are concerned. Research has shown that there seems to be a link between child care facilities and the spread of certain diseases such as infectious hepatitis, diarrhea and other intestinal infections, some types of influenza, and respiratory ailments (Kendall, 1983).

There are several reasons for the high incidence of infectious diseases in child care settings. These are closely associated with the specific nature of child care centers. Risk factors in centers are increased by a greater chance of exposure due to larger numbers of people; by a high turnover rate among both staff and children (thus increasing opportunities to introduce infection); and by intermingling of groups within the facility, which could allow infection to travel from one group to another (Packer, 1983).

While the risk of infection may be increased in child care, it is important to remember that young children are generally more susceptible to infection than older children and adults. This can make the incidence of sickness in child care centers with infants and toddlers higher than in other types of facilities. Children do not have a well-developed immune system before the age of two and are therefore more likely to become infected. The anatomy of a child is small, and disease can spread faster. The construction of a young child's ear, with its horizontal eustachian tube, allows nose and throat infections to reach the middle ear more quickly.

Young children are, therefore, physiologically more vulnerable to infectious disease. Moreover, their very nature and behavior enhance the risk (Packer, 1983). They tend to put their hands into the mouth or into the mouths of other children. They may "taste" toys and then let other children taste them. They like to be very close to other people while snuggling, playing, and talking. Young children know and care little about personal hygiene and cleanliness. They like to play in dirt and sand where they can pick up infections quite easily.

Controlling Infectious Diseases

Question Starter: What techniques can we use to reduce infectious diseases in child care? (Responses may include: awareness; knowledge; sanitation policies and practices; handwashing; immunization.)

As careproviders, we play a significant role in taking measures to limit disease among children in our care. We can help reduce the risks by understanding what causes infection and how it spreads, by taking steps to control the transmission of disease, and by learning to recognize the signs and symptoms of various infectious ailments. When we understand the infectious process, we are alert to disease symptoms; we may be able to avert and limit disease; we can communicate effectively with parents and medical professionals; we know when to separate or exclude sick children; and we can understand and advocate the need for immunization (Reinisch & Minear, 1978).

Reinisch and Minear define several factors that facilitate the infectious process. First of all, an infectious or causative agent must exist. This is in the form of tiny living organisms called microorganisms. Bacteria and viruses cause most infectious diseases in children. Bacteria can cause whooping cough, tetanus, conjunctivitis, and scarlet fever, while viruses cause measles, mumps, poliomyelitis, smallpox, infectious hepatitis, and the common cold. Infectious agents are specific to each disease. Their potency depends on a person's susceptibility or the way the disease is treated. The degree of infectiousness may also vary.

The place where the infectious agent resides, and from where it can be transferred to a susceptible person, is called the reservoir. Human beings and animals are common reservoirs for infectious diseases. In some cases, nonliving reservoirs can harbor infection.

Transmission of infection can occur in several ways. It may occur through the nose and mouth of the infected person—that is, through breathing, sneezing, and coughing. Chickenpox, diphtheria, influenza, measles, mumps, and poliomyelitis are among the diseases that can be transmitted in this way. Transmission can also occur by way of the intestinal tract—through unwashed hands, flies, and improper waste disposal. Diseases spread in this way include dysentery and various intestinal infections, typhoid, hepatitis, and poliomyelitis (which can be transmitted by both the respiratory and intestinal route). Infection is also spread through scales and discharges of infectious skin, mucous membrane lesions, and blister liquid (as in the case of chickenpox). Disease may be transmitted directly, such as through breathing or physical contact, or indirectly, through the use of common towels, handkerchiefs, utensils, or intermediate carriers such as flies.

When the infectious agent leaves the reservoir and is transmitted to a susceptible host, a pattern of development, usually consisting of four stages, follows. During the incubation period the infectious agent settles down and multiplies. Generally, no visible reaction is seen in the host. Most diseases have their own specific incubation period. A brief prodromal period follows, and the first symptoms appear. Then comes the acute period, when the illness is evident. Characteristic or typical symptoms of each disease are obvious, although fever and rashes may be common to many infectious illnesses. Symptoms and the course of the disease may vary from person to person. Furthermore, not all symptoms are always present. The final stage is the convalescent period. This can be a dangerous time in that complications might develop if proper care is not taken.

The communicability period of different diseases varies. But as long as an infectious agent is present, it is communicable. The problem is that infection is communicable not only when a person is obviously sick, but often before we know of the sickness. This makes it difficult to keep children from being exposed to most childhood diseases.

Some children are more susceptible to disease than others. Susceptibility may be influenced by several factors: length of exposure to the disease; amount of exposure to the infectious agent; age—infants and toddlers are often more susceptible; malnutrition; exposure to cold; tiredness; and the presence of chronic disease. Understanding the effect of these factors on a child's resistance will help us to realize which children are more at risk.

According to Reinisch and Minear, four general areas exist for the control of infectious diseases. Control of the reservoir is very difficult and often impossible. Control of transmission can be achieved by controlling the infectious agent's exit from the reservoir. This can be accomplished through good sanitation and personal cleanliness and hygiene. However, it is often hard to control transmission because most children's diseases are communicable before they are detected and identified. The infectious agent can be controlled in the host through immunizations and, in the case of actual sickness, through antibiotics and other medication. Finally, control can be enhanced by legal means, that is, by scrupulously following public health laws and regulations.

Question Starter: What steps can we take to prevent and control the spread of disease in child care facilities? (Responses may include: implement stringent cleanliness measures; teach proper handwashing; emphasize sanitary habits and proper nutrition; establish and implement health policies.)

Understanding the infectious process is only the first step toward protecting children from disease. Highberger and Boynton (1983) list various strategies or precautions child care staff can practice regularly to prevent and control disease. For example, we can maintain a clean, dry environment, since microorganisms flourish in warm, wet, dark, and dirty places. The diapering area requires special care. Disposable surfaces, such as newspapers, waxed paper, or paper bags can be effective for laying infants on during changing and for picking up soiled diapers. Meanwhile, permanent surfaces should be washed and disinfected often.

Cribs and strollers should also be frequently cleaned and disinfected. However, disinfectants that leave harmful residue should be avoided. Young children tend to put toys and rattles in their mouths, so play equipment should be cleaned and disinfected regularly. Moreover, we should try to prevent toys that have been put in a child's mouth from being used by other infants before cleaning or wiping.

Proper handwashing is, of course, one of the most essential factors in disease control. Detergent is usually more effective than soap, and liquid soap is considered more sanitary than bar soap. Our nails should be cleaned regularly. Faucets and sinks should be kept clean, and if possible, elbow control devices rather than regular faucets should be used. Handwashing is also important for children, especially for those who feed or are learning to feed themselves.

Utensils, food equipment, feeding bottles, high chair trays, tables, and floors should, of course, all be thoroughly cleaned to deter the growth of microorganisms. We should remove spilled food and crumbs from floors and other surfaces, since insects are attracted by food and food particles.

There are, in fact, many effective and practical measures we can take to prevent or reduce the spread of infectious diseases. Aronson (1983) suggests that by "altering" the host, the environment, and the transmission of the infectious agent, we can greatly decrease the risk of the spread of infection. For example, to reduce the risk of respiratory illnesses, we can see to it that children (the hosts) in our care get a balanced and nutritious diet, with adequate amounts of vitamin C. We can see that they drink plenty of fluids and get proper rest and adequate exercise. We can lessen opportunities for the infectious agent to be transmitted by teaching children sanitary habits and the essentials of personal cleanliness. We can encourage them not to cough or sneeze on their hands, which can become agents of infection, but toward the floor. We can use disposable personal items such as combs, washcloths, and tissues. We can maintain a healthy environment by providing adequate fresh air, appropriate ventilation, and a cool temperature. The transmission of infectious agents can be minimized by appropriate spacing between cots and other equipment used by children at resting time.

The spread of intestinal diseases can also be limited by adopting many of the procedures already described. We can take additional precautions, such as consulting health professionals and authorities when outbreaks are feared, by strictly enforcing and following standards of cleanliness, by excluding staff and children with diarrhea or other intestinal infections, by keeping the diapering area at a distance from food and drink areas, and by encouraging the use of flush toilets rather than potty chairs.

The host-agent-environment measures can work to prevent skin infections and other types of infectious disease as well.

One way of preventing or reducing the spread of disease is through immunization, which is available against diseases such as diphtheria, measles, mumps, rubella, tetanus, and poliomyelitis. Immunization can either eradicate disease or diminish its force. Vaccines do not exist for all infectious diseases. But where they do exist, we should attempt to see that all public regulations and requirements are met. We can also try to educate parents about the advantages of immunization that, on the whole, outweigh the disadvantages and dangers that some parents fear.

We need to have adequate knowledge and information about the signs and symptoms of children's infectious diseases. While some symptoms are disease specific, others are common to many diseases. Fever and rashes, for example, may appear in several diseases. We need to know something about rashes, to be able to give useful information to parents and health professionals. We need to be able to recognize whether a rash is infectious, allergic, or due to some other cause that we can alleviate (Aronson, 1985). Moreover, different diseases may have different kinds of rashes and different associated symptoms, and we need to learn to recognize and understand them.

Learning Activity: Divide into small groups and have each group devise a plan for preventing and controlling the spread of disease in their child care facilities. Share small group responses with the larger group.

Safety and Accident Control

Our responsibility and concern for children in general require that we do everything in our power to protect the safety of children in our care. Accidents can happen in any setting, even when safety precautions are observed, but accidents have less chance of occurring when we are aware of, and alert to, sources of danger and hazards, when we understand what constitutes danger and what rules and regulations exist to minimize it, and when we are prepared for all eventualities.

A study carried out in 1973 by the National Safety Council listed playground equipment, ingestions and poisonings, and burns as some of the serious contributors to injuries among young children. Certain general factors may make it easier for accidents to occur in child care settings. These include the characteristics and nature of children, the environment, and human nature itself (Reinisch & Minear, 1978).

The very nature of young children—their liveliness, curiosity, and adventurousness—can be a source of extreme danger to their health and safety. They tend to put things that attract them into their mouths to taste and perhaps to swallow. Therefore, we must be very careful to keep small objects and dangerous substances out of their reach. They are eager to try out their developing skills. They enjoy opening and shutting doors and drawers and can pull things down on themselves. While encouraging their development and independence, we must protect children by removing hazards and by guiding children to safety and safe behavior.

Hazards for children can abound in our surroundings. Building structures, room and playground equipment, appliances, cleaning materials, and chemical substances are examples of dangerous objects in the environment. Poisonous plants and insects can also present danger.

Human beings are not perfect and may at times be responsible for accidents. Stress, fatigue, ignorance, faulty judgments, and failure to recognize hazards may contribute to the danger. We must, therefore, be constantly on guard against mistakes and human factors that could be hazardous to a child's well-being and safety. We should, for example, be absolutely sure that the materials and substances we give children to use—such as glue or paints—are not harmful in any way. We know that children use adults as models, and for this reason we should avoid taking medicines or drugs in front of them. Our handling of potential hazards can increase or decrease risk factors for children, who are always ready to imitate us.

We cannot risk allowing our human characteristics to become dangerous for children. Often accidents caused by human factors can be avoided by "education, planning and practice" (Reinisch & Minear, 1978).

Accident Prevention

Question Starter: What specific steps can we take to prevent injuries and accidents to children in our care? (Responses may include: indoor and outdoor safety checks; precautions on the playground; careful supervision; safety education for children; preparedness; and first aid knowledge.)

In *School Safety Policies* (1968), the American Association for Health, Physical Education and Recreation recommends several measures for accident prevention. Sources of danger must be recognized, identified, and removed as soon as possible. If they cannot be removed, an attempt should be made to make them safer. Of course, new hazards should not be added to the environment.

There are, in fact, several general and specific measures we can take to prevent accidents. We can cooperate with authorities in the matter of official inspections, as well as carry out frequent inspections of our own to identify safety hazards. We can work actively to reduce the very real risk of poisonings and other injuries caused by environmental hazards. We can examine and, if necessary, rearrange our indoor and playground settings to reduce danger. We can teach children to behave and play safely. We can be prepared for emergencies and disasters. Finally, we can take steps to learn the principles and practical applications of first aid, which is an essential skill for all teachers.

Official inspections, as well as our own frequent safety checks, can contribute significantly to safety and accident control. Single room and environment inspections should take into account the following factors: electrical wiring; fire prevention; floors, walls, and ceiling; heating equipment; windows and clear glass panels; hazards, such as plastic bags, trunks, empty refrigerators, and lids and covers, which could cause suffocation; stairs; the kitchen area; bathrooms; storage places, cellars, and attics; classrooms; and, of course, the playground area (Reinisch & Minear, 1978).

We need to be extremely alert to the risk of poisoning in our center. We should read the labels on all drugs, cleaning substances, and other materials to learn how dangerous they are not only when swallowed but also when brought into contact with eyes or skin. All dangerous substances should be carefully locked away. They should be discarded safely, so that children cannot find and retrieve them.

It is better to avoid taking medicine in front of children. Nor should we court danger by referring to medicines as candy. Most children will be very eager to eat as much "candy" as they can lay their hands on. Thus, if it is necessary to have medicines in the room, they should be out of the reach of children.

The playground should be checked to ensure that poisonous plants are absent. The area should also be kept free of poisonous and stinging insects.

It is extremely important that we be aware of the need to maintain safe playgrounds and safe play equipment. According to a 1981–82 insurance study undertaken by Forrest T. Jones and Company, nearly two-thirds of all injuries in which locations are specified occur on the playground. The most severe injuries are caused by climbers. Other contributors to injuries are slides, swings, pebbles, and rocks. Indoor hazards include floor surfaces, hard toys, blocks, and pencils, while motor vehicles are another outdoor peril.

Some useful preventive strategies are recommended by the U.S. Consumer Product Safety Commission. Maximum climber height can be limited, thus lessening the distance from the top to the ground. Climbers can be mounted over eight-inch-deep filler materials such as pine bark, pea gravel, or shredded tires. These materials should be constantly checked and maintained, because their cushioning effect may wear off in time. Moreover, the number of children who use such equipment at one time should be limited.

Play equipment should, of course, be appropriate to the developmental level and size of the children using it. Hence, older children will need to be separated from infants and toddlers when using gross motor play apparatus such as slides, steps, and ladders, the height of which depends on the age and size of the children (Aronson, 1983).

All playground equipment should be in good repair. Dangerous parts should be eliminated or covered. Some parts that could be dangerous are screws, bolts, anything with sharp edges, rings through which a child's head might pass, open hooks, ropes, and some hand-gripping equipment. We should also watch out for splinters, rust, and loose nuts and bolts.

Playgrounds can be designed to prevent accidents. For example, all play equipment should be spaced to prevent collisions, and should be at a safe distance from paths, walls, and areas of frequent traffic. Children should not have access to vehicle traffic areas: some sort of barrier should be set up, since young children are apt to wander around or run into traffic while chasing after a ball.

It may be impossible to make playgrounds entirely safe for children. However, if we train ourselves to be vigilant and efficient supervisors, if we limit or eliminate hazards, and if we provide safety education for children, we can go a long way toward preventing accidents and injuries.

Our vigilance should extend to the condition a child is in at a particular time. Accidents occur, it seems, more often when children are tired, hungry, or in a new environment and surrounded by strangers. We need to be extra alert and cautious at such times and can act to alleviate the situation by getting the child to rest, eat, or relax and become more comfortable and confident.

One way to reduce accidents is to teach children how to play safely. We can explain ways in which they can take better care of themselves and look out for others. We can teach them to follow safety rules and to understand what type of play is hazardous. We can develop appropriate play behavior in children through modeling and role playing, and can discuss the consequences of unsafe play and behavior. We can teach them the Dos (and thereby the Don'ts) that go with the use and handling of play equipment.

Learning Activity: To develop the concept of accident prevention, divide participants into small groups and ask each group to devise a plan for preventing accidents in a child care facility. Share small-group responses with the larger group.

Disasters and Emergency Preparedness

While it is in our power to prevent many kinds of accidents, the occurrence of certain emergencies and disasters is beyond our control. Therefore, we should be prepared to deal with emergencies caused by natural disasters or fire. In fact, we should develop a feasible plan and frequently rehearse it before any disaster strikes. The telephone numbers of the fire department, police, ambulance, and hospital should be posted at convenient locations. A diagram indicating the location of the main shutoff for electric, gas, and water valves should be posted conveniently. Exits should be indicated and known, as well as alternative routes. Procedures to be followed in the case of particular emergencies such as fire, an earthquake, or a tornado should be carefully planned and often rehearsed.

Dealing with disasters, emergencies, and day-to-day accidents and injuries implies a practical knowledge of first aid on the part of staff in a child care facility. First aid should, in fact, be an ongoing training concern at all facilities. General guidelines should be established regarding who is in charge in the event of an emergency; how prepared everyone ought to be; emergency phone numbers; transportation to obtain medical aid; knowledge of each child's background and medical history; reports to be made; supplies to be kept, and so on.

When emergencies do occur, certain general rules should be kept in mind (Reinisch & Minear, 1978). We need to stay calm, and project confidence and reassurance to the sick or hurt child. We can make an attempt to understand the nature of the problem or the extent of the injury. We should, of course, make immediate efforts and arrangements to help the child. We should handle the child as little as possible and in most cases avoid diagnosing or giving medication, even though we should give first aid when it is required. We should attend to the most important things first and leave reports and records until later, although a record should be kept. Naturally, we should call the parents of the child as soon as possible.

Some emergencies are more serious than others and require more urgent action. Stoppage of breathing, severe bleeding, and poisoning are some examples of serious occurrences that need immediate action on our part. First aid training should include these and other eventualities.

While we should be competent to deal with serious injuries and emergencies, we should also be able to handle problems such as sunburn, heat stroke, and dehydration, all of which could become more serious if proper care is not given. Most of us probably know what to do in cases of lesser injuries such as cuts, scrapes, scratches and other small wounds, and insect bites.

Individual Needs of Children

Sometimes individual children have problems requiring special attention. In such situations, the cooperation of parents, teachers, and professionals is an asset. Parents should be aware of, and open about, their child's condition and provide what background information they can. The teacher can share relevant information about the child's day-to-day behavior with parents and professionals. The professional can provide useful information about the child's condition and discuss possible treatment or guidelines that could help parents and teachers care for the child. Thus, all concerned will be aware of the state of the child's general health, family history, growth, development, social and developmental skills, nutrition, and special needs.

Specific care needs to be given to children who become sick while in our care. Therefore, we need to know not only first aid techniques but also how to deal with conditions involving abdominal pain, diarrhea, earache, fever, toothache, and vomiting. If a child becomes sick while at the facility, or is not sick enough to stay at home, we should follow specific plans and procedures that have previously been formulated and made known to parents. These plans should include information about sick child care and available alternatives. For example, the giving of medication should follow a consistent policy, and the staff may need some training in how to provide medicine and how to handle children who require it (Aronson & Smith, 1985).

Feeding infants and young children may be considered among individual health needs. We should be aware of what is nutritionally essential for all children, but each child's individual requirements, allergies, or other problems should be known and understood. For example, Jenny may be allergic to milk and has to take a substitute. Mark may be unable to digest cereal of any kind. We must serve them according to their needs.

Cleanliness and hygiene should, of course, be strictly observed in the feeding area, and in connection with food preparation and feeding procedures. If snacks are provided, they should be nutritious, and as in the case of regular meals, each child's individual needs should be kept in mind. While this may seem a difficult, inconvenient, and cumbersome policy to follow, it is in the best interests of the children in our care.

Summary

In this chapter we have examined the importance of protecting the health and safety of children. We have seen how we can safeguard children and adults in child care by formulating and establishing good health programs and policies. We have discussed strategies for reducing the risk and spread of infectious diseases. We have also reviewed precautions that can be taken to reduce or eliminate accidents and injuries and have stressed the need for general preparedness and a knowledge of first aid.

It is, in short, important for us to remember that if we protect the physical health and well-being of children, we will also be contributing to their developmental, intellectual, and emotional well-being.

Enrichment Activities

1. Make a list of all the conditions and practices in your child care facility that

contribute to the prevention and control of disease, and of all those that hinder it. Identify changes you can make to correct any conditions and practices that hinder and prevent disease control.
2. Make a list of all the conditions and practices in your child care facility that are potential safety hazards. Specify how these problems can be corrected.
3. Organize a team of parents, teachers, and health professionals to examine and revise, as needed, your facility's policies and practices regarding health and safety.
4. Develop a checklist that can be used to do daily health checks for children in your facility. Devise a plan for conducting these daily health checks.
5. Develop a checklist that can be used to monitor the health and safety issues in your child care facility.

Bibliography

Aronson, S. S. (1983, March/April). Infection and day care. *Child Care Information Exchange,* pp. 10–14.

Teachers and parents will find this an extremely helpful article. The author discusses ways of preventing and reducing common respiratory and gastrointestinal illnesses among young children in group care. Many diseases can be avoided by altering certain factors conducive to the spread of infection. Immunization is also advocated.

Aronson, S. S. (1983, May/June). Playground safety: An ongoing challenge. *Child Care Information Exchange,* pp. 32–35.

A variety of strategies for making playgrounds safe for children are reviewed. Play areas should be designed, and play equipment chosen, with safety in mind. Teaching children to play safely is also stressed.

Aronson, S. S. (1983, July/August). Teaching children to be safe. *Child Care Information Exchange,* pp. 26–29.

Among the chief strategies for preventing accidents and injuries is teaching safe behavior and habits to children. Safety education should focus on how to be safe on the playground and indoors and on simple first aid techniques that children as well as adults need to know.

Aronson, S. S. (1983, September/October). Health policies and procedures. *Child Care Information Exchange,* pp. 14–16.

Administrators and child care staff will find this a useful article that brings together the various areas that should be kept in mind when formulating health policies and procedures.

Aronson, S. S. (1984, January). What routine health care should every child receive? *Child Care Information Exchange,* pp. 12–14.

A useful article that outlines the important issue of routine care necessary for all children. General considerations include the health history of children and their parents, physical measurements, sensory screening, developmental assessment, physical examinations, immunization and testing procedures, anticipatory guidance, and dental care. A guidelines chart for health supervision is also provided.

Aronson, S. S. (1984, March). Why is adult health an issue in day care? *Child Care Information Exchange,* pp. 26–28.

The peculiar nature of the child care setting implies the maintenance of adult health. The author suggests regular health examinations for personnel during employment. The issue of payment for such assessments is also discussed.

Aronson, S. S. (1984, August). Summer safety and first aid. *Child Care Information Exchange,* pp. 13–15.

Summer is a time of increased injury risk for children. Parents and teachers are provided with practical and useful tips on how to prevent and reduce accidents and how to deal with them when they occur. Drowning, sunburn, heat exhaustion, insect bites, cuts, scrapes and bruises, are summer risks with which the article deals.

Aronson, S. S. (1984, November). How sick is sick? Managing minor illnesses. *Child Care Information Exchange,* pp. 22–24.

The author discusses policies concerning sickness and its management. Factors examined are infection communicability, staffing needs, medication, illness symptoms, managing minor illnesses, and seeking health professional advice. Some useful activities for sick children are also provided.

Aronson, S. S. (1985, March). Infant feeding in child care. *Child Care Information Exchange,* pp. 22–25.

The author presents certain general but important principles to be kept in mind when feeding infants in child care. Feeding programs, funding, and nutrition concerns are discussed.

Aronson, S. S. (1985, May). What to do about rashes. *Child Care Information Exchange,* pp. 26–28.

The author provides practical information and insights into the problem of rashes, which can be symptoms of several diseases or the result of allergies. Teachers need to know and recognize different types of rashes. They also need to know whether certain rashes are infectious, dangerous, or due to allergy or poor hygiene. Some good skin health practices are listed. The chart describing diseases and accompanying rashes is helpful.

Aronson, S. S., & Osterhold, M. T. (1984, December). Prevention and management of infectious diseases in child care. *Child Care Information Exchange,* pp. 8–10.

Practical information is given on policies that can be formulated to reduce the risk of disease in child care. The interaction of child care workers and professionals and the importance of training and education are also discussed. Controversies such as who is responsible for sick children and whether they should be excluded from school are reviewed, and directions research can take are outlined.

Aronson, S. S., & Smith, H. (1985, January). Medication administration in child care. *Child Care Information Exchange,* pp. 27–29.

The authors examine the problem of policies and facilities for administrating medication to young children in child care. Factors that centers should consider include staff training to handle the task, preparing the situation and children, procedures related to giving medication, and safety measures. Both administrators and teachers will find the information provided thought-provoking and useful.

Denk-Glass, R., Laber, S. S., & Brewer, K. (1982). Middle ear disease in young children. *Young Children, 37* (6), 51–53.

Middle ear disease, when it strikes young children, can have adverse effects on their cognitive and language development. Parents and adults who work with children should therefore be alert to the appearance of this disorder. The authors describe methods that are being used to assess hearing loss in children, and urge parents, teachers, and professionals to work together to ensure adequate screening, detection, and treatment of the disease.

Highberger, R., & Boynton, M. (1983). Preventing illnesses in infant/toddler day care. *Young Children, 38* (3), 3–8.

Practical recommendations are offered on basic techniques effective in reducing disease in child care settings. The authors discuss essentials for disease control, such as a clean environment, good personal hygiene for both adults and children, sanitary conditions related to food and feeding, and a responsible attitude toward sanitation and health.

Iverson, D. C. (Ed.). (1981). *Promoting health through the schools.* New York: Human Sciences Press.

A collection of articles dealing with various aspects of health education. Policies, funding sources, organization, and planning programs are some topics discussed.

Kendall, E. D. (1983). Child care and disease. *Young Children, 38* (5), 68–77.

The author addresses the serious issue of the linkage between child care and the spread of infectious diseases. Recent research is cited and reviewed, and recommendations for prevention are made.

Packer, B. (1983, April). Communicable diseases in day care. *Mothers Today Preschooler,* pp. 17–18.

The author identifies common causes of infectious diseases in child care and outlines practical strategies for prevention.

Peterson, R. M., & Cleveland, J. O. (Eds.). (1976). *Medical problems in the classroom: An educator's guide.* Springfield, IL: Charles C. Thomas.

The book deals with various medical problems faced by teachers of exceptional children. How to manage the medical and educational needs of handicapped children and what effects disabilities have on the behavior of children are among the topics discussed.

Reinisch, E. H., & Minear, R. E. (1978). *Health of the preschool child.* New York: John Wiley and Sons.

The book provides a comprehensive look at factors related to various aspects of the health of young children. The authors stress the need for policies, procedures, and strategies to prevent and reduce the risk of disease and accidents. Staff at centers should be prepared for emergencies and disasters, and should have a sound knowledge of first aid. The need for professionals and parents to work together for the health, safety, and well-being of the child is constantly stressed.

Scott, D. K. (1985). Child safety seats—they work! *Young Children, 40* (4), 13–17.

This in-depth analysis of the importance of transportation safety focuses on the need for centers and educators to feel responsible for this aspect of children's well-being. Parent and community involvement and safety education for children are advocated. An annotated bibliography on preschool child transportation safety adds to the value of the article.

Scott, L. C. (1983). Injury in the classroom: Are teachers liable? *Young Children, 38* (6), 10–17.

The author provides an insightful and informative look at the responsibility of teachers in cases of injury in the classroom. Immunity, liability insurance, intentional injuries and those caused by negligence, and implications for early childhood education are topics discussed.

Wishon, P. M., Bower, R., & Eller, B. (1983). Childhood obesity: Prevention and treatment.

Young Children, 39 (1), 21–27.
The health of overweight children is endangered both physically and psychologically. This informative article examines the causes of obesity and states what can be done to avert or treat it. Infant care, eating habits, nutrition, exercise, and family life-styles are discussed.

12
Integrating Physical Care and Developmental Care

THE need to provide quality care for children in all settings has been recognized and emphasized in recent years. Quality care includes many different factors that make a child care setting advantageous to a child's growth and development. In this chapter we will focus on two particular concepts—physical care and developmental care—that provide the basis for understanding the integrated nature of quality care.

Objectives

In this chapter we will define and differentiate between physical care and developmental care. We will specify ways in which we can transform physical care into developmental care and evaluate the effectiveness of certain developmental efforts. We will also examine Maslow's Needs Hierarchy and demonstrate how Maslow's theory can be applied to child care tasks. Finally, we will identify some common barriers to developmental care.

Key Ideas

Although physical care and developmental care are distinct entities, they are both essential to a child's well-being and development. When caring for children, we can transform physical care into developmental care and thus optimize the development of children in our facility. To do this, we must be aware of the basic needs of children and of various barriers that can prevent us from giving appropriate developmental care. Some of these barriers are our own and other people's attitudes toward child care, the demanding nature of our work, lack of time to fulfill all of our goals, and a lack of understanding of child development. If we can overcome these obstacles, we will be able to provide quality care to children and facilitate their development.

Physical Care and Developmental Care

Physical care (sometimes labeled custodial care) is defined as tasks that an adult performs to meet the basic physical needs of a child. Such acts as feeding, dressing or undressing, bathing, serving meals or snacks, tending to spills, physical shepherding, and giving first aid are examples of physical care. This type of care is absolutely essential to meet the basic needs of children.

Developmental care begins with sound physical care plus efforts on the part of the adult to stimulate the child's physical/motor, cognitive, language, and social/emotional development. Developmental care is physical care enriched with verbal and nonverbal communication that educate a child about a topic, object, care act, or other people. Developmental care is sometimes spontaneous and does not always require deliberate preplanning of an educational experience. More often than not, however, developmental care is purposeful and, when practiced deliberately, becomes a natural part of the caregiving functions. The goal is to enrich the child's development. While developmental care requires cuddling, holding, touching, it also includes the provision of digestible learning experiences (Honig, 1981).

Like physical care, developmental care is essential to the child's optimal developmental growth. Without loving, developmental care children do not prosper as they do when such care occurs (Gregg & Knotts, 1980). Thus, physical care and developmental care address the basic needs of children. Both are absolutely essential to the well-being of the child. Quality child care programs should address both aspects of caregiving with equal seriousness and dedication (Caldwell, 1984; Cataldo, 1984).

It is not only necessary to differentiate between developmental and physical care but to understand how they are related to each other. We can perhaps best understand this relationship by visualizing care activities on a continuum (fig. 10).

Using the continuum, we can start with acceptable/appropriate physical care at one end, and acceptable/appropriate developmental care at the other. As we move to the right side of the continuum and provide developmental care, we increase the possibility that children will get the best care possible. It is important not to assign a negative value to the left side of this continuum, since acceptable and appropriate physical care is critical and essential to the health, safety, and happiness of children.

It is possible to extend this continuum to the left of that point, and add substandard physical care, which is, indeed, negative. Such care is characterized by less quality and is, perhaps, even below approved health standards with little or no nurturance on the part of the adult. A few examples of substandard physical care include washing the faces of fifteen children with the same washcloth; cleaning up a child's juice spill while complaining about all the trouble the child has caused; and talking to another adult about soap operas while attending to the child's needs.

For purposes of our discussion, we could also extend this continuum to the far right, beyond acceptable/appropriate developmental care to excessive developmental care. It is possible to bombard children with too much developmental—especially cognitive—stimulation, to the extent that little is simple, or quiet, or left to the imagination. Sometimes self-discovery or self-directed learning is not possible because all interactions between adult and children are delib-

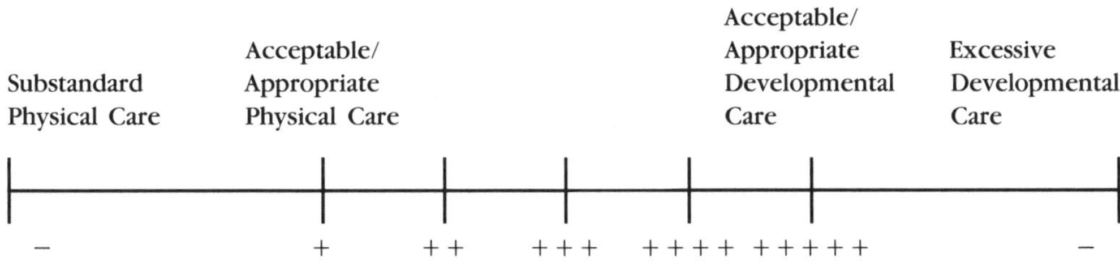

Figure 10. *Care activities continuum, from substandard physical care to excessive developmental care*

erate and stimulating educational efforts. For example, there is no time to enjoy eating a meal because the adult constantly talks about nutrition.

We are interested in interactions which fall between acceptable/appropriate physical care and acceptable/appropriate developmental care. Interactions that fall at either end of this continuum are positive, with interactions at the acceptable/appropriate developmental care end being the most positive.

By defining interactions in this manner, we are assuming that there is quality control over the physical care given to children. Parents assume basic quality care will occur when they leave their children in a care facility. Licensing agents monitor and require basic quality physical care of children. Therefore, our task is to start at acceptable/appropriate physical care and work toward making it acceptable/appropriate developmental care.

Learning Activity: In the larger group ask participants to take one caregiving task and move it through a progression on the continuum from acceptable/appropriate physical care to acceptable/appropriate developmental care. Participants should describe each progression in some detail, so that they clearly demonstrate how a physical care task becomes a developmental care task.

Transforming Physical Care into Developmental Care

How, then, do we get from one point (physical care) to the other (developmental care)? The answer lies in turning physical care tasks into developmental experiences for the child. That is, while children's physical needs are being served, their interests and development can be fostered and supported (Cataldo, 1984).

As the definition of developmental care indicates, any physical care task that assists a child in growing physically, mentally, socially, or linguistically becomes developmental in nature. The physical tasks of eating, washing, and toileting can all be exploited (Stewart, 1982). For example, when we select food that reflects a well-balanced diet and encourage children to make sound food choices, we engage in developmental care. In this manner, we are teaching children food choice habits that sustain them physically. When we model appropriate manners at mealtime, we assist children in the socialization process. When we discuss the foods we eat, we teach children about the correct names of foods. As a result, we have turned a physical task into a developmental experience.

Question Starter: Can you provide other examples of ways in which routine physical care tasks can be turned into developmental care tasks? (Responses may include: singing to a baby while diapering; discussing the color of clothes as a child helps fold the laundry.)

To apply the process to any (or all) physical care tasks, we can ask ourselves the following questions: As I perform this physical care task, what do I (could I) do to: (*a*) help the child advance in social development? (*b*) increase or perfect the child's use of new words or concepts? (*c*) add to the child's knowledge base? (*d*) encourage physical/motor development?

Learning Activity: Divide participants into small groups. Each group should explain how three physical care tasks can be turned into developmental care tasks. Participants should include enough description to explain what they would do and why they would do it. The why rationale can be formulated in terms of developmental goals for children.

Most physical care tasks can become developmental when deliberate attention is given to ways in which these tasks can be developmentally oriented. When a conscious effort is made to provide experiences that help children develop in the four developmental areas, the caregiving experience becomes more rewarding for children and for the adult (Honig, 1981). Even though deliberate efforts to transform physical care into developmental care may seem awkward at first, practice will make the procedure almost automatic.

When we transform physical care into developmental care, we can systematically evaluate our efforts by responding to the following questions: (*a*) Did we help the child's social development? (*b*) Did we increase or perfect the child's use of new words or concepts? (*c*) Did we add to the child's knowledge base? We can use the questions to gauge how successful we are at integrating physical and developmental care.

Applying Theory to Practice

Maslow's theory (1970) of human needs can be used in the caregiving situation to exercise judgment about the type and extent of developmental care provided. This theory can help us decide which area of development (social/emotional, language, physical/motor, or cognitive/learning) to emphasize and how much developmental enrichment to integrate into the physical care task. We can translate the four areas of development into Maslow's Needs Hierarchy (fig. 11), and can see a logical order in addressing the specified needs, thus making decisions about what kind of enrichment to attempt through physical care.

Very simply, the diagram illustrates that our physical needs are the most basic. If a child is hungry, tired, sick, or uncomfortable, we will not be able to teach him to share until these needs are satisfied. It is critical to feed, shelter, clothe, and provide rest opportunities for children first. Physiological needs are at the bottom in

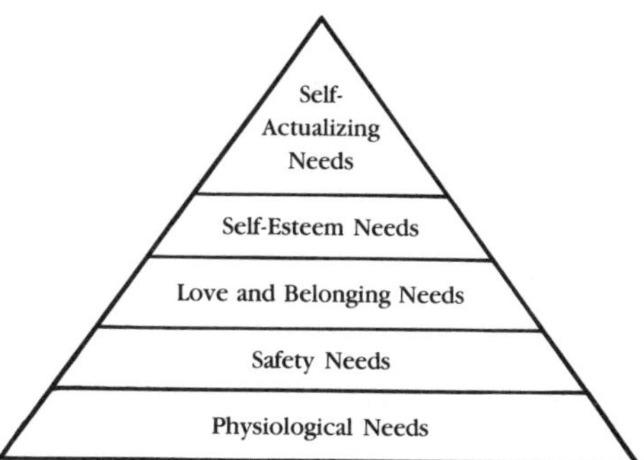

Figure 11. *Maslow's Needs Hierarchy. From* Motivation and Personality, *2d ed., by Abraham H. Maslow © 1970 by Abraham H. Maslow. Reprinted by permission of Harper & Row Publishers, Inc.*

the broadest section of the triangle, because the largest portion of our time is spent in satisfying physiological needs.

The quality of our attention to the physical task is important. For example, candy may stop hunger, but will the physical needs of the child be met if candy is the only food provided? Of course not. We must provide nutrients that will maximize the growth and development of the body and tissues. That means we must give the child protein products, dairy products, fruits, vegetables, and whole grains. Thus, physiological needs that are attended to in ways that promote optimum human growth are the most important of all needs. If this need level is ignored, we will be unable to attend to other needs in the hierarchy.

Safety needs must also be addressed. A child who is fed and rested must also be protected from abuse or a dangerous environment. If a child stays in an environment where she is not safe, she will soon get the message that no one really cares.

Whenever physiological and safety needs are being met, nurturing gestures, calm caring voice tones, consistent human guidance, and frequent adult-child interactions can also be used to demonstrate to the child that she is loved and belongs. Security in the knowledge of being loved and cherished makes it possible to be social and to develop intellectually.

In succession, this theory tells us that a human being who has sufficient self-regard can cope with life's varied situations. The individual with self-esteem feels knowledgeable and capable of taking on family responsibilities and caring for self and others. Self-confident children can cope with stress so that it is not overwhelming.

All developmental areas of the child (the physical/motor, cognitive, language, and social/emotional) can be attended to in a prescribed manner beginning with the physiological level. It is impossible to accomplish four without three, or three without two, or two without one.

Learning Activity: Using small groups, ask participants to select a physical care task and demonstrate at each level on Maslow's model how they would make each task developmental in nature.

In essence, we can assess what the child's status is with respect to these needs, and address unmet needs first. In implementing Maslow's theory, developmental care efforts are not artificial, nor wasted in a situation where a child cannot benefit. Once the teacher begins thinking about interactions with children in this manner, there is very little need to formalize the evaluation process. The overarching goal of child care is to facilitate the optimum development of children, and when the momentum of interactions is moving in that direction it is fair to conclude that time is not being wasted, and opportunities to work toward the ultimate goal are being used.

Barriers to Developmental Care

Although we may all agree that developmental care is necessary and best for children, there are several conditions that can prevent such care from occurring. One significant cause is the general unspoken attitude in the child care field that children are to be watched. Child care first came into existence when parents needed someone other than themselves to watch a child when they had to be absent. Parents were satisfied as long as the child's basic needs were met while they were away. Child care was and still is viewed by many as merely babysitting (Hostetler, 1984).

Only recently has the extensive use of the term child care become routine. Frequently, we now see a child spending more waking hours with a careprovider than with parents. The attitude and behavior of this adult is thus very important (Jacobson, 1978). The increased use of child care time makes us responsible for using this time to the child's best advantage. However, the shift in responsibility can be overlooked and sometimes feared. Unless we, along with parents, assume primary responsibility, we may neglect the developmental work we can do with children.

Another reason why developmental care is sometimes overlooked is because providing care for children is a personally demanding and stressful job. The human tendency is to perform one's job in a manner that addresses one's own needs. Thus, we sometimes find that psychologically removing ourselves from concentrating on a child's developmental needs diminishes the pressures we may feel. It is easy to justify this removal when there is so little monetary reward for our services.

Furthermore, group care can make it difficult to attend to each child's individual needs. A large proportion of our time is spent in physical care of children. Because of limited amounts of time, each interaction must be as efficient and meaningful as possible. The quality of interactions thus becomes more significant than the quantity.

Finally, lack of understanding of the critical nature of child development during the early years of life can cause us to ignore the role of the responsible adult. The skills, attitudes, and knowledge base needed for quality developmental care are not quickly or easily acquired. Extensive study and training in child development provide the means by which we can analyze a child's developmental status and react to it appropriately. Awareness of the magnitude of the situation, and an opportunity to develop the knowledge base needed to serve as an effective child development specialist can help remove this barrier to developmental care (Silin, 1985).

Summary

A large proportion of our time is spent in providing physical care to children. Quality physical care is basic and is, perhaps, the essential mandate of our jobs. Quality physical care alone, however, is shortsighted and deficient, because many opportunites to help children develop optimally are missed.

Isolating the concepts of physical care and developmental care helps us to adjust our perspective of the child care role. Once we realize the power of developmental care, we can take deliberate action to transform child care into a developmental mode.

Analyzing the developmental needs of a child and addressing them through the opportunities provided in daily living routines is the principal difference between physical care and developmental care. Transforming physical care into developmental care makes the job of caring for children most rewarding. Once developmental care becomes a standard operating procedure in day care, the benefits are obvious. Developmental care is one of the avenues to a rewarding career in child care.

Enrichment Activities

1. Identify five routine physical care tasks you perform frequently. Specify how you can transform the physical care act into a developmental care act, and how it can benefit the child.
2. Record all the physical care acts you do for a week. Specify how you transformed each physical care task into a developmental care task. Indicate which developmental area was positively affected and how. If you did not turn the physical task into a developmental task, indicate why you did not.
3. List specific steps your child care facility can take to transform routine physical care tasks into developmental care tasks. If changing routine procedures is involved, specify what these changes are.
4. Use Maslow's Needs Hierarchy model to demonstrate how a physical care task can become a developmental one.

Bibliography

Alston, F. K. (1984). *Caring for other people's children: A complete guide to family day care.* Baltimore: University Park Press.

A well-written and well-organized reference guide that deals with developmental needs and levels, activities and ideas to stimulate development, first aid, nutrition, and the relationship between families and teachers. It is interesting to note that the author sees child care workers as individuals possessing various and interrelated skills connected with a variety of other professions.

Ames, L. B., & Chase, J. A. (1980). *Don't push your preschooler.* New York: Harper and Row.

A controversial work in many respects, this book nevertheless presents an important idea. The authors believe that children should be allowed to develop at their own rate—both physically and cognitively, and that teaching should be a relaxed, enjoyable process for parents (and teachers). While the preschooler's growing intelligence and curiosity should be encouraged and stimulated, the child should not be pushed to learn.

Bailey, R. A., & Burton, E. C. (1982). *The dynamic self: Activities to enhance infant development.* St. Louis: C. V. Mosby.

The motor development of young children can be encouraged and reinforced through planned movement and other activities. At the same time a supportive environment and loving, positive contact can enhance learning experiences and development.

Curits, S. R. (1982). *The joy of movement in early childhood.* New York: Teachers College Press.

The author believes that movement is as important in a child's life as adequate care, love, rest, and good nutrition. The movement education advocated here includes physical, environmental, and instructional aspects; involves creativity and problem solving; and is aimed at stimulating the growth of the whole child. It is suggested that teachers observe the movement and play of young children to understand, facilitate, and guide their development successfully.

Flinchum, B. M. (1975). *Motor development in early childhood: A guide for movement education with ages two to six.* St. Louis: C. V. Mosby.

The author presents a useful taxonomy as guide to the motor skill and learning development of young children. A variety of activities and experiences that the teacher can provide are also listed.

Gonzalez-Mena, J., & Eyer, D. W. (1981). *Infancy and caregiving.* Palo Alto, CA: Mayfield.

A readable and informative book for teachers and parents of very young children. The authors describe the physical, intellectual, emotional, and social development of infants, and discuss ways in which adults can stimulate and encourage development in these areas.

Gulley, S. B. (1982). The relationship of infant stimulation to cognitive development. *Childhood Education, 58,* 247–52.

This comprehensive article reviews and discusses major research on the effects of quality child care—which should be developmental in nature—on the cognitive growth of infants. Among the topics covered are caregiver responsiveness, adult-child interactions, and environmental influences on children and on learning. Implications for infant education programs are also analyzed.

Honig, A. S. (1981). What are the needs of infants? *Young Children, 37* (1), 3–10.

Focusing on adult responses to the needs of infants, Honig states that caregiving is more than the following of an organized daily routine. It entails "cuddling, holding, touching," the realization that individual differences exist, an understanding of the importance of attachment, the provision of space for freedom of movement and development, and the planning of learning experiences that are "digestible." In such situations caregiving becomes more meaningful and valuable for both the child and the caregiver.

Honig, A. S., & Lally, J. R. (1981). *Infant caregiving: A design for training.* Syracuse, NY: Syracuse University Press.

A valuable book offering helpful and practical information on infant caregiving. Various aspects of children's development are explained, and numerous ideas and activities for stimulation and growth are provided. Training ideas and realistic caregiver experiences are also described. Excellent appendixes and an annotated bibliography add to the book's usefulness.

Humphrey, J. H. (1980). *Child development through physical education.* Springfield, IL: Charles C. Thomas.

The author analyzes ways in which physical education influences not only the physiological but the emotional, intellectual, and social development of children.

Jacobson, A. L. (1978). Infant day care: Toward a more human environment. *Young Children, 33* (5), 14–21.

A penetrating and thought-provoking study on the necessity of maintaining the human element in day care centers. Major research is cited on attachment and on adult influence on infant competence, vocalization, perceptual-cognitive development, play behavior, social development, and happiness. A chart is included, depicting desirable caregiver characteristics specifically related to personality, attitudes, values, and behavior.

Julius, A. K. (1978). Focus of movement: Practice and theory. *Young Children, 34* (1), 19–26.

The article relates theories of child development to various movement activities that can be carried out with ease in the classroom. Movement comes naturally to children and is part of development, both physical and intellectual. Movement facilitates expression of moods, feelings, emotion, and self-awareness; it promotes self-confidence; and it can be integrated with a variety of learning and skill development activities. Laban's movement system is described, and suggestions for teachers are offered.

Maslow, A. H. (1970). *Motivation and personality* (2nd. ed.). New York: Harper & Row.

The author views science and human nature in a humanistic and holistic way. Thus, the total environment of individuals, as well as the context of their life situations, must be examined in relation to what they are. To understand human beings, their highest aspirations as well as their most basic physiological needs must be taken into consideration, because a deprivation of certain needs can lead to neurosis and lack of fulfillment. Judging the motivations of people depends on an understanding of the gratification of their needs and metaneeds. However, need gratification does not automatically lead to human satisfaction. Striving to achieve can be satisfying as well. Maslow's disussion of self-actualizing or fully human persons and of the society in which it is possible for them to develop and function will be of special interest to educators.

Raines, S. C. (1984). Who are we in the lives of our children? *Young Children, 39* (3), 9–12.

This thoughtful and thought-provoking article focuses on the perceptions teachers have of their role in child development, and on the fundamental principles of development they must convey on behalf of children. Specifically, the caregiver has several roles in addition to that of provider of basic care: the caregiver is role model, leader, advocate, documenter, messenger, researcher, interpreter, and family friend.

Robinson, H. F. (1977). *Exploring teaching in early childhood education.* Boston: Allyn and Bacon.

The author examines the history and philosophical foundations of early childhood education and discusses various areas of motor and other skills. Art, music, and play are emphasized as significant factors aiding development and should be included in child care programs. Resources, activities, materials, and effective teaching strategies are also presented.

Weiser, M. G. (1982). *Group care and education of infants and toddlers.* St. Louis: C. V. Mosby.

A practical book that offers realistic guidelines for quality day care. The importance of interactions between adults and children is stressed. Suggestions are made for enhancing development, and practical applications of theory are presented. References and resource information add to the value of the book.

Zaichkowsky, L. D., Zaichkowsky, L. B., & Martinek, T. J. (1980). *Growth and development: The child and physical activity.* St. Louis: C. V. Mosby.

The authors emphasize the necessity of integrating physical activity and child development strategies to achieve maximum motor, cognitive, and affective development.

13

Interacting with Parents

THE overall goal of our work with children is to take care of them in the most effective way we can. Since children are an extension of their homes, effective work with them means that we must build strong relationships with their parents. We can best accomplish this goal when we deliberately plan for, and execute, a well-conceived parent involvement and parent education program.

Parenting is one of the most important roles any adult can assume, as well as one of the most awesome responsibilities. This fact is especially true when the goals of parenting include helping children to develop in optimal ways. Parenting does not occur naturally but must be learned, and as child care professionals we are probably in the best position to help parents in this lifelong role.

Since our overall goal is to meet the needs of children, we must form a partnership with parents by incorporating a parent involvement and parent education program in the child care facility. The child care setting is the one place where parents have regular contact with professionals, and a number of strategies can be designed to take advantage of this built-in contact.

In light of the many responsibilities parents have, a parenting program can be a substantial benefit offered by child care staff. In fact, it is quickly becoming our responsibility as we attempt to provide better care for children. We can offer a tremendous support system for parents in their primary role of parenting.

Objectives

The primary purpose of this chapter is to examine ways in which we can play a role in strengthening the bond between child, parent, and child care staff. We will assess the need for parenting education programs provided by child care facilities. We will identify some of the problems associated with providing this service. We will specify the primary goals of a parenting program and examine various approaches that can be used to provide parent education.

Key Ideas

One of the best ways to meet children's needs is to assist parents in their caregiving roles. This can be accomplished through parenting programs that include parent education and parent involvement. Since parenting skills must be learned, all parents can benefit from having more information about children. Child care programs offer excellent opportunities to provide parent education.

The goal of any parenting program is to increase parents' awareness of the crucial role they play in their child's development. Since limited funding and parent/staff time, capabilities, and motivation pose barriers to a parenting program, it is necessary to first develop a sense of trust and positive relationships with parents. A conscious and deliberate effort to implement a parenting program must be made. When implemented, an effective parenting program should improve staff-parent, parent-child, and staff-child relationships.

Rationale for Parenting Programs

Any discussion of incorporating a parenting program in child care facilities undoubtedly makes us wonder how anyone has the time to add a parenting component to an already full and busy schedule of caring for children. Since we will probably not get more time, the answer, of course, lies in the manner in which we conceptualize ways to assist parents in their children's growth and development.

The basic assumption underlying the need for parenting programs is an understanding of the crucial role that parents play in their children's development. A good home environment is important and basic for human development, especially in the early years when so much learning occurs during the first three to five years of life. These early years are also the critical times for establishing enduring, healthy parent-child relationships.

The intense involvement and mutual attachment of parents and children during the early years make this period a particularly teachable time for parents. New parents especially are eager for information and are in great need of support. Early contact with sources of information and support can help them to establish a pattern for continued use of parenting resources.

In addition, the child is more adaptable to change and more influenced by parents in the early years than at any other time. Therefore, the years in which the child is likely to be in child care are the years when parents have optimal opportunities to positively affect their child's development.

It is apparent that parents need help in creating the most effective learning environment for their children. It is also obvious that parenting skills are not acquired automatically but must be learned. Still, we might wonder why we should be the ones to help parents in their parenting roles? There are several responses to this basic question. First, we probably have more contact and more accessibility to parents than any other professional. In addition, we are trained in child development and child care and in general know what is best for children. Furthermore, we have a basic concern for the welfare of children that can easily extend beyond the child care facility. Finally, when the child is best served by all those individuals who care for her, the job of caregiving is made easier.

In summary, parenting is an art, not a gift. All parents can benefit from additional information about children, and as teachers of young children we appear to be in the best position to offer this service. In fact, helping parents is one of our primary responsibilities.

Obstacles to Parenting Programs

Even when we recognize that parent education and involvement are critical, we could encounter obstacles when we try to provide parenting programs. The degree of resistance is dependent upon a number of different factors.

Question Starter: What problems have you encountered or can imagine encountering in your attempts to implement parenting programs? (Responses may include: limited time and resources; parent disinterest; lack of staff-parent communication.)

Most child care facilities operate on a very limited budget, frequently without a single dollar to spare. Yet we know that many free materials and services exist. Professionals in the field are often willing to donate time or materials if they think it will benefit the community. Local libraries, schools, and local merchants are good resources for obtaining materials or additional funds for parenting programs.

Limited staff time is another major problem. Few child care facilities have enough staff to release even one individual to work exclusively on a parenting program. Instead, child care facilities must use staff time efficiently, which can mean using time during child rest periods to develop and discuss approaches to developing such programs. In general, once the notion of a parenting program is accepted as important, time for it must be built into the schedule when those rare free moments occur.

In addition to limited staff time, parents are busy and spend little time in contact with child care staff. We must therefore make the best use of time when parents come to the facility to deliver and pick up their children. There are many ways in which we can utilize this time to disseminate important information to parents.

Perhaps the most difficult problem to overcome is lack of parental motivation and interest in being involved in a parenting program. Such a program must be designed as carefully as the children's educational program, therefore we must involve parents as much as possible in the kinds of activities in which they will engage. We should begin by finding out what their needs and interests are. We can help them set their own goals and objectives based on their needs and on sound developmental care. We can build on their interests, provide relevant learning experiences, and reinforce appropriate behavior by providing feedback.

Goals of Parenting Programs

The primary goal of any parenting program is to increase parents' awareness of the crucial role they play in their child's development. This includes helping them to realize and accept their responsibility as the primary teachers of their child.

To be successful as teachers, parents must first develop a close, trusting, and respectful relationship with the child. To be successful initiators of that relationship, we must develop a trusting and respectful relationship with the parents. It is necessary to emphasize that we and the parents have the same goal—the child's welfare—and that we can best achieve that goal by working together, helping each other, and teaching each other.

Prior to implementing a parenting program, we must first build a positive relationship with parents, if one does not already exist. We must spend time with them in friendly conversations about their child. Once a friendly and trusting relationship is established, we can begin to develop the educational potential. During the process we must provide support, boost confidence, and inform parents of community resources.

The building of a positive relationship begins with the first contact a parent has with the child care facility. During initial phone calls and/or visits we should make parents feel that they are an important and a necessary part of the program. We should encourage them to visit frequently and unannounced. It may well be through these visits that parents learn the most about appropriate care of children.

We can try other strategies, such as recommending that parents spend time in the center and establishing a variety of interviews and conversations with staff and other parents. We can require a parent orientation prior to the child's entrance into the program. In this way, we can know that parents are familiar with the program's philosophy, goals, and policies.

Strategies for Implementing Parenting Programs

Since there are a number of different approaches to parent education and involvement, the child care staff should assess resources that are available to help them fulfill their roles effectively. First, and most primary, is the capability and know-how of the teachers. Not only are knowledge, skills, and appropriate attitudes about child care and development required, but the parent educator must be a teacher, counselor with helping skills, and manager as well. Professionalism is the key to success in positive parent education and involvement.

Although there are many ways to educate and involve parents, we will concentrate on a few that have proven to be successful in a variety of child care facilities. Since time is a critical consideration, full utilization of staff-parent contact time is assumed no matter what strategies are selected.

Parent Involvement

Parents who volunteer to work in a child care facility can learn a host of parenting tips. They observe not only specific applications to a single child but parenting for children of different ages as well. Parents learn by observing other adults as they teach, play with, respond to, and discipline children. For example, a parent who observes the successful handling of a disagreement between two children learns that there are various approaches to disciplining children.

Parents also have opportunities to learn about child development when they observe appropriate activities that are planned for a particular child's stage of development. We can introduce them to many new toys, materials, creative ideas, and activities that are suited for children of various ages. Exposure to other children gives parents many opportunities to reflect upon their own child's growth and development.

Parent involvement can also be beneficial to staff. Teaching someone else means that we have to reflect upon how and why we do something. Confidence in our own abilities can be increased, or the need to change the way we are doing things may become apparent to us.

Question Starter: How do we begin to involve parents in the child's education? (Responses may include: identify interests and talents; encourage active participation in experiences; share information; hold conferences and group meetings; sponsor family gatherings; do home visits.)

There are many ways to involve parents, but we should begin by finding out what parents are interested in doing. One way to get this information is to develop a questionnaire that will help identify what they would like to do.

A parent talent file that identifies hobbies, occupations, and interests can be developed. When in need of a guest speaker or advice in a particular area, we can use the talent file to get the help we need. Most parents appreciate being asked to help if they are approached in a positive manner.

Parents learn more about children when they understand the objectives and participate in the implementation of a learning experience. A parent who is asked to design a learning experience for a child is more likely to discover that there is a wealth of information in everyday life that children need to learn. For example, if a parent has access to a farm setting, he could host a field trip to see lambs, calves, and gardens. That same parent could help children plant seeds of their own to grow.

Parent Bulletin Board

One of the most common methods of disseminating information to parents is by using a bulletin board. The bulletin board can contain much more than the menu, fee notes, and facility notices about holidays. It can be a very important tool in improving parent-child relationships. One corner can be used as a Parenting Tips Corner. In this spot parents, as well as staff, can post suggestions on any aspect of parenting: toilet training, child guidance, safety hints, and so on.

Another corner can be designed as a Parent-Child Activities Corner, where parents and staff post ideas for activities that parents and children can do together. Places to visit, photos, pamphlets, maps, descriptions, and instructions for activities and games for use at home can be included. Common resources for free or inexpensive materials available in the community for parent-child activities at home are additional possibilities. The list can continuously be added to and changed.

Photos of children, parents, and staff can be an integral part of the bulletin board. Photos of each staff person with name, position, qualifications, past experience, and other personal information can be an excellent way of helping promote better relationships between parents and staff. When parents feel that they know the staff better, they are more likely to build a cooperative, enjoyable relationship.

Pictures of children involved in activities are excellent tools for parent education. Such photos stimulate interest, comments, and questions. They also help parents to see and better understand what their child does in the facility during the day. Pictures provide opportunities to discuss specific developmental activities, how children learn, and how parents can extend the learning at home.

Messages such as "Have You Hugged Your Kid Today?" can be parent education tools. We can create single-phrase messages to impact parents, with a weekly changing motto posted on the bulletin board.

The bulletin board can be expanded into a Parent Exchange Corner. It can become a place for parents to leave messages and announcements of interest to other parents, including lists of people who care for children, places to get free immunizations for children, or special programs in the community. We should make it convenient by providing pads and pencils nearby and responding promptly to parents' written communication.

Parent Library

Home libraries are likely to be scanty with respect to parenting literature. Popular literature is filled with parenting advice but may be unscreened and ill advised. A library that is compiled by child care professionals can be more extensive and selective. A place to read, a system to check out readings, and the assurance that the readings are valid is a service that many parents will treasure.

The library can include materials that help parents deal with a dilemma, a question, or a difficult decision. It can contain consumer information, commercial or self-made cassette tapes, filmstrips and slide/tape presentations on child rearing, and pertinent journal articles and books on parenting. In addition to parent education materials, the library can also contain materials for children, including a supply of good books that can be checked out on a regular basis. A toy lending system with instructions for the use of each item can be incorporated in the library.

Newsletter

A newsletter can further the philosophy, commitments, and goals of the child care program. It is an excellent place to communicate the importance and the characteristics of quality child care. A periodic newsletter can, moreover, be a valuable source of parenting information. The newsletter should contain material that keeps parents informed of facility activities, announcements, and parenting issues. A newsletter that is parent education oriented includes activities children are doing at the facility and suggestions for additional activities that can be done at home.

The newsletter can also be used not only to show appreciation to parents who have contributed time and materials but also to encourage further involvement of parents in specific activities. Parents are more likely to read a newsletter if it contains interesting information about themselves and others they know. It can also include a vast array of other information: recipes for nutritious snacks children like to make; rainy day activities; words to songs children sing; stories written by children; and pertinent segments of books and articles.

Child Logs

An excellent way to inform parents about their child's development is to use a communication system that details the child's activities and behaviors while the child is at the facility. Child logs can provide parents with current information about their child and can serve as a tool for parent education. Child logs are designed to provide both parent and teacher with critical information about the child before and after he arrives at the facility. Each day, on arrival, the parent records some basic information about the child's most recent activities on the child log: time of arrival at the center, latest feedings, and sleep periods. In addition, conversation between the arriving parent and teacher is focused on the child, not on the weather or other trivial matters. While coats, hats, and personal belongings are being transferred, critical information that can make a difference in the day's activities is shared.

Once the log is started and the parent has left, the careprovider records additional information about the child's day. Time and content of feedings at the site are recorded throughout the day. Sleep and elimination patterns are also recorded. Developmental play and special excursions are noted. Individual comments about the child are specified on the log.

The child log is considered a parent education tool because it is a means of providing continuity of care between home and child care facility. It is also a focal point for discussion of the child's basic physical and developmental needs and provides an excellent means of teaching parents about the developmental needs of the child. Stimulation activities that are matched to the age and stage of the child's development, and that are recorded on the log, help parents judge which activities are appropriate for their child. The recorded activities also provide a focal point for conversation about development and encourage parents to continue to do these same activities at home with their child.

Recording nutritious meals and snacks served at the facility can be a means of educating parents about nutrition. Parents are encouraged to use snack ideas—such as apples with peanut butter or celery with cream cheese instead of chips and cookies—for a more nutritious diet.

The comment section of the log allows the teacher the opportunity not only to share anecdotes of the day but to lead the parent to synthesize the events with developmental expectations and theory. For example, reassurance of normal progress is one of the benefits when a teacher can say that 18-month-old Susy's refusal to cooperate is to be expected, since she is approaching a stage of development where she should and will say "no" many times. In this manner, parents can be reassured that their child is developing normally.

The child log encourages discussion between parent and teacher at the end of the day and keeps that discussion focused on the child's development. Since parents are often rushed, critical choices of words, generalizations, and advice must be made. The child log offers these choices and communicates what we do not get a chance to say. Day by day, the most relevant issues of parenting unfold.

Parent Group Meetings

Another way to involve parents is through conventional workshops or seminars. It is wise to plan topics around issues in which parents themselves express interest. It is important to select times for group meetings when the largest number of parents are able to attend. An informal survey can be used to gather information about topics of interest and times that are best for parents to meet.

The group meetings can be designed in several ways. For example, if it takes several sessions to cover a particular topic, a series of workshops over a period of time can be planned. Other topics can be covered adequately in one session. Whatever the circumstances, it is best to determine at the beginning the length of each session and the number of sessions needed to cover the topic.

When parents attend workshops, it is important to make them feel as comfortable as possible. Informal seating arrangements, name tags, and get acquainted games help participants relax. Open-ended, friendly questions about the topic promote sharing and discussion.

In addition to presentations the staff makes, other resources can be used. Guest speakers who are experts in a particular area can add a needed dimension. An entire workshop devoted to children's activities that parents can do at home can be planned. In addition, excellent audio visual materials on parenting can be utilized.

Some parents are interested in teaching a workshop. They may have specific skills to share, special knowledge in one area, or experience that is of interest to some of the other parents. For example, a mother who has toilet trained three children, using a different approach with each child, could share these experiences with parents of toddlers.

Workshop topics should originate from the group. Some of the topics that arise in groups are: issues related to the child's entrance into the program; separation issues; changes in behavior; chronic problems such as toilet training and temper tantrums; program issues such as curriculum goals; seasonal issues; termination of the program year; parents' expectations for their children; and current issues and concerns (Kelly, 1981).

An entire workshop can be devoted to making nutritious snacks, and parents can actually prepare the snacks during the workshop. Other sessions could focus on selection of good books for children and making inexpensive learning materials, which can either be kept for use at the facility or taken home.

Whatever topic is selected, the manner in which it is executed is equally important. A poorly taught and ill-prepared session can kill any parenting education effort. A parent group meeting should include several components, such as topics to be covered, clearly stated objectives, activities to accomplish objectives, resource persons and materials to be utilized, and a way to evaluate the success of the meeting.

Family Support Groups

Teachers of young children can be leaders in the establishment of parenting support groups among the parents of their children. The Minnesota Early Learning Design (MELD) is a prototype for parenting support groups that can be modeled. Such support groups encourage parents to talk with each other about the normal problems and issues of parenting and to aid each other in such ways as establishing telephone trees to pass on messages more easily. We are in a good position to instigate a support group of this sort.

Social Activities

Social activities involving families and child care staff are excellent ways to establish the foundations for better rapport between the two groups. More than one problem has been solved over a cup of coffee and a piece of pie. Parents learn about parenting in a relaxed setting where there are common interests.

The help of families can be enlisted in a group project. For example, when a playground needs additional work, a weekend can be set aside as a day for families to come together to clean up the playground and make needed repairs. Everyone benefits, and many interchanges between parents and staff are made.

Parent Conferences

Parent conferences provide staff and parents private time to discuss individual concerns. They offer opportunities to initially state or reiterate the goals and objectives of the child care program to parents. Discussion of the child's progress can provide additional ways to educate the parents about how to encourage optimal development. Addressing specific aspects of each child's development and behavior lends itself to teaching parents about the stages of child development, realistic expectations for behavior and responsibilities, and the importance of parental stimulation and involvement in all areas of their child's development.

Plans for the child can be constructed as a cooperative effort between the primary and auxiliary teachers. The evolution of development can be profiled so that total understanding will guide those plans. Special problems introduced by the day care situation can be aired, and adjustments that may be needed in practice or policy can be identified.

These sessions can also be used to help parents identify a need to secure services that are beyond either the home or the child care facility to provide. For instance, a suspected hearing impairment, wherever discovered, needs the attention of a specialist. The adult who is intent on supporting the family and helping the child will know where audiologist services can be found in the community and can guide the parent into securing assistance, predicting costs, finding resources to help finance special services (when needed), and provide data from the child care setting to assist the specialist in diagnosing the problem.

Learning Activity: Using role play, ask several volunteers to enact a parent conference that incorporates the principle of establishing a strong bond between the child care facility and the home.

Home Visits

When parents are agreeable, and when staff have time, home visits are a very rewarding parent education opportunity. We can also observe the child in the home setting where interactions are unique between adult and child. Such insight can be stored and utilized later if needed. Explanations for behavior often are evident when a family is observed at home. If we are truly to be a source of support for the family and child, understanding the total environment is necessary. The conversations in and around such a visit can be invaluable.

It is important to remember that the parent must solicit and volunteer for such a visit, but we must first make ourselves available. Frequently, there is hesitation to open up one's home to outsiders. Professional insight and skills are required to execute a home visit successfully. But the bond established by such visits can be a most valuable base on which to build a parent education program.

Open House

Periodic open houses in which families visit the child care setting are excellent ways to promote parent education opportunities. Open house times can be used to highlight program activities, children's products, and appropriate methods of teaching children.

At such times children can provide entertainment or a demonstration of what they do and learn about in the facility. Creative art experiences like painting with shaving cream, modeling with clay, or playing with water can be set up for parents to join in with their children. In this manner parents learn about the program, their children, and appropriate activities, all at the same time.

Extended Family Activities

Grandparents in child care are special resources. They can be incorporated into an ongoing program. Exposure to older citizens may be novel to children and could be an educational experience for younger parents as well. Older people who are not part of a family can sometimes help young families learn how to incorporate their elders into the family constellation.

Learning Activity: Using small groups, ask participants to design an ideal parenting program that would reflect the goals of increasing positive parent-child relationships.

Summary

One of our major concerns is to recognize child care as a parenting education opportunity that is frequently overlooked. The implementation of parenting programs into child care must be a conscious and deliberate effort and requires a professional stature and a commitment to the endeavor. Finding the time and starting small will make parent education and involvement through child care a reality.

Parenting programs through child care can be very powerful tools in promoting better parent-staff relations and optimum developmental growth for children. If executed properly, such programs can and will improve day care, staff-parent relationships, parent-child relationships, and staff-child relationships.

Enrichment Activities

1. Devise a plan for incorporating parenting education activities into a child care program for one year. Include all objectives and activities and describe how they would be implemented and evaluated. Specify follow-up activities that you would attempt.
2. Design a parent newsletter for one month for a child care program. Circulate it and solicit feedback about its effectiveness as a parent education tool.
3. Design a child log that can be used in your child care facility. The child log

should reflect the ages of children with whom you work.

4. Plan a parent group meeting that incorporates the following: topic; objectives; activities; resources, including people and materials; and an evaluation system.

Bibliography

Auerbach, A. B. (1980). *Parents learn through discussion: Principles and practices of parent group education.* New York: Robert E. Krieger.

A helpful book dealing with strategies developed by the Child Study Association for the training of group leaders to assist parents in improving their parenting skills.

Bell, T. H. (1976). *Active parent concern: A new home guide to help your child do better in school.* Englewood Cliffs, NJ: Prentice-Hall.

Parents are a child's first teachers, and certain skills, concepts, and types of knowledge are needed for effective parenting. All of these, however, stem from active concern for the child's welfare and success. Ways in which parents can help their children and understand how to work with schools, educators, and systems are outlined.

Berger, E. H. (1981). *Parents as partners in education.* St. Louis: C. V. Mosby.

A stimulating, readable, and comprehensive book. The author cites research, outlines the history of parent involvement, discusses home-school-community relationships, describes existing programs, examines current issues such as child abuse and child advocacy, and provides a detailed resource guide.

Brandt, R. S. (Ed.). (1979). *Partners: Parents and schools.* Alexandria, VA: Association for Supervision and Curriculum Development.

The book includes a variety of articles that underline the necessity of constant interaction and cooperation among schools, parents, and communities. Research findings about the characteristics of successful parent programs are presented. These include: effective communication; direct parent involvement in what interests them; friendly attitudes of school personnel; ongoing programs for both parents and teachers; and the sharing of decision making.

Bromwich, R. (1981). *Working with parents and infants: An interactional approach.* Baltimore: University Park Press.

Different problems need different solutions, and the author suggests that parents use problem-solving techniques to decide how best to deal with a particular problem or crisis. Interaction and support are emphasized.

Core, M. (1982, July/August). Parent communication: Making the most of transition time. *Child Care Information Exchange,* pp. 33–39.

A critical look is taken at daily parent-staff interactions, and the need for communication and communicative attitudes is stressed. Various means of achieving this communication are suggested. These include parent bulletin boards, newsletters, effective use of transition time, parent orientation sessions, and family meals and picnics.

Gordon, I. J., Olmsted, P. P., Rubin, R. I., & True, J. H. (1979). How has follow through promoted parent involvement? *Young Children, 34* (5), 49–53.

Discussing the Follow Through Parent Education Model, the authors describe the roles of parents as decision makers, adult learners, audience, and classroom volunteers. The positive effects of the model on the school, the community, and the career development of parents are also pointed out.

Gross, B. D., & Shuman, B. J. (1980). *The essentials of parenting in the first years of life.* New York: Child Welfare League of America.

The book synthesizes current theories and research and presents applicable ideas and relevant information that can be discussed in parent education groups.

Heimberger, M. J. (1978). *Continued focus on families for cultural appreciation, curriculum planning, and tutoring in reading.* Paper presented at the annual meeting of the International Reading Association World Congress on Reading, Hamburg, West Germany. (ERIC Document Service No. 162 290)

The paper stresses the importance of educating parents to help their children understand cultural values and encourage reading and learning. Various school-parent programs are described, and a variety of practical suggestions are offered.

Heinicke, C., Carlin, E., & Given, K. (1984). Parent and mother-infant groups: Building a support system. *Young Children, 39* (3), 21–27.

The authors describe ways in which group discussions and self-help programs can support and encourage predelivery parents and mother-infant groups.

Honig, A. S. (1979). *Parent involvement in early childhood education.* Washington, DC: National Association for the Education of Young Children.

This book includes many ideas for working with parents to ensure a high-quality program. It goes beyond many of the typical ideas and suggestions usually given for ways to involve parents.

Kelly, F. J. (1981). Guiding groups of parents of young children. *Young Children, 37* (1), 28–32.

Child care centers and teachers need to initiate parent guidance and discussion groups. The functions and purposes of such groups are explained. Useful tips are given for starting and maintaining the group process, and certain problems and concerns that are frequently expressed in parent groups are examined.

Laosa, L. M., & Sigel, I. E. (Eds.). (1982). *Families as learning environments for children.* New York: Plenum.

The book consists of a variety of articles that explore the family and home environments of children and study the impact of these factors on children's development.

Manburg, A. (1985, January). Parent involvement: A look at practices that work. *Child Care Information Exchange,* pp. 9–11.

Encouraging and maintaining parent involvement requires strong commitment to the concept of equal parent participation in a child's education. A variety of programs at child care centers around the country are examined, and a set of practical working ideas and rules are derived and explained.

Margolin, E. (1982). *Teaching young children at school and home.* New York: Macmillan.

The book provides helpful information for teachers on how to work with parents of young children. It emphasizes the need to be aware of the social environment in which both teachers and parents operate, and points out the effect of societal attitudes on children. Interesting activities and programs are also presented for the enhancement of school and home learning.

Morrison, G. S. (1978). *Parent involvement in the home, school, and community.* Columbus, OH: Charles E. Merrill.

Current theories and programs for parent involvement are examined in detail, and various strategies to generate more active participation are presented.

Sigel, I. E., & Laosa, L. M. (Eds.). (1983). *Changing families.* New York: Plenum.

The authors study the individual, ethical, moral, and social aspects of family and community life in relation to their impact on children and on child development.

Stevens, J. H. (1978). Parent education programs: What determines effectiveness. *Young Children, 33* (4), 59–65.

The author reviews the characteristics of effective parent education programs and discusses relevant research on the changes such programs bring about in parent-child behavior and interactions. The types of parents who benefit from certain programs and the effects of different kinds of programs are also examined.

Taylor, K. W. (1981). *Parents and children learn together.* Hagerstown, MD: Teachers College Press.

The author discusses parent-parent and parent-child interactions, parenting by fathers, growing conflicts encountered by career-oriented mothers, parents rearing children alone, and needed community resources. The book also contains a logical and cohesive plan for developing, maintaining, and extending parent cooperative nursery schools and for understanding the dynamic interactions involved between cooperating parents, parents and teachers, and parents and communities.

Thibault, J. P., & McKee, J. S. (1982). Practical parenting with Piaget. *Young Children, 38* (1), 18–27.

Written specifically for parents, this informative and interesting article explains child development in terms of Piagetian concepts and stages. Each stage is discussed in detail, and practical information is given about appropriate activities, toys, literature, and equipment that can enrich the environment and make it conducive to development and learning. Teachers of young children will also find this a helpful article.

Tizard, B., Mortimore, J., & Burchell, B. (1981). *Involving parents in nursery and infant schools.* London: Grant McIntyre.

Various approaches and attitudes to parent involvement are examined. A research project carried out on teachers and parents in Britain is reported, and practical suggestions for activities designed to encourage and support involvement are offered.

Wallat, C., & Goldman, R. (1979). *Home/school/community interaction: What we know and why we don't know more.* Columbus, OH: Charles E. Merrill.

In education, the roles of family, school, and community interweave, often generating complications and problems that the book dramatically highlights. Practical solutions are proposed, and useful information on resources, organizations, and various programs is also given.

14 Understanding Child Abuse and Neglect

ONE of the most perplexing problems we can encounter when we work with young children is that of child abuse and neglect. It is a major concern because child abuse and neglect can be difficult to detect, and once detected, it can be even more difficult to manage.

Yet it is apparent that as long as we work with children and families we undoubtedly will at some time encounter cases of child abuse and neglect. Therefore, we are in a better position to handle the problem when we are familiar with exactly what abuse and neglect is, how we can identify it when it has occurred, what steps we can take to report it, how we can approach the problem with the child and family, and what resources are available to assist the child and family.

Objectives

In this chapter we will define child abuse and neglect. We will clarify the teacher's role and responsibilities in reporting suspected cases, and will specify the correct procedures in reporting such cases. We will identify the indicators of abuse and neglect and the characteristics of adults who maltreat children. We will also specify ways in which we can assist children and families in these situations. Finally, we will describe ways in which maltreatment can be prevented in child care facilities.

Key Ideas

Defining child abuse and neglect is difficult because a commonly agreed-upon definition does not exist. Each state has formulated its own definitions of child abuse and neglect and, in so doing, has a mandate for reporting suspected cases.

In general, child abuse is repeated maltreatment or neglect of a child by adults and results in physical or psychological harm. The abuse may be physical, verbal, emotional, or sexual. Reasonable cause to believe that a child has been maltreated in any of these ways is sufficient justification to report a suspected case.

As teachers, we play an extremely important role in providing assistance to children and families where abuse has occurred. The task of handling these problems is easier when a set of procedures for detecting and reporting suspected cases exists in child care facilities.

Child abuse can also occur in a child care facility. Policies can be established to minimize the potential for abuse occurring within the center, and steps can be taken to reduce stressful situations which could lead to abuse.

Defining Abuse and Neglect

Child abuse and neglect is difficult to identify because different definitions exist. What constitutes abuse and neglect to one person or one segment of society may not be abuse and neglect to another person or another segment of society.

In addition, there are several levels of abuse and neglect. There is cultural abuse, which encompasses all the attitudes and beliefs about children that the society has. For example, the traditional saying, "Spare the rod, spoil the child," is commonly accepted by a majority of people in our society. There is also institutional abuse, which includes the attitudes, beliefs, and practices that are adhered to by institutions. For instance, it is still a widespread and commonly accepted practice to spank children in public schools. Finally, there is individual abuse and neglect which includes the attitudes, beliefs, and practices to which an individual adheres. For example, an adult may use extreme physical punishment to discipline a child.

Learning Activity: Working in small groups, ask participants to develop a definition of abuse and neglect. Have each group explain its definition and respond to questions from other groups. This activity should stimulate initial reactions to the difficulties involved in addressing this problem.

Legal Definitions

Although there are problems inherent in defining child abuse and neglect, some definitions do exist. Each state has legal definitions of child maltreatment, even though they may be broad in nature. These definitions may be subdivided into the following categories: physical abuse; sexual abuse; emotional abuse; emotional neglect; and physical neglect.

Physical abuse is any act or failure to act by an adult that causes physical injury or impairment of the child's future growth or development. Sexual abuse ranges from molestation that includes fondling, exposure, and masturbation, to intercourse that includes incest and rape; it can also include sexual provocation.

Emotional abuse is the failure to provide a positive emotional atmosphere for the child by not giving love and proper direction, not encouraging a child's normal development, and downgrading, blaming, belittling, or ignoring a child. Emotional neglect is passive and includes not showing any feelings for the child. Physical neglect, on the other hand, is the failure by the adult to provide adequate food, clothing, medical attention, shelter, care, supervision, protection, or education. Emotional abuse and neglect can sometimes be more damaging than physical abuse and neglect.

Reporting Suspected Cases of Abuse and Neglect

Question Starter: What would you do if you suspected that a child in your child care facility was being abused or neglected? (Responses will vary depending upon state laws and participants' knowledge about them.)

All states have laws requiring certain individuals to report suspected cases of child abuse and neglect to an appropriate agency. However, these laws vary. In some states all persons are required to report suspected cases of abuse and neglect. In other states responsible persons are limited to physicians, hospital personnel, social workers, law enforcement officers, and other individuals in social service positions who work with children and families.

As teachers of young children, we are

responsible for reporting suspected cases of abuse and neglect. We are required to report our suspicions to the designated child protective services agency in our state. We do not need to have conclusive evidence to make a report. We must only have reasonable cause to believe that maltreatment has occurred. It is not our responsibility to investigate a case; it is only our responsibility to report our suspicions. As reporters we also have immunity from any liability of prosecution.

However, in most states we could be held liable for failure to report a suspected child abuse case. Under any circumstances, and no matter how difficult it is, it is always in the best interest of the child to report our concerns, even when we fear further actions against the child.

The first step in dealing with a suspected case of abuse or neglect is to report it to the appropriate child protective services agency. Once a report is made, the child protective social worker or law enforcement officer will take steps to investigate the case. Usually a visit is made to the home for the purpose of assessing if abuse or neglect has occurred. The investigator will make every attempt to find out from the parents and child if the alleged abuse or neglect has occurred.

The major goal of all child protective service agencies is to assure protection of the child within his home environment. If it is determined after the investigation that abuse or neglect has occurred, the investigator must determine whether there is considerable risk to the child if left in the home. If there is considerable risk, then the child is usually removed from the home temporarily, and a court order is obtained so that there can be a hearing within a specified period of time.

Sometimes the investigator will determine that the child is not in immediate danger but that the family needs help to improve the situation. Counseling and other supportive services to the family may then be provided.

As part of the child care center staff we may, in fact, be part of the supportive services provided for the family. That is, child care provides relief for parents who may be overburdened by pressures caused by the demands of caring for children and other stressful circumstances. Child care also includes the teaching of social skills and use of play materials that may be vital to children of such families. Child care can provide emotional support for the child and also for the parents.

Every child care facility should have a set of procedures for detecting and reporting suspected cases of abuse and neglect. Types of information that should be included in a child maltreatment policy are:

1. A brief rationale for involving personnel in reporting.
2. The name and appropriate section numbers of the state reporting statute.
3. A statement indicating support for reporting child abuse and neglect.
4. Who specifically is mandated to report.
5. The exact language of the law defining reportable conditions of abuse and/or neglect. Explanations or expansions beyond the state definition may sometimes be necessary.
6. The person or agency to receive reports.
7. The information required of the reporter.
8. Whether or not there is immunity from civil liability and criminal penalty for those who report child abuse and neglect.
9. The action that will be taken by the child care facility for failure to report.
10. Any provision of the law regarding the confidentiality of records pertaining to reports of suspected abuse and neglect.
11. Copy of form to be used in filing reports.

12. Whether employees reporting child abuse and neglect may inform parents of the action they have taken.
13. Actions that the child care facility will take following reporting of suspected abuse or neglect to ensure feedback to the reporter on the findings of the investigation and any further action to be taken.
14. The role of the child care facility in multidisciplinary community efforts to provide service to abused and neglected children and their families.
15. The child care facility's policy regarding corporal punishment as a form of discipline.
16. The child care facility's role in providing parent training, public awareness programs, or other activities devoted to preventing child abuse and neglect.
17. Other community resources that child care facilities can draw on in responding to child abuse and neglect.
18. Any special instructions regarding removal of children from the child care facility and instructions for contacting police or other agencies with responsibilities for placing children in protective custody.

One person in the child care facility should assume primary responsibility for handling child abuse cases. This person should: serve as a liaison to the child protective services agency and other agencies; inform parents and staff of the state and local laws regarding child abuse and neglect; know community resources available to families with child abuse and neglect problems; discuss the report with the family, as appropriate; inform the rest of the staff of the process for identifying and reporting; and report suspicions of child abuse and neglect on behalf of the program.

Reporting suspected cases of child abuse and neglect is critical. If they are not reported, the cases cannot be investigated. One does not have to be positive that abuse or neglect has occurred before reporting. All that is needed is a reasonable cause to believe that maltreatment has occurred. All staff can participate in making that decision. It may not be wise to report every child who comes in with a bruise, but it may be equally unwise to ignore a child who frequently comes to the center with varying or multiple injuries. We should discuss and examine the indicators with other staff and report the incidences that give us reasonable cause to believe that abuse or neglect exists.

Question Starter: Given the situation presented here, ask participants to respond to the following questions. The situation is: A child is extremely withdrawn and will not become involved in any activities. She is very shy, and often goes unnoticed by the other children. What would you do first? What information would you try to obtain? To whom would you report your suspicions? (Responses should demonstrate an understanding of how a report is made.)

Indicators of Abuse and Neglect

There are specific behaviors and physical signs that we should learn to recognize as indicators of child abuse and neglect. Some signs are obvious, such as long, straight welts across the child's back or buttocks, which would almost certainly be the result of having been whipped with a belt, cord, or similar object. Other signs are much more subtle, and to recognize them it is necessary to be aware of the child's normal state of attitude and disposition. For example, a child who is emotionally maltreated may act unusually quiet and withdrawn or unusually aggressive.

Learning Activity: One way to become more sensitive to indicators of abuse or neglect in children is to examine more closely the feelings and behaviors associated with various forms of maltreatment.

Divide participants into at least three groups and assign each group one of the following case histories. Ask each group to respond to three questions: What they would expect the child to feel in the situation? How they would expect the child to behave? What type of maltreatment is indicated?

Sample Case 1: Jason, aged 1 1/2, lives with his mother, father, and older sister, Amy, aged 8. Their mother, who is employed full time, expects Amy to help in caring for Jason because she is so much older than Jason. Amy is often put in charge of watching Jason, changing his diapers, feeding him, and comforting him when he cries. But Amy, who is only 8 years old, often gets involved in playing games outside and forgets to keep track of Jason. Sometimes she is too busy playing to attend to Jason when he cries. She also does not like to change Jason's messy diapers, so she often ignores the fact and postpones changing them. Mother usually makes sure that Jason gets enough to eat but is too busy cleaning and cooking in the evening to give much personal attention to him. (Responses may include: child feels lonely, ignored, unimportant, and without influence in his environment; child behaves withdrawn, stays to himself, has low expectations; type is physical and emotional neglect.)

Sample Case 2: Cindy is 4 years old. Her mother frequently holds and hugs her 2-year-old sister Sarah but does not usually give Cindy much physical affection, for she believes she is getting too old for that. Cindy is expected to help in caring for Sarah but is often inadequate at her assigned tasks. She frequently trips and spills and breaks things. Her mother gets annoyed at her clumsiness and yells at her quite often, calling her stupid, dumb, and clumsy. (Responses may include: child feels dumb, clumsy, and worthless; has low expectations; lacks self-esteem; child is quiet and withdrawn; type is emotional abuse.)

Sample Case 3: Steven is 3 years old. His parents insist they love him very much and want him to be a well-mannered and good boy. They feel it is very important for children to behave, to follow instructions, and to obey their parents. When Steven misbehaves, he is always punished by being spanked and sent to his room for a couple of hours. For example, if he talks back, his face is slapped and he is sent to his room. If he crosses the street without an adult, he is whipped with a belt and spends the rest of the day in his bedroom. If he throws a temper tantrum, he is tied to his bed for an hour. (Responses may include: child feels fearful, insecure, hateful, revengeful; child becomes passive or overaggressive; type is physical abuse.)

Child Indicators

Although there are many ways in which a child can be abused, there are common signs that we need to be aware of.

Physically abused children have repeated injuries, such as bruises, welts, and burns on their bodies. Their parents may seem unconcerned, and often deny that anything is wrong or give an unsatisfactory explanation. Physically neglected children are often badly nourished and inadequately clothed. They are frequently left unsupervised and sometimes held responsible for the care of younger children. Sometimes abused children exhibit very aggressive, negative behavior in an effort to gain much-needed attention. In some cases abused children may be very withdrawn and without friends. Such indicators may be a sign that these children's basic needs for love and affection are not being met at home. Children who are unwilling to participate in activities, particularly sports, may be experiencing some form of sexual abuse at home. Their unwillingness to participate may be

Table 5. Physical and Behavioral Indicators of Maltreatment

Type of Maltreatment	Physical Indicators	Behavioral Indicators
Physical abuse	Unexplained bruises and welts on body	Fearful of adult contact
	Unexplained burns, including rope burns	Extremely aggressive or withdrawn
	Unexplained fractures	Frightened of parents
	Unexplained lacerations or abrasions	Not worried about adult authority
		Cries frequently or shows little emotion
Physical neglect	Consistently hungry, unclean, inappropriately dressed	Arrives early for school and leaves late
	Unsupervised	Consistently tired
	Unattended medical needs	Drug and alcohol use
	Inadequate and unsafe housing	Chronic absences from school
	Inconsistent school attendance	
	Abandoned	
	Given adult responsibility	
Sexual abuse	Sitting or walking is difficult	Lack of participation in gym activities
	Bruises and bleeding or itching and pain in private areas	Withdrawn or infantile behavior
	Venereal disease	Unusual sexual behavior
	Pregnancy	Poor adjustment of peers
		Delinquent or runaway
Emotional stress	Speech delayed	Sucks, bites, or rocks
	Physical growth delayed	Antisocial
	Failure to thrive	Sleep disorders
	Skin disorders	Hysterics, phobias
		Passive, aggressive
		Hyperactive
		Inappropriate behavior for age
		Learning problems
		Discipline problems

a sign that they are uncomfortable or embarrassed.

We should be especially sensitive to children who are considered different by their parents. For example, children at high risk for abuse may be: handicapped; unattractive; the wrong sex; learning disabled; slow in development; mentally retarded; born prematurely; hyperactive or precocious; adopted or a stepchild; or delayed developmentally.

A summary of physical and behavioral

indicators for each type of maltreatment is provided in table 5.

Adult Indicators

Recognizing adults who may be abusing or neglecting children is equally important, especially since we have significant contact with both children and their parents on a regular basis. When we can associate child indicators with adult indicators, we are in a better position to make a realistic assessment of the situation to determine if maltreatment is occurring.

Several typical themes can be associated with adults who may be abusing children. Maltreating adults are often immature and fail to understand the child's behavior and needs. They typically expect children to behave like adults even when they are very young. They are unable to relate well to other adults and consequently look to the child to satisfy their unmet needs. Stressful situations in the home, such as loss of job, divorce, or death, can cause an adult to take it out on the child. In addition, maltreating parents often lack the appropriate knowledge and skills to raise their child and, typically, have few friends or family to support them in the job of child rearing.

Many abusive adults were abused themselves as children. Most maltreating parents are insecure themselves and suffer from low self-esteem. Some maltreating parents are supercritical and may severely punish their child when their expectations are not met. Moreover, some parents are so disorganized and unable to attend to life's demands that they are unable to attend to their child's needs. Finally, an alcoholic or drug-abusing family is at high risk for child abuse, since such problems limit the parents' ability to care properly for their child.

The abusive adult differs from the neglectful adult in several ways. These distinctions are identified in table 6.

These adult indicators of abuse and neglect alone are not enough to determine if maltreatment is occurring. Parents who share these characteristics are simply at higher risk of being abusive. If we become suspicious that a child is being abused, we can refer to the indicators and try to assess if maltreatment is occurring. Several indicators together can indicate that maltreatment could be taking place.

Table 6. Characteristics of Abusive and Neglectful Adults

Abusive Adult	Neglectful Adult
1. Volatile and impulsive	1. Lacks emotional and physical support as child
2. Conditioned to violence	2. Views child as not very important
3. Often abused as child	3. Unstructured life
4. Possessive of children	4. Poor sense of responsibility
5. Anxious when dealing with child's problem	5. Views children with hostility
6. Rejects offers of advice	6. Needs of child are not apparent or are unimportant
7. Has unrealistic expectations of child	7. Discourages dependence of child-desire to escape responsibility
8. Fears spoiling or coddling the child	8. Remains isolated, lacks friends
9. Views physical punishment as positive	

Helping the Child and Family

Child care staff play an extremely important role in providing assistance to the child and family. Frequently, we are the most likely people to have contact with the family on a consistent basis. We may also be the only people whom the parents trust. Therefore, our role in detecting, reporting, and helping the family becomes even more critical.

If we suspect that child abuse or neglect has occurred, we have a responsibility to report our suspicions to a person who can help—usually a child protective services worker. If we are not sure whether a situation justifies a report, we should discuss the matter with the appropriate individuals in our facility. It is better to make an error by reporting a situation in which the evidence is not available than by failing to report possible abuse or neglect.

Once a report has been made and the situation has been investigated, we should be prepared to provide support for both the child and the family. In addition, there are a number of local service agencies that provide support: mental health agencies, school nurses, public health authorities, homemakers, Parents Anonymous, school counselors, child protective service agencies, and private family counselors. Each community will have different yet similar services. A list of local services should be on file in the child care facility at all times.

Once a report is made and the parents are aware of it, we can offer assistance to the family. We should be as honest, direct, and professional as possible. In any conversation, we should not show anger, repugnance, or shock. We can, on the other hand, assure the parents of our interest in the child and of the support of the child care facility.

The parents may try to convince us of their innocence. We can be understanding but should not get entangled by trying to judge the situation. We are not in a position to prove their guilt or thoroughly accept their explanation. Our task is to stick to facts and observation and offer ways to improve the parent-child relationship in the future.

Learning Activity: Divide participants into small groups. Ask each group to respond to the following questions after they have read the case study presented here: John is extremely aggressive, and becomes excessively involved in activity. He is hostile and is not liked by other children. He frequently becomes physically violent when games are played. Questions: What would you do first? What information would you try to obtain? Would you contact the parents? What would you say to them? Would you call the child protective services agency in your locale? How would you relate to the child and family if a report is made?

Meeting with parents to discuss a problem may be in order. If a conference is necessary there are several points to consider. Before the meeting, we must deal with our own anxieties. When we request a meeting, we should explain its purpose. We should define clearly the objectives for the meeting and come prepared with pertinent information. We should think ahead of questions to ask. Questions should be open-ended and asked in a supportive manner. The place for the meeting should be as comfortable and private as possible.

During the meeting, we should be frank, open, and honest while, at the same time, exhibiting a positive and supportive attitude. We should be ready to listen and observe and decide on a plan of action with parental input. After the meeting, we should document factual observations and follow up on any plan of action decided on in the conference. We should continue to be supportive of any efforts the parents make and record observations of progress.

Children react to maltreatment in varying ways. Some become withdrawn, some more aggressive. Their behavior will define how they are responding to the maltreatment, thus suggesting what type of special attention they need. But they most surely need some type of extra attention in the child care facility.

There are various ways in which we can help the child depending on the nature of the problem. For example, when aggressive behavior occurs we can respond in several appropriate ways. It is, first of all, important to consistently verbalize limits and explicitly define unacceptable behavior. We should state forcefully why the behavior is unacceptable and encourage the child to verbalize anger. We should separate the child from the group when the aggression is too much, acknowledge the child's fear of rejection, let her know that it is her behavior and not she herself that is unacceptable, and redirect destructive behavior.

When passive and withdrawn behavior occurs, we can provide a protective environment for the child and help him develop relationships with other children. We should provide additional one-to-one contact, express warmth and affection, and encourage the child to engage in activities for which he can be praised.

Preventing Abuse in the Child Care Facility

Child abuse can also occur in child care facilities if appropriate steps are not taken to prevent it. Because the task of caring for individual children is stressful, child care staff is as much at risk as other adults for abusing children.

We can take several steps to minimize the risk of abuse in our facilities. For example, we should make sure that children are constantly supervised. This means that several adults are in eye contact with children at all times; that is, one adult is not left alone with several children for an extended period. In addition, we should not leave children alone for certain tasks, such as going alone to the toilet when it is not within the range of eye contact.

Every effort should be made to alleviate stress among staff. We should plan our work schedules so that there are not too many hours with children in one day. We also need to take sufficient breaks away from children for short periods during the day. Staff-child ratios should always be maintained, since they are established to assure that an adequate number of adults are available to provide appropriate care for children. Moreover, the ratios help minimize stressful situations, since they allow an adult who is under stress to briefly leave the situation to regain composure.

Policies and procedures for handling discipline and other responsibilities should be clear and in writing. Every staff member, child, and parent should be aware of the acceptable forms of discipline, which should not include physical punishment or verbal assault. Clear policies help define the limits of our behavior.

Every staff member should have primary responsibility for the same small group of children for the majority of time spent at the facility. When this arrangement exists, staff and children are more likely to establish a bonding relationship that strengthens the care and concern each has for the other. Young children need to have one-to-one relationships that address their basic developmental needs.

When we all work together and take precautionary measures, child abuse is less likely to occur. When we learn to recognize the stressful signs in ourselves, other adults, and children, our ability to prevent abuse is strengthened.

Summary

It is important to remember that child abuse is a symptom of adult problems. It will not go away if ignored. For the sake of children and their parents, we can best assist by understanding the facts about child abuse, by learning how to recognize signs of abuse and neglect and how to report our suspicions, by knowing how to help victims and their parents, and by supporting all efforts to prevent child maltreatment in our facilities. We should remember that more than any other group of professionals we are probably in the best position to help children.

Enrichment Activities

1. Develop a plan that your child care facility can follow in dealing with suspected cases of child abuse and neglect. In your plan include: (*a*) the staff person(s) who will assume primary responsibility for reporting the case and contacting the family regarding the concern of the staff; (*b*) the procedures that the facility will follow; (*c*) the staff person(s) who will confer with the family; (*d*) the steps that will be used to follow up; (*e*) community resources available to the family; (*f*) approaches that will be used to help the child victim; and (*g*) the facility's plan for prevention of maltreatment within the center.
2. Plan an imaginary interview with parents who are suspected of abusing their child. Include the following: (*a*) clearly stated purpose of the meeting; (*b*) objectives of the meeting; (*c*) content of the meeting (including background information); (*d*) factual observations of the meeting (types of responses you might observe); (*e*) plan of action; and (*f*) follow-up procedure.
3. Develop a plan for helping a child who has been abused. Include the following points: (*a*) statement of the problem; (*b*) specific ways to assist the child; (*c*) ways to monitor the child's progress; and (*d*) follow-up procedures.
4. Identify practices in your child care facility that could lead to abuse. Specify ways to correct the practices so that the potential for abuse is minimized.

Bibliography

Adams, C., & Fay, J. (1981). *No more secrets: Protecting your child from sexual assault.* San Luis Obispo, CA: Impact Publishers.

Teachers and parents can make children aware of ways to recognize and protect themselves from sexual abuse. Various strategies for prevention are presented, along with suggestions on how to talk to children about this sensitive and delicate matter.

Broadhurst, D. D. (1979). *The educator's role in the prevention and treatment of child abuse and neglect.* (Dhew Pub. No. 79–30172). Washington, DC: National Center for Child Abuse and Neglect. (ERIC Document Reproduction Service No. ED 182 882)

This manual stresses the fact that educators should play a dominant and active role in detecting, preventing, and seeking help in cases of child abuse and neglect. Schools should have specific policies to deal with abuse and neglect. Various steps schools and educators can take to combat the problem are suggested.

Dayee, F. S. (1982). *Private zone.* Edmonds, WA: Charles Franklin Press.

Written in a simple, readable style that can be understood by children, this pamphlet suggests ways in which children can be taught to recognize and prevent sexual abuse. It also tells what they can do if such abuse takes place.

DeCourcy, P., & DeCourcy, J. (1973). *A silent tragedy: Child abuse in the community.* New York: Alfred Publishing.

Written at a time when child advocacy had not gained the momentum it possesses at present, this book is nonetheless a significant work and should be read by all concerned community members and teachers. The authors take a realistic and sobering look at several case studies that highlight the phenomena of child abuse and neglect in society. They stress the need for parent education, legal protection of children, and acceptance of moral responsibility by educators and community.

Fairorth, J. W. (1982). *Child abuse and the school.* Palo Alto, CA: R and E Research Associates.

The characteristics of neglected and abused children are described to help teachers recognize such children. Information is provided on how schools can prevent and detect abuse, and intervene when it is evident. The psychological and socioeconomic causes of abuse are also briefly surveyed.

Fontana, V. J., & Besharov, D. J. (1979). *The maltreated child: The maltreatment syndrome in children—a medical, legal and social guide* (4th ed.). Springfield, IL: Charles C. Thomas.

This comprehensive book describes the causes and characteristics of child abuse. Prevention and intervention are also discussed.

Freeman, L. (1982). *It's my body-a book to teach young children how to resist uncomfortable touch.* Seattle: Parenting Press.

A sensitive book that can be used with very young children to help them understand how they can discourage and prevent sexual abuse.

Hart-Rossi, J. (1984). *Protect your child from sexual abuse: A parent's guide.* Seattle: Parenting Press.

This book gives parents and teachers information and suggestions on how to teach children abuse prevention techniques and how to encourage them to express their feelings.

Kelly, J. A. (1983). *Treating child-abusive families: Intervention based on skills training principles.* New York: Plenum.

Parents who abuse their children require special treatment and training. The book presents a behavioral skills model of training that deals with child management, anger and emotion control, and management of life-styles that contribute to stress and abuse.

Kinard, E. M. (1978). *Emotional development in physically abused children: A study of self-concept and aggression.* Palo Alto, CA: R and E Research Associates.

An important work on the effects of physical abuse on children's personality and behavior. Abused children are more outwardly aggressive, unhappy, nonconforming, and low in self-concept than unabused children. Strategies for intervention are also proposed.

Koblinsky, S., & Behana, N. (1984). Child sexual abuse: The educator's role in prevention, detection, and intervention. *Young Children, 39* (6), 3–15.

The article deals with what to tell children about sexual abuse and how they can prevent and report it. Staff and parent education is stressed, prevention programs are advocated, and various resources are listed.

Leavitt, J. E. (1981). Helping abused and neglected children. *Childhood Education, 57,* 267–70.

The moral and legal responsibility of teachers to act where suspected child abuse or neglect is concerned is emphasized and discussed. The writer enumerates signs and characteristics of physical abuse and neglect, sexual abuse, and psychological abuse and neglect. Suggestions are offered on how teachers and schools can help parents eliminate some kinds of abuse. Other, more serious cases must be reported. Useful bibliographical and resource information is also provided.

Mazur, S., & Pekor, C. (1985). Can teachers touch children anymore? *Young Children, 40* (4), 10–12.

A sensible article that should be read by parents, teachers, and administrators. The authors ask some timely and relevant questions about the outcry and issues arising out of sexual abuse in day care and the impact on physical contact between adults and children. Nurturance, loving physical touch, and routine physical care are essential for normal, healthy development, yet many caregivers now fear to provide them. The dangers to child development if these factors are denied or lacking are many and real.

Pelton, L. H. (Ed.). (1981). *The social context of child abuse and neglect.* New York: Human Sciences Press.

The book focuses and elaborates on the relationship of socioeconomic factors, specifically poverty, to child abuse.

Peterson, K. L., & Roscoe, B. (1983). Neglected children: Suggestions for early childhood educators. *Childhood Education, 60,* 2–5.

There are many ways in which teachers can reach out to interact with neglected children. Teachers should, first of all, be aware of the needs and sense of inadequacy of such children: they can then provide them with opportunities and activities to enhance self-esteem, skill development, and learning. A variety of activities designed especially for neglected children are recommended.

Polansky, N. A., Chalmers, M. A., Buttenweiser, E., & Williams, D. P. (1981). *Damaged parents: An anatomy of child neglect.* Chicago: University of Chicago Press.

The authors deal with neglect as a facet of child abuse that often gets less attention than the violent, more evident forms. Current research and policies are reviewed, the characteristics of neglected children and neglecting parents are studied, and the serious implications of neglect are pointed out. An informative and enlightening book for educators and professionals concerned with children's welfare.

Stolk, M. V. (1974). Who owns the child? *Childhood Education, 50,* 259–65.

A discerning article in which the causes and consequences of child abuse are discussed. The importance of adult modeling is stressed, since it is likely that those who are abused in childhood will in turn become abusers. The historical and anthropological roots of child abuse are examined, and the need for society to accept responsibility is emphasized.

Williams, G. J., & Money, J. (Eds.). (1980). *Traumatic abuse and neglect of children at home.* Baltimore: John Hopkins University Press.

A valuable and informative book that explores the various aspects of child abuse. A variety of articles deal with the history of abuse; society's sanctions for abuse; characteristics of abusive parents and abused children; the psychological effects of abuse, deprivation, and incest; and intervention programs.

15

Communicating with Staff

EFFECTIVE communication in group settings is one of the keys to a well-functioning child care facility. It promotes cooperation and positive interaction among staff and children. Lack of effective communication, on the other hand, leads to confusion and tension, which is reflected in the way we perform our duties and is evident to those with whom we interact. It is therefore very important that staff communication in child care centers be efficient and effective.

Objectives

The primary purpose of this chapter is to examine the importance of communication within an organization. We will analyze the causes of communication gaps and problems and will discuss how these can be reduced or eliminated through the acquisition of effective communication skills. Finally, we will review ways in which clear and flexible organizational patterns and relationships can be established to facilitate communicaton flow.

Key Ideas

Communication means to be in contact with another person. It can be described as a meeting of meaning between a sender and a receiver. Thus, communication is essentially a two-way, rather than a one-way, process.

Staff communication problems arise from assorted causes. Power struggles between director and staff, or among staff, can be a major cause. Some other causes are unclear policies and objectives, clash of interests, unequal treatment of staff members, and the lack of problem-solving mechanisms and communication skills.

There are, however, ways to improve communication among group members. We can pay attention to certain types of behaviors that foster better communication. Attending behavior, using behavior descriptions, paraphrasing, and parafeeling are examples of communicating behavior. Other ways of improving group communication include organizing efficient communication networks, adopting effective leader-staff relationship patterns, clarifying role expectations, and agreeing or contracting for specific performance statements.

Defining Communication

One of the fundamental principles of human communication is that "one cannot not communicate" because one cannot not behave, and all behavior has message value, verbal and nonverbal (Faules & Alexander, 1978; Galloway, 1976; Miller,

1981). Therefore, we constantly communicate with each other (whether we want to or not), which makes it very difficult for us to understand the process. We cannot stand outside communication exchange and see it whole—analyzed, defined, categorized. We define communication as we see it from where we stand—inside it—and wherever we stand is for us the heart of the process. We have to understand communication while participating in it.

Thus, we must become active observers in our own communications. We must learn to communicate and watch and listen to ourselves communicating at one and the same time. Our watching and listening help us to develop maps or models of our experience in communicating that, hopefully, will enhance our ability to speak and listen. These maps or models help us to imaginatively stand outside by presenting us with a pattern or copy of the communication process that can be imitated or re-created. For example, when making a dress, the pattern tells the dressmaker where to cut and how to arrange the material in order to get the desired product. So in communication, a model serves as a pattern that can help us to make educated guesses about those factors on which our success or failure in communicating will hinge. And it helps us know where to look when communication breaks down.

To communicate is to make contact with another, to inspire and receive response. The goal of the contact is the meeting of meaning among the communicators. Thus, we can say that communication is composed of three components: (*a*) gesture; (*b*) response; and (*c*) shared meaning.

In this view, we know what we have said only when we know how others respond to it (Timm, 1985). Even a simple statement may elicit an unexpected, perhaps unwanted response. For example, we may make a spoken gesture toward a colleague by saying, "How are you this morning?" Perhaps our intention was simply to go through the motions of a social convention, expecting the colleague to reply with a routine "Fine, thank you." The gesture, however, elicits from her quite a different response. She has a bad headache and her neighbors had a party that kept her awake all night. This morning someone backed into her car and dented a fender on her way to work. And she is worried about her sick mother. She describes at length how she is.

From this exchange we have learned something about the colleague—perhaps a lot more than we really wanted to know. But we have also learned something about ourselves, namely, that our spoken gesture conveyed an altogether different message in the communication process than we thought it would. We may be surprised and embarrassed to see that this routine question was taken as a gesture of genuine caring. But if we listen to her response, we may hear in it the message that she hears the question as coming from a person who cares, and on that morning she needs someone to care. Communication, that is, knowing what we have said, has taken place when our spoken gesture and her response lead to shared meaning.

Of course, colleagues may respond to questions routinely, as we expected in the first place. Then meaning is still shared but at a lower level of significance. The relationship has been mutually defined by social convention rather than mutual care. In turn, we can turn off a response, refuse to hear questions as gestures of caring, and pay no attention to another's troubles. In this latter case, there is no shared meaning but rather two people who have missed making contact with each other.

This view of communication insists that it is a two-way rather than one-way process. Too often, a speaker assumes that a word means just what he chose it to mean. Such a speaker sends out a message with no regard for how it is to be received; this is one-way communication. When what the speaker says is not heard in the way in which it was intended, frustration and confusion result.

Effective communication must be two-way; there must be a meeting of meaning between sender and receiver. If a person asks for an apple and gets a lemon, no meeting of meaning has occurred. Two-way communication involves listening and responding to what is heard.

Ineffective Communication

Question Starter: What are some of the causes of ineffective staff communication in child care facilities? (Responses may include: power struggle; clash of interests; unclear policies and objectives; lack of support; inconsistency; and lack of problem-solving mechanisms and communication skills.)

Communication problems in child care facilities sometimes arise because of the way in which authority is structured. In some organizations the director has all of the authority and the teachers have none. They merely carry out the directives of the director. When the autocratic pattern of leadership is exercised, the director or leader does not seek or allow adequate input from staff. All decisions are made without consulting other staff members. The net result is that individuals within the organization have little commitment to carrying out the objectives of the program.

In other instances the director has authority but fails to execute it. She may not be clear about what the job expectations are or may be unable to provide direction to achieve the objectives of the program. Sometimes the director is not even present for the most part.

When the lines of authority are not clear or when they are so rigid that there is little flexibility or input from staff, effective communication does not occur. Feelings of powerlessness or lack of direction often lead to conflicts among staff and management.

Conflicts among staff can arise when staff members are unable to differentiate personal needs and interests from professional needs and interests. For example, when several members of the same family work in an organization owned by a family member, they sometimes find that it is difficult to separate the family structure from the organizational structure. That is, they may expect certain privileges that other staff members do not have. This arrangement can arouse feelings of resentment in other staff members.

Some conflicts arise because of lack of clear personnel policies. That is, either written job descriptions and job responsibilities do not exist, or they are so vague that they do not provide enough clarity to allow workers to meet their responsibilities or others' expectations. The net result is role confusion and resentment about conflicting expectations concerning the job. Moreover, when clear, written personnel policies are not available, problems can arise concerning unanswerable questions and resolutions to questions such as absenteeism, coffee breaks, vacation days, sick days, hiring, and firing. Lack of such policies can lead to confusion or abuse of privileges, which in turn leads to a breakdown in communication.

In addition to unclear personnel policies, conflicts can arise when there are no clear objectives and operating policies. When facility objectives are unwritten and/or unclear, staff can be unaware of the overall concerns of the child care program and are less likely to work to accomplish the same objectives.

Vague operating policies can lead to confusion and conflicting ways of functioning. For example, in the absence of a clear discipline policy, teachers may discipline children according to their own notions. Such inconsistent practices frequently lead to conflicts among staff about the best way to handle situations that require discipline procedures.

Failure to support, praise, and show appreciation for a worker's efforts can lead to feelings of resentment and bitterness. Conflicts can arise in child care facilities when staff members feel they are being taken advantage of and are not appreciated. This condition can lead to staff gossip, peer criticism, negative self-concept, and a lack of respect for others.

Conflicts can also arise when there is inconsistency or inequality in the treatment of staff. Inconsistency is more likely to occur when there is uncertainty about roles and expectations. When staff do not feel as if they are treated equally, they are more likely to be resentful and bitter.

When conflicts do arise and there are no mechanisms for resolving them, they are likely to increase rather than decrease. Conflicts that continue to be ignored generally become bigger problems. Regular staff meetings or some other mechanism for airing grievances and differing opinions can generally help to minimize the level of conflict. Group problem solving allows everyone to confront and resolve issues.

Improving Communication

Teachers of young children should work together to acquire basic problem-solving skills (Kostelnik, 1982). There are specific ways in which we can act to enhance our ability to receive messages from others. We can indicate our willingness to listen to others through our use of attending behavior. We can describe what we see them doing by using behavior description. We can reflect what we hear them saying by using a paraphrase. We can reflect what we sense them to feel by using a parafeel. Each of these skills can help us make contact with another and share their meaning (Wallen, 1971).

Attending Behavior

A helping relationship is formed if readiness to help another person is communicated through attentiveness. Attentiveness is a powerful tool that promotes self-respect and a sense of security because it reinforces and facilitates communication.

Attending behavior has three requirements. First, the listening person must relax physically. A comfortable and relaxed person will find that it is easier to listen, which in turn encourages the speaker to communicate better.

The second requirement is the use of eye contact. Eye contact lets the speaker know that the other person is listening. Observing the speaker also clarifies the message to the speaker.

The third requirement involves verbally following what the other person is saying. The listener's remarks should be related to those of the speaker. Interrupting or changing the subject severs communication. Statements and questions should address the topics and feelings provided by the speaker. These responses help develop the discussion and reinforce free and open communication.

Behavior Description

When two colleagues discuss the way they work together, both should be able to talk about what each does that affects the other. However, most people find it quite difficult to describe another person's behavior clearly or objectively. What we usually do is to comment on what we infer to be the other's attitudes, motivations, traits, and personality characteristics. Our statements are more expressive of how we feel about another's actions than about describing what those actions are.

A behavior description reports specific, observable actions of others. It is nonevaluative; it is nonblameful, that is, it does not imply that what happened was good or bad, right or wrong (Lloyd, 1985). It is noninferential; it does not make accusations or generalizations about the other's attitudes, feelings, motives, or personality traits (Kostelnik, 1982). A behavior description states what is observed; it does not infer why. We can see that these skills are similar to the skills we use when we do formal observations of children in child care settings.

An example of a behavior description is: "Ron, you've taken the opposite view of nearly everything Susan has suggested today." It is not: "Ron, you're just trying to show Susan up," which is an accusation of undesirable motivation, or "Ron, you're just being stubborn," which is name calling.

Learning Activity: Using role play, ask two or three participants to demonstrate how they could improve communication in the following situation: A colleague tells you that you are rude or that you don't care about her opinion (your motivation). She even points out that several times in the past few minutes you have interrupted her and have overridden her before she could finish what she was saying.

Paraphrasing

Question Starter: Can you identify ways in which we can check to make sure that we understand another person's ideas, information, or suggestions as she intended them? How can we know that the sender's remarks mean the same to the listener as they do to her? (Responses may include: repeat what the speaker says; check for the meaning behind the words.)

Paraphrasing is a useful skill to enhance understanding of what another person says. Paraphrasing is any means of showing the sender what her idea or suggestion means to the receiver. It focuses on objective verbal content and requires that the receiver state in her own way what the other's remark has conveyed, so that the other person can determine whether her message is coming through as she intended.

Paraphrasing, then, reveals and tests one's understanding of another person's comments. It lets the other know that the listener wants to understand what the speaker is saying. A good paraphrase can even help the other by crystallizing her comments in a more concise manner. When one person is satisfied that the other person really understands, the chances of mutual understanding will increase.

Paraphrasing is crucial in attempting to bridge the interpersonal gaps in our work relationships. It increases the accuracy of communication and thus the degree of mutual or shared understanding. The act of paraphrasing itself conveys feeling—interest in the other and concern to see how she views and feels about things.

The skill of paraphrasing is more than swapping words—saying the same thing in different words. Instead of rewording, we should ask ourselves what a person's statement means. Effective paraphrasing is not a trick or verbal gimmick. It comes from an attitude, a desire to know what the other wants to communicate. Skill in understanding others can be developed by using personal pronouns (you, yourself) and by trying different ways of conveying interest in what the other person's statement implies.

Parafeeling

Carl Rogers (1961) says that the chief barrier to mutual interpersonal communication is the human tendency to judge, evaluate, approve, or disapprove the statement of other people and other groups. Although this tendency to make judgments is common in almost all conversations, it is greatly heightened in those situations where feelings and emotions are deeply involved. So the stronger our feelings, the more likely it is that there will be no mutual element in the conversation. There will be just two ideas, two judgments, and no communication!

Rogers believes that true communication occurs, and the tendency to evaluate is avoided, when we listen to others with understanding. This means that we must pay attention to the other person's feelings and point of view in the context of the conversation.

Listening to another and understanding the other's frame of reference can best be accomplished by recognizing and following the pattern of the other's feeling and reflecting that feeling back to her. Parafeeling responses express in fresh words the essential feelings stated or strongly implied by the other person.

Three essential skills are needed to parafeel responses. First, we should listen for feeling. What the other is saying is only part of the message being communicated. How she says what she says is extremely important. A change in breathing or in the speed of talk, a sigh, a blush, a stammer, an extra emphasis upon a particular word—any of these can be important cues to feelings of the other. Words that communicate emotions and feelings should be noted. As teachers and as individuals in a group we need to be intensely aware of the importance of nonverbal behavior (Faules & Alexander, 1978; Miller, 1981).

Second, we should time comments. It is not necessary to respond to every statement. A smile or nod will do until there is an opportunity to reflect the feelings of the other. Interruptions should be avoided, particularly when the other is expressing strong emotion with intensity, so that the nature of the feeling is mutually obvious.

Third, we should reflect feeling. As we listen for, and find instances of, expressions of feeling, we can reflect the speaker's feeling by restating what she is expressing in our own words. If the other should say, "I wish I could talk to the director about things like this, but I never seem to have the nerve," a reflecting response might be, "You are a bit afraid of the director?" We can describe the other's behavior and name the feelings it suggests. Person words such as "I," "me," "you," "yours," are appropriate. We should respond to the underlying feeling as well as the expressed feelings and reflect them in the present tense.

The goal is to understand what the other is experiencing. Being alert to, and responding to, the feeling is a skill that is appropriate at any time, regardless of the nature of the feeling (positive, negative, or ambivalent) and regardless of the direction of expression (toward self, others, the leader, or a particular situation or incident).

Resolving Communication Problems

Question Starter: What are some ways in which communication problems can be decreased? (Responses may include: better systems of communication; better staff relationships; role clarification; contracts.)

Communication Networks

Like the relationship between two people, the relationships among members of a group are limited by the kinds of communication that occur. Group members can use one-way (one person) or two-way (several persons) communication no matter what they talk about. The flow of communication in groups usually follows structured patterns called networks, which tell us how the group is organized.

Communications Networks

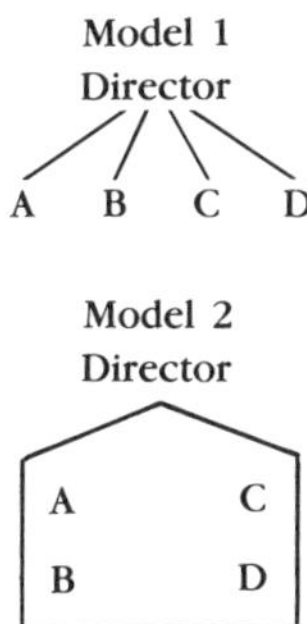

Figure 12. *Flow of communication based on group organization*

Two different models (fig. 12) provide clues about the type of organization and communication patterns used in child care settings. The lines represent communication paths. The diagrams tell us nothing about the people involved, just something about the organizational system.

Question Starter: Given both communication patterns, what differences would the two patterns make in the leader's flow of information? If each group was given a problem to solve, which group would solve the problem faster? (Responses may include: the first network would be faster, because it is a one-way communication system—the leader is the only one to whom anyone talks. There are no extra messages. On the other hand, the second system would foster higher morale because people can talk to almost anyone. This model offers greater flexibility, more checkpoints for error, more opportunity for participation and responsibility.)

Communication structure affects a group's efficiency. Some communication networks allow for faster operation than others, but the advantage of speed may be gained at the cost of accuracy and morale. Thus, it is important to choose the structure carefully.

Leader Behavior

The role of the leader can strongly influence a group's cohesion and communication. In addition to following a specific pattern of communication, organizations often adopt a particular pattern of manager-staff relationship without recognizing the range of possibilities available. There are at least seven different types of leader behavior that can influence group behavior. Each type of behavior generates its own consequences (Napier & Gershenfeld, 1983).

The leader makes the decision and announces it: In this case, the leader identifies a problem, considers alternative solutions, chooses one of them, and then reports this decision to the staff. The leader may or may not consider what the staff will think or feel about the decision; in any case, no opportunity is provided for them to participate directly in the decision-making process.

The leader sells the decision: Here the leader, as before, decides. However, rather than simply announcing the decision, she takes the additional step of persuading the staff to accept it. Recognizing the possibility of some resistance, the leader seeks to reduce this resistance by indicating, for example, what the staff has to gain from the decision.

The leader presents ideas and invites questions: Here the leader who has arrived at a decision and seeks acceptance of it provides an opportunity for the staff to understand more fully the thinking and intentions behind the decision by inviting them to raise questions. This give-and-take enables all involved to explore more fully the implications of the decision.

The leader presents a tentative decision subject to change: This kind of behavior permits the staff to exert some influence on the decision. The initiative for identifying and diagnosing the problem remains with the leader who, before finalizing a decision, presents the proposed solution and invites the reaction of those who will be affected by it. Nonetheless, the leader will make the final decision.

The leader presents the problem, gets suggestions, and then makes a decision: Up to this point the leader has come before the group with a solution. In this case, however, the staff gets the first chance to suggest solutions to a problem identified by the leader. The group increases the leader's repertory of possible solutions to the problem; the leader then selects the most promising solution.

The leader defines the limits and requests that the group make a decision: At this point, the leader passes to the group (possibly including herself as a member) the right to make a decision. Before doing so, however, she defines the problem to be solved and the boundaries within which the decision must be made. In this case the leader becomes a facilitator rather than a boss (Neugebauer, 1984).

The leader permits the group to make a decision within prescribed limits: This approach represents an extreme degree of group freedom only occasionally encountered in formal organizations, as, for instance, a research group consisting of highly trained professionals who have worked together for some time. Here the team identifies and diagnoses a problem, considers alternative solutions, and chooses one. The only limits are those imposed by the leader's superior. If the leader participates, she does so as an equal, committing herself in advance to assist in implementing whatever decision the group makes.

Many relationship problems between leader and staff occur because the leader fails to make clear how she plans to use her authority. For example, if she actually intends to make a certain decision herself, but her staff gets the impression she has delegated this authority, considerable confusion and resentment are likely to follow. Problems can also occur when the leader uses a democratic facade to conceal the fact that she has already made a decision that she hopes the group will accept as its own. If effective communication is to occur, it is important that the nature of the relationship between leader and staff in decision making be clearly understood.

Learning Activity: Divide participants into small groups. Ask them to identify the communication pattern that is most characteristic of their child care facilities. They should also evaluate the benefits and consequences to their colleagues, to their leaders, and to themselves.

Mutual Role Expectations

It is important for each of us to develop a clear understanding of our roles in a child care facility if we are to work effectively. One way to clarify our roles is to develop a written or verbal contract (or agreement) that specifies what functions we are to perform and how the performance fits in with that of our coworkers (Neugebauer, 1984). Contracts can specify what work or services will be performed and for what reward, what each party to the contract will pay attention to and what they will ignore, what feedback they will offer each other, and so on. For example, if staff are expected to attend staff meetings once a month, this expectation should be stated in a contract at the beginning of employment.

Work teams that operate effectively consist of members who know what contribution each makes to the whole operation. This idea, called differentiation of function, means that all employees are usually not expected to do the same tasks; rather, the work is divided into tasks that are differentially assigned to staff. For example, only one person on a baseball team pitches at a time: the rest field the ball.

It is also important to know who is in charge of the organization. There is a leader who has a leader who has a leader, just as lieutenants report to captains, captains to majors, and so forth. When conflicts arise, it is better not to circumvent the leader by appealing to the leader's leader without her prior knowledge, unless we are willing to pay the consequences of bypassing her authority. Some situations may require such drastic action, but under normal circumstances, it is best to work within the established hierarchy to affect the desired changes.

Summary

Effective communication is essential to successful operations of any organization. Effective communication consists of a meeting of meaning among communicators. Moreover, the meaning of communication is the response it elicits, independent of our intention. This is why two-way communication is essential to effectiveness. We can enhance our ability to accurately receive messages from others by improving our skills of attending behavior, behavior description, paraphrasing, and parafeeling.

The communication pattern within a center strongly influences communication flow, efficiency, accuracy, and morale. In addition, leadership style affects staff communication and efficiency. Recognizing the range and consequences of each leadership model can enable greater flexibility and improve staff morale. Finally, staff communication is enhanced when mutual expectations regarding role performance are clear and written, usually in the form of contracts.

Enrichment Activities

1. Analyze the communication network used in your child care facility by responding to the following questions: What typically occurs when the communication pattern is used? Does it promote or hinder communication? What are the benefits of the communication pattern? What problems, if any, are associated with this communication pattern? Can you identify ways to improve the level of communication in your child care facility?
2. What type of leader behavior is used in your child care facility? Describe the behavior and its effects on staff-leader communication.
3. Analyze your own communication skills. Identify specific ways in which you can improve communication with others. Make a chart that includes these skills in the left column and the days of the week across the top column. Put a check mark in the appropriate column each time you exercise one of these communication skills.
4. List all the causes of communication problems in your child care facility. Next to each cause propose a solution.
5. Analyze the difference between one-way and two-way communication by using both in various situations. Record the effects of each on listeners and on yourself.

Bibliography

Faules, D. F., & Alexander, D.C. (1978). *Communication and social behavior: A symbolic interaction perspective.* Reading, MA: Addision-Wesley.

Symbolic interaction, which includes negotiation, process, emergence, and holism, is closely related to communication and social behavior. The book looks in depth at factors such as sign systems, nonverbal behavior, role behavior, and purposes and strategies of communication. Part 4, "How Organizations Use Communication," is especially interesting.

Galvin, K., & Book, C. (1975). *Person-to-person: An introduction to speech communication.* Skokie, IL: National Textbook Company.

An easy-to-read, enjoyable book that defines communication and its various aspects. The reader is directly addressed and involved in the subject matter. Illustrations, photographs, and humorous drawings highlight the text.

Kostelnik, M. J. (1982, July/August). A practical approach to resolving interstaff conflict. *Child Care Information Exchange,* pp. 7–12.

A useful article presenting strategies that help to stimulate interstaff communication. These strategies include delivering complaints in terms of feelings rather than as criticisms, utilizing personal and group problem-solving approaches, and establishing guidelines and policies to be followed during times of interpersonal conflict.

Kostelnik, M. J. (1984, August). Real consensus or groupthink? *Child Care Information Exchange,* pp.25–30.

Staff participation and group decision making bring organizations together, reduce strife and dissension, help ensure worker commitment, and "generate . . . creative solutions to problems." But one danger stemming from cohesion is "groupthink" in which unanimity and peace are sought at the expense of realism and a scrupulous search for solutions. Ways of avoiding groupthink are detailed.

Lloyd, S. R. (1985, May). Managing would be easy: If . . . *Child Care Information Exchange,* pp.5–8.

The author suggests that investing in relationships leads to success. Some practical tips are offered on how to manage people problems as a means of lessening conflict. Topics discussed include: recognizing types of behavior and nonverbal signals; communication styles; understanding behavior choices; choosing appropriate words; focusing on body language; and facing challenges.

Napier, R. W., & Gershenfeld, M. K. (1983). *Making groups work: A guide for group leaders.* Boston: Houghton Mifflin.

This book will be helpful for those who wish to promote cohesion and communication in their organizations through team work. Topics dealt with include: leadership, group design, conflict situations, and evaluation.

Neugebauer, R. (1984, June). Step by step guide to team building. *Child Care Information Exchange,* pp. 9–13.

The author advocates developing staff into an efficient team whose members support, satisfy, and stimulate each others' work and efforts. The team-building process is described and explained in detail, common problems are identified, and a variety of practical suggestions are offered.

Schuler, J. R. S. (1979). Effective use of communicating to minimize employee stress. *The Personnel Administrator, 24,* pp. 40–44.

Employee stress can be reduced by supervisors with good communication skills such as effective listening, receiving and providing feedback, giving meaningful nonverbal signals, and diagnosing situations correctly. Managerial behaviors effecting or reducing stress are: achievement communication behavior; ego deflation communication behavior; contingent approval communication behavior; contingent disapproval communication behavior; participative communication behavior; directive communication behavior; and, supportive communication behavior.

The Child Care Staff Education Project. (1982, March/April). Shared decision-making: Including all staff in the process. *Child Care Information Exchange,* pp. 27–30.

Centers where decision making is shared are centers where staff and administrators communicate and form a cohesive group. Developing communication skills and learning to share responsibility should be an essential part of teacher-training programs. Many helpful suggestions on how to involve staff in decision making are offered.

Timm, P. R. (1985, January). Driving out the devils of communication. *Child Care Information Exchange,* pp. 5–7.

The article identifies seven deadly sins of management communication that must be avoided for effective interaction. These are: failing to adjust misunderstood messages; attempting to impress rather than express; choosing the wrong medium; not listening to feedback; sending contradictory nonverbal messages; not clarifying messages; and perceiving communication to be a fringe benefit.

Index

Beverly Gulley, Ph.D., is an associate professor and coordinator of early childhood programs in the Department of Curriculum and Instruction at Southern Illinois University. She has taught courses and done research in the field of early childhood for approximately ten years. Dr. Gulley has been active in providing training for day careproviders in centers and homes for many years. She has written numerous training materials for child careproviders that have been used extensively. She is currently involved in a Family Day Care Provider CDA training program. Dr. Gulley has made numerous presentations and written a number of articles on early childhood. She has been active regarding early childhood issues at the national, state, and local levels. She is currently serving as regional vice-president for the Illinois Association for the Education of Young Children.

Jacqueline Eddleman, Ph.D., currently serves as an associate professor of early childhood programs in the Department of Curriculum, Instruction and Media at Southern Illinois University at Carbondale. In addition to teaching for many years in child and family life education, she has spent much of her professional career in teacher education supervision. Dr. Eddleman was the major local administrator of the in-service training projects that developed and validated the training materials inherent in this book. She has been cited as a child advocate. She is motivated in her work by a philosophy that envisions a child's optimum development in the context of a caring family, which chooses to interface with competent and significant support systems such as high-quality child care services.

Douglas Bedient has been director of Learning Resources Service at Southern Illinois University at Carbondale since 1982. Prior to assuming that position, he served as assistant director and as an instructional developer in the same office. He received M.S. and Ph.D. degrees from Southern Illinois University at Carbondale. He received his undergraduate degree from the University of Wyoming in Social Studies. His professional career has included teaching at the secondary level, consultation about instructional materials, instructional development, teaching at the higher education level, and administration. His responsibilities at SIUC involve him in working with faculty from numerous disciplines. Many teaching and learning issues have been addressed in a variety of innovative ways in the programs that are supported by Learning Resources Service. *Training for Professional Child Care* is one example of what can result when systematic approaches to teaching and learning are applied to a particular discipline.